AF470656

THE
PRIME MINISTERS

THE
PRIME
MINISTERS

*Stories and anecdotes
from Number 10*

Edited and with an Introduction by
William Douglas Home

Written and researched by
Jennifer Browne

W.H. ALLEN · LONDON
1987

Copyright © Victorama Ltd and William Douglas Home, 1987

Set in Concorde by
Phoenix Photosetting, Chatham, Kent
Printed and bound in Great Britain by
Mackays of Chatham Ltd, Chatham, Kent
for the Publishers, W.H. Allen & Co. Plc
44 Hill Street, London W1X 8LB

Reprinted July 1987

British Library Cataloguing in Publication Data

The Prime ministers: stories and anecdotes
   from Number 10.
   1. Prime ministers——Great Britain——
   Anecdotes, facetiae, satire, etc.
   I. Home, William Douglas
   941.07′092′2   DA28.4

ISBN 0 491 03067 3

CONTENTS

page

MONARCHS

George I	1714–27
George II	1727–60
George III	1760–1820
George IV	1820–30
William IV	1830–7
Victoria	1837–1901
Edward VII	1901–10
George V	1910–36
Edward VIII	1936
George VI	1936–52
Elizabeth II	1952–

ACKNOWLEDGMENTS

Sources of material quoted in each chapter are given at the conclusion of the book. We are grateful to the authors, editors and publishers of all the works referred to and acknowledge with thanks the permission kindly given to reproduce copyright material from the following books:

Sir Robert Walpole, (vol. 1), by J. H. Plumb (Cresset Press, 1960).
Memoirs, by Lord Harvey, edited by R. Sedgwick (William Kimber, 1952).
George III, by Stanley Ayling (Collins, 1972).
Correspondence of Horace Walpole, edited by W. S. Lewis (Oxford University Press, 1973).
The Younger Pitt: the Years of Acclaim, by John Ehrman (Constable, 1969).
Addington, by Philip Ziegler (Collins, 1965).
Disraeli, by Robert Blake (Eyre & Spottiswoode, 1966).
The People from the Horizon, by Philip Snow and Stefanie Waine (Phaidon, 1979).
Gladstone, by Philip Magnus (John Murray, 1954).
Autobiography, by Margot Asquith (Butterworth, 1920).
Rosebery, by R. R. James (Weidenfeld & Nicolson, 1963).
Great Contemporaries, by Winston Churchill (Butterworth, 1937).
Lloyd George, by Richard Lloyd George (Frederick Muller Ltd, 1960).
Lloyd George, A Diary by Frances Stevenson, edited by A. J. P. Taylor (Hutchinson, 1971).
Recollections of Three Reigns, by Lord Sysonby (Eyre & Spottiswoode, 1951).

Diaries and Letters, by Harold Nicolson, 3 vols (Collins, 1966–8).
Ramsay Macdonald, by David Marquand (Jonathan Cape, 1977).
Balfour, by Max Egremont (Collins, 1980).
The Letters of Sidney & Beatrice Webb edited by N. Mackenzie, 2 vols (Cambridge University Press, 1978).
The Second World War, by Winston Churchill (Cassell, 1948).
Chips, The Diaries of Sir Henry Channon (Weidenfeld & Nicolson, 1967).
Clementine Churchill, by Mary Soames (Cassell, 1979).
Winston Churchill as I Knew Him, by Violet Bonham Carter (Weidenfeld & Nicolson, 1965).
Memoirs, by Lord Ismay (Heinemann, 1960).
Winston Churchill, Four Faces and the Man (Allen Lane, 1969).
Attlee, by Kenneth Harris (Weidenfeld & Nicolson, 1982).
Another World, by Anthony Eden (Allen Lane, 1981).
The Art of the Possible, by R. A. Butler (Hamish Hamilton, 1971).
The Blast of War, by Harold Macmillan (Macmillan, 1967).
Wyndham and Children First, by Lord Egremont (Macmillan, 1968).
Enemies of Promise, by Cyril Connolly (Routledge, 1938).
The Diaries of a Cabinet Minister, by Richard Crossman, 3 vols (Hamish Hamilton and Jonathan Cape, 1975–7).
Heath and the Heathmen, by Andrew Roth (Routledge & Kegan Paul, 1970).
Heath, by George Hutchinson (Longman, 1970).

INTRODUCTION

THIS BOOK IS intended to be an informative if selective anthology of British Prime Ministers from the first, Sir Robert Walpole, who held the post for twenty-one years right through to Margaret Thatcher who – well, your guess is as good as mine!

It was Beachcomber, of course, who thought up a bizarre volume entitled *The List of Huntingdonshire Cabmen* (which I don't suppose he ever wrote and which, certainly, nobody ever saw) and some may rate this conception as no less ambitious and, perhaps, even more bizarre, when one takes into consideration the eccentric sidelights that it casts on all our First Lords of the Treasury.

It does not, of course, provide a full portrait of each and every Prime Minister between Sir Robert and the present incumbent of Downing Street. How could it? – unless the publisher were to demand, and the writer possess stamina to provide, a volume equivalent in weight to sixty or seventy lives of Lord Mountbatten rolled into one.

Its purpose is to allow any reader requiring information about any of our Prime Ministers to open up the book at the appropriate page, learn the date of birth and the duration of life of the Prime Minister he, or she, is interested in and then, as an added bonus, get the low-down on that particular statesman's achievements, failures, eccentricities and loves, within the marriage bed or out of it. Indeed, a total perusal of the book – taken at leisure – provides a panoramic view of British history, not, I would imagine, to be found in any other publication of this size.

When I had finished editing it my overall impression was a sense of deep-seated thankfulness that men or women (or, to be precise, one woman) like these should have been in charge of our affairs from the late eighteenth century right through until the very day on which I pen these words.

And that thankfulness is not, in any great measure, due to the fact that some of them were *great* people, but rather to the realization that, whether they were great or not, it didn't matter all that much. And, for the good reason that, in normal circumstances, the democratic process soon corrects any damage automatically.

In other words, a profound feeling of good health pervades one as one wanders down the centuries and notes the merits and the weaknesses of each and every Premier, with no feeling of panic or despair, but rather, with affection and an understanding smile.

And that, of course, is the true beauty of democracy – the knowledge that a nation – never mind who leads it – can remain in health and happiness, regardless of the failings of those at the top, provided that the base is sound and *that*, in a democracy, goes without saying. Whereas, a dictatorship or an undemocratic monarchy has no such safeguard against the madness which inevitably presages disaster taking over. Only a democracy can ride the storm. And within a democracy a storm need not happen.

For example, Lord Chatham was just a touch daft. According to Thomas Whitely writing to Lord Grenville, 'the physicians say there is nothing in his disorder which he may not recover but do not pretend to say there is any prospect of it being soon.' But no harm came of it, whereas Hitler in his craziness destroyed a nation.

What I love about this collection of anecdotes is the gossip, the outspokenness, the total lack of reverence, the down-to-earthness and the domestic details, such as Chatham's report to his wife by letter on the state of his son William's bowels – 'Our sweet little boy passed the night well, and is quite easy this morning, having had, before going to bed, a copious motion.'

Imagine Ghengis Khan penning a letter like that! These things, surely, are what make democracy so picturesque and comforting, because they tell us that the people who direct our lives are only people like ourselves who, when they have attained the heights, remain like us and do not change their personalities. Unless, in wartime when occasionally the democractic process is, to all intents and purposes suspended – more's the pity – thus allowing leadership to overreach itself a shade.

But normally, in peace time, we can look upon our leaders with indulgence and forgive them all the things they say and all the minor irritations, like their Party Broadcasts, that they visit on us, and regard them with affection, tolerance and even admiration. We can even ignore them altogether, as one might a neighbour or a relative, according to his personality and one's assessment of him as an individual.

I know this to be true because I have a relative who figures in this book. He was Prime Minister some twenty years ago, albeit for a short time, but for long enough to prove to me that Premiers, like leopards, do not change their spots. They stay precisely as they were, before they got the job and, when they lose it, they revert with ease to former life (with minimal exceptions) since democracy has seen to it that their boots stay the same size as they were when they first entered Downing Street. If they were modest when they went in, they are still that when they leave. If bossy on arrival, they will still be bossy when they come out – indeed, such a quality no doubt, provides the reason for their exit, premature or late, according to the tolerance displayed by the electors.

A word or two about this relative might not be out of place here, because Sir Alec (as I fondly call him) was the perfect prototype for a British Prime Minister. That is to say he is a modest, self-effacing man with an integrity of steel, a sense of the ridiculous, a sense of humour, an unending tolerance and, above all, a certain eccentricity.

He wrote his speeches, for example (and still does), with grand-children around him on the floor, undoing his shoe-laces and oc-casionally, emboldened by the silence of their prey, removing the shoes altogether. He would then deliver the speech, perhaps to the United Nations, where another shoe-remover (name of Kruschev) left him just as unmoved as he had been with his grandchildren.

And he pursued his private interests – nature, fishing, racing, gardening, as keenly, though with less time for them, as he had before (and has since), thus preserving sanity. This was interpreted by some as unprofessional, as lacking dedication, as a hang-over from feudalism – old Etonian, aristocratic! Indeed, every insult that the ignorant or jealous, or plain stupid, level at a man who is himself and will not be diverted from that station by any pressure or false counsel since, to be himself, as nothing else is, is his *raison d'être*.

And, as I say, he has his eccentricities – one is that he enjoys the racing form-book rather more than he does Bagehot and another is that sometimes he forgot exactly where he was when he was Foreign Secretary (though never where his country ought to be). These foibles, let me emphasize, are not unique to him, but shared by many of his predecessors – though not all of his successors.

Every Premier – not just my brother – gathers tales about him.

Indeed such titbits are scattered through this book like children's Easter eggs around a garden and are just as intriguing to find and consume.

Before repeating some of them (if only to afford myself the pleasure) let me record some statistics that I have compiled concerning the whole outfit.

First of all, a study of this book, asssisted by some amateurish mathematical deductions, leads me to the theory that, broadly speaking, twenty-one Prime Ministers attended Eton College whereas only seven went to Harrow. (The rest were scattered among other educational establishments such as Winchester, Charterhouse, Haileybury and Glasgow High School.) I say 'broadly speaking' to allow for any error there may be in my addition, having been myself at Eton, at which school we never thought that an addiction to unarguable accuracy was necessarily required of a broad-minded, mature individual.

By the same token, forty went to Oxford and ten or so to Cambridge.

One cannot detect much difference between any of these variously educated little boys in their approach to life when they grew up, although some were more unequal in the field of eccentricity than others.

One Prime Minister, to get down to a more detailed analysis, had two unique achievements to his credit (or discredit perhaps), namely Walpole. He went to the Tower (the only one that has to date!) as well as running up a wine bill for £1,100 at, so to speak, one sitting – each of those distinctions one would guess, being dependent on the other.

Two more Premiers – Pelham and the Duke of Newcastle – shared a single distinction, that of being brothers. This feat, like Walpole's, was not achieved by any others – though, of course, I live in hope!

In this book it is the minor detail which is most informative. Read, for instance, the section on Lord Bute, possibly the most unpopular Prime Minister in British history, with especial note of his long letter to George III outlining, most effectively, all the disasters that tend to befall Prime Ministers and detailing the sad effects that such setbacks would have on him, leading inevitably to his resignation. I can think of many a Prime Minister since Lord Bute who would echo what he writes with a most feeling 'Hear, Hear.'

It intrigued me, too, to note one reason that he gave for his retirement (echoing Lord Chatham's letter to his wife) which he described as 'a great relaxation of my bowels in many years standing'. Poor man, to have such trouble, if indeed trouble it was!

Yet, one is glad to note that his liaison with Princess Augusta was not interfered with by the constant movement of his bowels if Horace Walpole is to be believed. He wrote of himself as 'being as convinced of amorous relations, as if I had seen them together'!

Nor, now we're on to a bit of character assassination, was a later Prime Minister, Lord Shelburne, very flattering to poor unhealthy old Bute when he said 'Lord Bute had a great deal of superficial knowledge, such as is commonly to be met with in France and Scotland,' – which insult to this writer's native land I am only too happy to be able to counter by quoting what Jeremy Bentham wrote of Lord Shelburne which ran as follows: 'His manner was very imposing, very dignified and he talked his vague generalities in the House of Lords in a very emphatic way, as if something good were at the bottom of it all when, in fact, there was nothing at all.'!

Now back to sample further titbits of intriguing fact. The Duke of Portland too suffered illness (though not in so diluted a form as did Lord Bute) and evidently from incompetence also since, according to the Opposition,

> *He totters on a crutch;*
> *His brain by sickness long depressed*
> *Has lost the sense it once possessed,*
> *Which isn't saying much.*

On the question of retirement, Lord Bute was not, of course, the only Prime Minister with an almost pathological desire to embrace it. Lord Grenville longed to retire due, no doubt, to the fact that he lived up to his own verdict on himself, namely that he was 'not competent to the management of men'. And then, when the hour of resignation did in fact come, in 1807, he wrote to his brother, Lord Buckingham, with an almost audible sigh of relief as follows: 'The deed is done and I am again a free man and, to you, I may express what it would seem to be affectation to say to others, the infinite pleasure I derive from my emancipation.'!

Superficially disquieting words, perhaps, bearing, as they do, the implication that the writer felt no shame in feeling as he did nor suffered from the mildest pang of conscience at abandoning his duty. Yet, to those addicted to democracy, it surely is a message of profound hope, showing us, as it does, that democratic leaders can be chosen – and frequently are – from people who lack ambition, thus pin-pointing yet again the safety barriers that circumscribe democracy.

Another Premier I found myself intrigued by was Lord North, whom I had always regarded, after admittedly gaining only a Fourth Honours degree at Oxford (me, not him!), as a rather dim and boring character.

But not at all – he comes out as a rather splendid fellow. I'm aware, of course, that the war with America did nothing for his reputation but, apart from that, he seems to me to have been quite a fellow and a bit of a wag.

For example, he besought a fellow member not to wake him up till Grenville got to 'modern times' in an interminable speech. And when the member eventually did so, North remarked, 'Zounds, you have waked me up a hundred years too soon.'

'The noble Lord is asleep' cried an outraged member of the opposition on the same occasion. 'How I wish to God I was,' said North, not opening his eyes.

He was not pretty, so it seems. 'Who is that plain-looking lady in the box opposite?' his neighbour asked him. 'My wife,' said Lord North. 'I don't mean her, I mean the lady next to her,' said his companion. 'She's my daughter,' said Lord North, 'we are considered to be three of the ugliest people in London.'

Who else shall I single out? The Duke of Wellington, I think, because the whole story of his life appeals to me, especially his mother's comment at the start of his career – 'I vow to God I don't know what I shall do with my awkward son, Arthur.'

Equally, I like his own remark in answer to the Duke of Bedford's statement that, in 1834, 'the nation's choice was between anarchy and despotism', and that he preferred the former. Said the Duke, 'I can tell Johnny Bedford, if we have anarchy, *I'll* have Woburn.'

I am also struck by the honesty with which he outlined the reasons for his less than successful marriage to Kitty Pakenham. And it intrigues me to think that the poor fellow, had he not been so honest, could have got out of it when, after proposing to Kitty by letter, he confided to his brother Gerald, on meeting her, 'She has grown ugly, by Jove!'

These sidelights on a great man and a great career show clearly on what lines this book is compiled. No long dissertations on his military conquests – though, of course, they get a mention – but intriguing stories, designed to illustrate his character – as well as his achievements.

What I like particularly about the Duke is that he served as Foreign Secretary and later leader of the Lords when he had ceased to be Prime Minister, reminding me of a more modern Premier who carried on in just the same unselfish way – no names, no pack-drill!

So much for the Great Duke, who has been immortalized in paint so often as to make us think we know him personally.

Yet the mention of the portraits of him reminds me of just one more story of him. He was counting out the notes to pay Sir William Allan who had painted Waterloo. 'Why don't you draw a cheque to save yourself the trouble?' asked Sir William, to which the Great Duke replied, 'Do you suppose I would let the clerk in Coutts know what a fool I've been?'

Reading of the Prime Ministers in the last two-thirds of the nineteenth century, the names of Grey and Melbourne, Gladstone and Disraeli seem almost contemporary.

Grey hated politics at the start of his career, writing to his wife, 'I feel more and more convinced of my unfitness for a pursuit which I detest. Do not think this is the language of momentary low spirits. It is really the settled conviction of my mind.'

Yet, twenty-six years later, he became Prime Minister and Creevey noted, 'Grey was all alive O' at the time of the Reform Bill.'

There are some – the individuals, eccentrics, statesmen, call them what you will – who are remembered to this day in detail.

Take William Lamb, Lord Melbourne. Melbourne was a lazy man by all accounts and yet a man of quite outstanding personality and perspicacity. His comments, quoted in this book, are a delight to the eye. For example, at his home, Brocket, he saw Landseer pause before a picture of Lord Egremont. Rumour had it that Egremont was Melbourne's true father.

'Aye, you've heard that story, have you?' Melbourne said. 'It's all a damned lie for all that. But who the devil can tell who's anybody's father?'

None the less, remarkably like Lord Egremont, he was a ladies' man, being involved in two court actions brought by angry husbands.

And, of course, his own wife, Lady Caroline Lamb, brought notoriety to both of them, while his avuncular relationship with Queen Victoria had, at the time, as now, an utterly unrivalled charm for those who contemplated it.

This aspect of his character I much prefer to that which Philip Ziegler (quoted in this book) brought up in his biography of Melbourne, namely, an addiction to beating or, flagellation – call it what you will, it still remains unpleasant. My view is that it was all talk or confined to letter writing or a rather laboured joke which misfired for all those who were not in the know. In any case one would have thought such an activity would have been far too strenuous for such a lazy man as Melbourne. May he rest in peace, unharmed by tittle-tattle and remembered for his honesty, outspokenness and tactlessness as illustrated in his answer to the Queen when she told him that one of the things she liked most about Prince Albert was the way that he paid no attention to other women. 'No,' said Lord Melbourne, 'that sort of thing is apt to come later.'!

As for Gladstone and Disraeli there are some interesting tales to tell about them.

For example, Gladstone's sister, Helen, was to say the least eccentric. She took opium, became a member of the Russian Orthodox Church and got engaged to a Polish Count, all of which her brother took quite well.

He also took her ultimate conversion to the Roman Catholic Church with equanimity, though his patience finally snapped when he found she was using leaves from the works of Protestant theologians in his library as lavatory paper!

Gladstone was a man of immense stature but as with all politicians, there were those who disliked him – perhaps, with all the more intensity because of that great stature. The Cecils, for example, rather than concede that the letters GOM stood for 'Grand Old Man' called him 'God's Only Mistake', which at the time of Khartoum was revised to MOG (Murderer of Gordon). Indeed a song was written on the subject at the time:

> *The* MOG, *when his life ebbs out,*
> *Will ride in a fiery chariot;*
> *And sit in state,*
> *On a red-hot plate,*
> *Between Pilate and Judas Iscariot.*

It was Benjamin Disraeli who, when asked the difference between a disaster and a tragedy, replied, 'It would be a tragedy if anybody were to push Mr Gladstone into the river and a disaster if anybody were to pull him out again.'

Quoted in this book is the exchange between Lord Melbourne and Disraeli, in his youth. 'Well, tell me what you want to be,' said Melbourne. 'I want to be Prime Minister,' said Dizzy. 'No chance of that in our time,' Melbourne said. 'It's all arranged and settled.'!

But it wasn't, was it? And of course it isn't now. That's why I sometimes think of Pelham and the Duke of Newcastle because I know the job would suit me fine since this book shows that any kind of man can be Prime Minister – mad, sane, rich, poor, eccentric, pompous, fond of racing, fond of drink, young, old, fat, thin, good-looking, ugly – the list is unending. And no matter which he is, the country will survive. That is the beauty of it.

In this century, of course, there have been giants like Churchill, for example, who can measure up to any predecessor, specially in wartime – others such as Stanley Baldwin, Chamberlain, Macmillan, Wilson, who, in their own way were colourful, though some of them more colourful than others.

I do not propose to comment on them, since their portraits are not yet completed – only to point out that, as the century progresses, stories of their private lives and eccentricities will multiply, as yet more information comes to light.

For instance, I heard one about Sir Winston Churchill which my eldest brother told me and with which, with his permission (or, indeed, without it!) I intend to close this introduction.

Over coffee at a dinner at Buckingham Palace at the end of the Second World War for the United States Heads of Services, the King's secretary saw an American Admiral putting a gold coffee spoon into the pocket of his tunic as a souvenir. The secretary approached Sir Winston and asked what he was to do to prevent the whole outfit being purloined.

'Leave it to me,' said Sir Winston, putting a gold dessert spoon into the breast pocket of his tailcoat, with half of it sticking out. He then walked round the table, tapped the American Admiral on the shoulder, removed his cigar from his mouth and said, 'We've been spotted. We'll have to give them back.'

Long live Diplomacy. Long live Democracy as well.

William Douglas Home
AUGUST, 1985

SIR ROBERT WALPOLE

First Earl of Orford (1676–1745)

'Thus was he formed to govern and to please;
Familiar greatness, dignity with ease,
Composed his frame, admired in every state,
In private amiable, in public great,
Gentle in power but daring in disgrace,
His love was liberty, his wish was peace.'

Works, SIR CHARLES HANBURY WILLIAMS (1708–59)

SIR ROBERT WALPOLE was born on 26 August 1676, the second son of Robert Walpole and his wife Mary. The Walpole family lived at Houghton in Norfolk where they had been established for many generations. He was educated at Eton and at King's College, Cambridge. After only two years there, his elder brother unexpectedly died and his father insisted that his new heir should return home to learn about the family estates.

In 1700, Walpole married the rich and passionate Catherine Shorter, daughter of a Baltic timber merchant and a few months later his father died. In 1701 he entered the House of Commons where he immediately displayed great abilities, winning the patronage of the influential Marlboroughs. In 1705 he was appointed one of the Council of Admiralty, in 1708 Secretary at War, and in 1709 Treasurer of the Navy. Walpole's power was so bound up with that of the Whigs that when they fell from favour he was actually committed to the Tower in 1712 for alleged corruption. On his release a few months later he returned to the House of Commons, and the accession of George I in 1714 brought him back into power as Paymaster of the Forces. From 1715 to 1717 he was First Lord of the Treasury and Chancellor of the Exchequer, and returned to the same position in 1721 having saved the ministry from ruin caused by the South Sea Bubble.

For the next twenty-one years Walpole successfully established his reputation as Britain's first Prime Minister. Prosperity at home was assured by avoiding war at all costs, and it was only after the death of Queen Caroline in 1737 had removed his loyalest ally that his supremacy was seriously threatened. Against his better judgement, Britain entered into a war with Spain, the number of his Whig opponents grew, and by 1742 he had resigned all his places and was created Earl of Orford. For the next few years his influence was still great but ill-health finally forced him to withdraw to Houghton. He died in March 1745 after enduring several operations.

Marriages

Walpole's first marriage to Catherine Shorter was a disaster. She had been selected as a good match by Colonel Walpole, Sir Robert's father, but the passion and sensuality evident in Kneller's portrait of her soon degenerated into jealousy and hysteria. Only one love letter from Walpole to his wife remains, dated 10 July 1702, and it already betrays the rift between them after only two years of marriage:

'*My dearest dear,*
For I will still use the same language to you, although you can soe easily change your style. I will not say what might be said upon this occasion for two soe very unkind letters, it must have been some satisfaction to me to have deserved it and would have been a great [_____?] to me to know how to account for soe great an alteration. But what can I say? What can I think?

'Am I to judge by my self? May I measure your heart by my own? O there I find that love, that tendernesse, for you, that are there any failings in you they are still perfections to me and doth my Dearest doe or omitt any thing that might seem better otherwise, I am blind, cannot, would not see any thing in my dearer self but what is most agreeable. Why then this difference betwixt us? Why soe hard to believe what I am fond of and most happy in thinking? Why so easy to entertain thoughts to me so distracting? I could have found a thousand excuses for you rather than have arraigned you of coldnesse, indifferency, neglect or want of love. Is this then the prologue to that delightful scene that I have been framing to myself?

Are the pleasures of promised joy and rapture to be clouded over with jealous and uneasy thoughts? Doe you thus prepare yourself for those dear embraces the hopes of which have been my only support for your absence? Are we then to meet with cold faint hearts and chideing complaining eyes? Noe, my dearest soul, think again, examine the life of him you so severely censure and you'll find cause enough to believe that the greatest surprise and concern I ever mett is your unexpected and unjust complaints, and reason enough to convince you that my obedient wife and humble servant has a most tenderly affectionate, and passionately loving husband, whom nothing, not your own unkindn[esse] can alter from being my dearest creature

most sincerely your
R. Walpole'

Walpole soon gave up the attempt to make his wife happy though he continued to finance her extravagances until she died in 1737. They led almost separate lives, Catherine immersing herself in a fashionable Chelsea existence, where her chief diversions were the Opera, a collection of exotic birds and buying expensive clothes and jewels. There was even a rumour that their youngest child Horace, who was totally unlike his father both in character and in looks, was really the son of Carr, Lord Hervey, a half-brother of the more famous John, Lord Hervey.

Until Walpole met Maria Skerrett, the daughter of Thomas Skerrett, in 1724 his affairs with other women were unimportant to him. Maria, though, he loved deeply. He provided for her out of public funds and lost little opportunity in marrying her after his wife's death. Tragically, she died in childbirth only a few months after their marriage.

The Queen and Mrs Skerrett

Lord Hervey, the diarist, recounted how the Queen was extremely concerned one day in 1735 to find Walpole in wretched spirits. Hervey had assured the Queen that the cause was not political but that Walpole's mistress was suffering from pleurisy to which the Queen replied:

'... she was very glad he had any amusement for his leisure hours, but could neither comprehend how a man could be very fond of a woman he only got for his money, nor how a man of Sir Robert's age and make, with his dirty mouth and great belly could ever imagine any woman would suffer him as a lover from any consideration or inducement but his money. "She must be a clever gentlewoman," continued the Queen, "to have made him believe she cares for him on any other score; and to show you what fools we all are in some point or other, she has certainly told him some fine story or other of her love and her passion, and that poor man – avec les gros corps, ces jambes enflées, et ce vilain ventre – believes her. My God! What is human nature!"'

Extravagance

His wife was not the only member of the Walpole family to be extravagant. Walpole himself lived continuously beyond his means and, until she died in 1711, his mother was an additional strain on his overstretched resources. A letter from her dated 29 April 1702 was typical of many:

> '*Dear son,*
>   it is with no small conserne that I torment you thus for money, but I am now put to those straights as I can no longer make shift.'

Walpole's own tastes were extremely expensive. In 1721 he decided to transform Houghton into a Palladian miniature palace set in a redesigned park. The scheme necessitated the wholesale removal of the local village to a new site. Nevertheless the work was virtually complete by 1730. Inside, the house was decorated and furnished to the highest standards, including furniture by William Kent. The gold trimmings for Kent's green velvet state bed alone cost almost £1220. Walpole's enthusiasm extended to pictures and wagon-loads of Raphaels, Rubens, and Rembrandts, etc. arrived at Houghton from all over Europe. In 1733 his wine bill from only one of the six or seven merchants he used amounted to about £1120. Little Horace as a small child of about seven had his own footmen and writing master, and wore French tailored silk suits.

Houghton Congresses

From about 1725 Walpole spent a fortnight in May and the month of November at Houghton where he entertained large numbers of people to what became known as 'Houghton Congresses'. Lord Hervey described one to Frederick Prince of Wales in July 1731:

> 'Our company at Houghton swelled at last into so numerous a body that we used to sit down to dinner a snug little party of about thirty odd, up to the chin in claret, strong beer and punch. We had Lords spiritual and temporal besides commoners, parsons, and freeholders innumerable. In public we drank loyal healths, talked of the times and cultivated popularity; in private we drew plans and cultivated the country.'

The Tower

Walpole managed to keep up appearances even when incarcerated in the Tower for several months in 1712. He had his own servants there, his own table, pen and ink, and a constant stream of visitors who treated him like a hero.

Corruption

It is unlikely that Walpole ever said 'every man has his price'. There is no doubt though that, following the standards of the age, Walpole lined his own pockets and those of his friends and relatives out of public funds. As a young man, together with his partner who happened to be Secretary of the Admiralty, he smuggled large quantities of claret, burgundy and champagne from Holland. Even when he was Chancellor of the Exchequer he had no scruples about buying contraband lace from Holland. In contrast, when George II offered him 10 Downing Street he was honest enough to admit that he did not need it for himself but accepted it as the official residence for the First Lord of the Treasury.

Coarseness

Walpole was a short dumpy man with a florid complexion and a disregard for filthy clothes. He had a coarse laugh and only appeared to stay awake during debates in the House of Commons by munching large numbers of Norfolk apples.

Vulgarity and Tactlessness

The effect of Walpole's coarse appearance was made worse by the
vulgarity of his manner and conversation. Acording to the Duchess
of Marlborough, the Queen once complained that Walpole had
tapped her on the shoulder during a service in chapel.

Lord Hervey described an incident which occurred in 1737:

'Sir Robert Walpole, with all his dexterity on some occasions,
and his knowledge of those he had to deal with, sometimes
made as gross mistakes as if his natural sagacity had given him
no share of the first of these qualities, nor his long experience
any proficiency in the last. An affectation of too much famili-
arity with pcople of the highest rank and a very coarse manner of being familiar drew him into these scrapes; and his way
of talking to and of the Princesses Emily and Caroline on
occurrences to which he should not only have shut his
mouth, but his eyes, went so far at this time that a message was
sent to him from them in form by the Duke of Grafton to
desire he would discourse no more in that strain. The Duke of
Newcastle's coquetry to the Princess Emily, and Her Royal
Highness's coquetry back again to him, as the only male
creature who made up to her, had been often the topic of very
ill-understood raillery, in very gross terms, uttered by Sir
Robert Walpole, and not very privately. He has often and
before many people in the expressions of a porter, told the
Duke of Newcastle he would certainly draw himself into
some scrape, for as the Princess Emily thought of nothing but
the main point and his Grace of nothing but the outwork Her
Royal Highness would certainly catch him alone one day and
ask him the question; upon which his Grace would be
frighted out of his wits and run away, whilst she would hate
him for so doing, and tell her papa and mama to be revenged
of him, that he had offered to ravish her.

'Sir Robert Walpole had not said this once or twice, or in
private only, but it had been almost his daily topic of conversation to and of the Duke of Newcastle for these last seven or
eight months; and often rather more than hinted by him in
mixed companies at dinner, even before servants.

'The last conversation of this nature, that occasioned the

messages which I have mentioned, was part of it in the Queen's morning drawing-room, and the rest in the apartment of the Princesses, where Sir Robert went to fetch the Duke of Newcastle away to dinner. If I were to relate all the particulars they would be incredible, considering by whom these things were said and to whom; but how strong they were may be guessed when Sir Robert, who loved hunting and often took his metaphors from that science, carried on an allegory on this occasion between the apartment of the Princesses and a dog kennel, in which he made the Duke of Newcastle one of the principal puppies of his parable and the two Princesses what, I believe, is as unnecessary as unfit to repeat, when I say he called them in plain terms, during this every way ill-understood raillery, what a hackney coachman would think the last affront he could offer in words to an applewoman.

'All this was told by the Princesses to the Queen, who was very angry with Sir Robert Walpole for what had passed, but never spoke to him about it, expecting, I suppose, what did indeed happen, that the message by the Duke of Grafton would suffice to reform him.'

Lord Hervey warmed to his subject:

'Nor was this the only subject on which Sir Robert Walpole at this time ruffled the temper of the Queen towards him; for whilst Her Majesty, with a little female and conjugal pride united, was every day telling Sir Robert Walpole in private how uninterruptedly kind the King's behaviour had been towards her ever since his arrival [George II had recently returned from a visit to Hanover where he had spent a lot of time with his mistress], Sir Robert used to shake his head, shrug his shoulders and laugh, and to tell her: "Madam, do not flatter yourself. For pleasure of the body there must be youth on one side; and believe me, marriage is never so properly called one flesh as after twenty years' marriage, for no husband then knows his wife's from his own."

'It was in vain for Her Majesty to give him instances of the King's expressions of kindness and affection towards her. Sir Robert still persisted, and told her: "Tis compensation,

Madam, for the sins of the summer; and he thinks to expiate the crime of real fondness to his mistress by putting it on to his wife."

'The King, having got a violent cold in his journey and taken no care of it at his first arrival, was extremely out of order, too, at this time, having at once the piles, a violent pain in one side of his head, and a little fever. This disorder, for which the King was at last forced to shut himself up and keep his bed, Sir Robert Walpole would insist to the Queen was principally occasioned by the disorder of his mind; that it was pining and fretting; and that he would never be well till she would send for Madam Walmoden [his mistress] to nurse him. . .

'Sir Robert Walpole continued every day plaguing the Queen, and whenever she told him the King was better than he had been, or better than people thought him, he used to answer her only with shaking his head and saying: "Do you flatter me, Madam, in telling me what you do not believe, or do you flatter yourself and believe what you say?" This often made the Queen peevish with him and complain of him to Lord Hervey, telling Lord Hervey at the same time: "You often pity me for the snubs and rebukes I meet with from the King, but I assure you the affronts I meet with there are nothing compared to what I receive from your friend Sir Robert. I cannot imagine what ails him, or who it is he listens to. In the first place, he wants to persuade me the King is dying; in the next, that he knows him better than I do; and what is more extraordinary still, is telling me every time he sees me that my being from morning to night in the King's room is owing to my forcing myself upon him, and that he had much rather be without my company." '

Sir Blue String

Walpole was extremely proud of the Garter, awarded to him in 1726. He had the Star and Garter painted into the new ceiling and carved into chimney pieces at Houghton, and he went to the trouble of having the Garter ribbon painted into old portraits of him done before that date.

In contemporary ballads he was an object of ridicule:

> *In Body gross, of Saffron Hue,*
> *Deck'd forth in Green with Ribband Blue.*

Retirement

Sir Robert always claimed that the Norfolk countryside was his first love. It is doubtful whether he always opened letters from his huntsmen first as is often claimed but he did write a letter of 24 June 1743 in which he described his retirement at Houghton:

> 'This place affords no news, no subject of amusement and entertainment to you fine Gentlemen. Men of wit and pleasure about town understand not the language, nor taste the charms of the inanimate world; my flatterers here are all mutes, the Oaks the Beeches and the Chestnuts seem to contend, which shall best please the Lord of the Mannor: They cannot deceive, they will not lie.'

Mrs Piozzi later painted a different view of his retirement in her Memoirs:

> 'When Sir Robert Walpole was dismissed from all his employments he retired to Houghton and walked into the Library; when, pulling down a book and holding it some minutes to his eyes, he suddenly and seemingly sullenly exchanged it for another. He held that about half as long, and looking out a third returned it instantly to its shelf and burst into tears. "I have led a life of business so long," said he, "that I have lost my taste for reading, and now – what shall I do?" '

SPENCER COMPTON
First Earl of Wilmington (1673–1743)

'See yon old dull important lord
Who at the longed-for money board
Sits first but does not lead,
His younger brethen all things make,
So that the Treasury's like a snake,
And the tail moves the head.'

Works, SIR CHARLES HANBURY WILLIAMS (1708–59)

SPENCER COMPTON WAS the second surviving son of James, third Earl of Northampton, by his second wife, Mary daughter of Viscount Campden. His father died whilst he was a child, and he was brought up by his brother and educated at St Paul's School. Later, he took a degree at Trinity College, Oxford, and began practising at the Bar. In 1698 he entered the House of Commons, joined the Whigs, and soon devoted all his time to politics.

With the restoration of the fortunes of the Whigs on the accession of George I, he was chosen Speaker, protesting in his first address that 'he had neither memory to retain, judgment to collect, nor skill to guide their debates.' Others rated his abilities higher; he was appointed Treasurer to the Prince of Wales, and in 1722 Walpole added Paymaster-General to his other offices.

On the death of George I in 1727 the new King George II told Walpole to go for his instructions to 'Sir Spencer Compton'. Whether the King intended that Compton should replace Walpole as Prime Minister is not clear, but Compton soon showed that he was unable even to draw up the new King's speech to the Council without Walpole's help. Once Walpole had assured his own continuance in office, he consoled Compton with a peerage, soon promoting him to Earl of Wilmington. He was appointed successively Lord Privy Seal and Knight of the Garter under Walpole, but by the late 1730s his loyalty to his leader was questionable. On Walpole's downfall in 1742 he was appointed First Lord of the Treasury, in reality little more than a cipher to Carteret. Lord Hervey satirized the ministry in a ballad (Carteret is addressing the King):

> *The Countess of Wilmington, excellent nurse,*
> *I'll trust with the Treasury, not with the purse,*
> *For nothing by her I've resolved shall be done:*
> *She shall sit at that board as you sit on the throne.*

By the end of 1742 he was too ill to transact business, and he died in July 1743. He never married, and the earldom passed to his nephew.

Lord Hervey

Lord Hervey considered Spencer Compton's failure to form a ministry in 1727 deserved contempt. When he became Lord Wilmington, Hervey observed:

> 'I think he might have said, like Agrippina, the mother of Nero, in Racine's *Britannicus*:

> *Tous ces présents, hélas! irritent mon dépit,*
> *Je vois mes honneurs croître, et tomber mon crédit.*

> But Wilmington did not seem to feel the ridicule or the contemptibleness of his situation. That snowball level of his, which had opened and that gathered so fast, melted away at as quick a pace; his visionary prospects of authority and grandeur vanished into air, and yet he seemed to be just as well satisfied to be bowing and grinning in the antechamber, possessed of a lucrative employment without credit, and dishonoured by a title which was the mark of his disgrace, as if he had been dictating in the closet, sole fountain of Court favour at home, and regulator of all national transactions abroad.'

HENRY PELHAM

(1696–1754)

'Lie heavy on him, land, for he
Laid many a heavy load on thee.'

Anonymous contemporary lament of Tory squires

BORN IN JANUARY 1696, the second son of Thomas, first Baron Pelham, Henry Pelham was educated at Westminster and at Oxford. Like his elder brother, the Duke of Newcastle, he served his King in the 1715 campaign against the Jacobites, and in 1717 was elected to the House of Commons as member for Seaford.

As soon as Walpole became Prime Minister, Pelham was given office, and from 1730 he held the post of Paymaster-General. On Wilmington's death he became First Lord of the Treasury and Chancellor of the Exchequer, remaining in office until his sudden death eleven years later. To George II, he had become irreplaceable: 'Now,' he declared forlornly, 'I shall have no more peace.' In 1726 Pelham married Lady Catherine Manners, daughter of the second Duke of Rutland. They had six daughters and two sons, both of whom died in 1739 from ulcerated sore throats, an affliction which became known as Pelham's disease.

A Good and Able Man

The notoriously sharp-tongued diarists of the time discovered no trace of scandal that could be attached to Pelham's name, nor indeed anything very uncomplimentary that could be said against him. According to Lord Hervey:

'... Mr Pelham ... was strongly attached to Sir Robert Walpole, and more personally beloved by him than any man in

England. He was a gentleman-like sort of man, of very good character, with moderate parts, in the secret of every transaction, which added to long practice, made him at last, though not a bright speaker, often a useful one, and by the means of a general affability he had fewer enemies than commonly falls to the share of one so high in rank.'

Horace Walpole too could find little fault with him:

'When his power was established, he assumed a spirit and authority that became him well. Though he first taught or experienced universal servility in Englishmen, yet he lived without abusing his power, and died poor.'

The worst he could say against him was that he was 'careless of his health, most intemperate in eating, and used no exercise.'

The Long-suffering Brother

Henry Pelham and the Duke of Newcastle are the only two brothers ever to have been successive Prime Ministers. In some ways, the Duke was more than generous to his younger brother, granting him half the Pelham estates on his marriage to Lady Catherine. Fond as he was of his younger brother though, it was quite impossible for the Duke not to quarrel or take offence, his whole life being spent in a constant state of anxiety and jealousy. His worst moments came when his brother rather than himself was made First Lord. He confessed as much to Lord Hardwicke:

'There is one thing I should mention to you, relating to myself. It must be touched tenderly, if at all. My brother has been long taught to think, by L..d Orford, that he is the only person fit to succeed him and that he has a credit with the King upon that foot, and this leads him into L..d Orford's old method of being the first person, upon all occasions. This is not mere form, for I do apprehend that my brother does think that his superior interest in the Closet, and situation in the House of Commons, gives him great advantage over everybody else. They are indeed great advantages, but may be counter balanced, especially if it is considered over *whom* those advantages are given.

In time, Newcastle was forced reluctantly to accept that there were good reasons for his brother's political dominance. Even so, there were still occasional querulous letters from Newcastle to which Pelham replied with great restaint, and Lord Hardwicke's son revealed that he had heard his father confess that he was tired with 'carrying water between the brothers.'

Esher . . . and White's

For the rest, not much is known about Pelham's domestic life. With the money received from his brother he bought Esher Place, near Claremont, in Surrey, where he lived the life of a country gentleman and landscaped the gardens to the designs of William Kent, as Alexander Pope mentions in his *Epilogue to the Satires*:

> *Pleased let me own, in Esher's peaceful grove,*
> *(Where Kent and nature vie for Pelham's love,)*

The only complaint made against his unblemished private life has been that, when in London, he spent a disproportionate amount of time at the picquet table at White's.

THOMAS PELHAM-HOLLES

Duke of Newcastle (1693–1768)

'You see I am compelled to take the Duke of Newcastle
to be my Minister, who is not fit to be the chamberlain
in the smallest Court in Germany.'

Attributed to GEORGE II (1727–60)

THOMAS PELHAM was born on 21 July 1693, the eldest son of another
Thomas Pelham and his wife Lady Grace Holles, the sister of the
Duke of Newcastle. He was educated at Westminster and at Cam-
bridge and in 1711 succeeded to most of the estates of his uncle, the
Duke of Newcastle. By 1715 he had himself been created the Duke of
Newcastle in return for providing troops against the Pretender.

Newcastle's political career lasted over forty years. He was Secretary of State under both Walpole and his own brother, Henry Pelham, and was himself First Lord of the Treasury twice, from 1754 to
1756 and from 1757 to 1762. It was then that his weaknesses were
most apparent. An industrious worker and competent manager of
electoral business, he had no political strategy and no capacity for
leadership. Having failed to find anyone to manage the House of
Commons for him he was forced first to resign, and then to return,
still nominally Prime Minister, but very much Pitt's underling. The
hostility of George III and of Bute caused his resignation in 1762 but
even then his political career was not over and he was Lord Privy
Seal for the closing months of Grenville's administration in 1765. In
1768 he suffered a stroke, and died on 17 November.

The Duke of Newcastle was married to Lady Henrietta Godolphin.
They had no children.

The Buffoon

The Duke of Newcastle was a figure more at home in the world of comic opera than in that of eighteenth-century politics. His bustling, fidgeting, pompous figure was everywhere to be seen, always late, always nervous, never achieving anything very much. Unfortunately for him, both Lord Hervey and Horace Walpole* had good reasons for disliking him and they were both merciless:

> 'He was Secretary of State without intelligence, a Duke without money, a man of infinite intrigue, without secrecy or policy, and a Minister despised and hated by his master, by all parties and Ministers, without being turned out by any.'

> '. . . those for whom he spoke generally wished he had been silent, and those who listened always wished so.'

Even those, like Lord Chesterfield, who tried to be kind could think of few redeeming features:

> 'The public put him below his level: for though he had no superior parts or eminent talents, he had a most indefatigable industry, a perseverance, a Court craft, and a servile compliance with the will of his sovereign for the time being.'

Hubble Bubble

Nicknames were inevitable for such a man. 'Hubble Bubble' was one of the favourites but another was 'Permis' because he always prefaced anything he said to the King with the question '*Est-il permis?*'

On the Death of his Brother

There were those who doubted the sincerity of Newcastle's grief on hearing about his brother's death in 1754. As usual with Newcastle, his hysterics were comic instead of tragic.

> 'Either grief for his brother's death, or joy for it had intoxicated him. He flung himself at the King's feet, sobbing and crying "God Bless your Majesty" and lay there howling and embracing the King's knees, with one foot so extended that Lord C______, who was luckily in waiting, begged the standers by to retire, with "For God's sake, gentlemen, don't

*Son of Sir Robert Walpole (Prime Minister 1721–42), and a noted diarist and wit.

look at a great man in distress," endeavoured to shut the door, caught his grace's foot, and made him roar out with pain.'

The Bedford House Ball

Newcastle's hypochondria and constant fear of catching cold made him an easy prey to the practical jokes of Horace Walpole and his cronies.

'The ball, at Bedford house, on Monday, was very numerous and magnificent . . . But the delightful part of the night was the appearance of the Duke of Newcastle, who is veering round again, as it is time to betray Mr Pitt. The Duchess [of Bedford] was at the very upper end of the gallery, and though some of the Pelham court were there too, yet they shewed so little cordiality to this revival of connexion, that Newcastle had nobody to attend him but Sir Edward Montague, who kept pushing him all up the gallery. From thence he went into the hazard room, and wriggled, and shuffled, and lisped, and winked, and spied, till he got behind the Duke of Cumberland, the Duke of Bedford, and Rigby; the first of whom did not deign to notice him; but he must come to it. You would have died to see Newcastle's pitiful and distressed figure, – nobody went near him: he tried to flatter people, but they were too busy to mind him: in short, he was quite disconcerted; his treachery used to be so sheathed in folly, that he was never out of countenance; but it is plain he grows old. To finish his confusion and anxiety, George Selwyn, Brand and I, went and stood near him, and in half whispers, that he might hear, said, "Lord how he is broke! how old he looks!" then I said, "This room feels very cold: I believe there never was a fire in it." Presently afterwards I said, "Well, I'll not stay here; this room has been washed today." In short, I believe we made him take a double dose of Gascoign's powder when he went home.'

At George II's Funeral

Newcastle, as we have seen already, was terrified of catching cold. At the funeral of George II, the Duke of Cumberland could not think why his robes felt so heavy. He looked down and found that Newcastle was standing on them to keep his feet warm.

At George III's Coronation

Again, Newcastle's instinct for doing the wrong thing was unerring:

> 'The Coronation is over: 'tis a more gorgeous sight than I imagined . . . Of all the incidents of the day, the most diverting was what happened to the Queen. She had a retiring-chamber, with *all* conveniences prepared behind the altar. She went thither – in the *most convenient* what found she but – the Duke of Newcastle.'

On Being Made a Freeman of Bristol

After over thirty years in political life, Newcastle was given the freedom of the city of Bristol in 1760. He still had to ask Lord Hardwicke how he should reply to the Town Clerk.

A Visit to Pitt

During one of Pitt's illnesses Newcastle visited him in bed to discuss vital matters concerned with the Seven Years' War. There was no fire in the room so Newcastle, to keep warm, eventually leapt fully dressed into another bed. When the Under Secretary came in he was astonished to find his two ministers both sitting up in bed shouting at each other.

WILLIAM CAVENDISH
Fourth Duke of Devonshire (1720–1764)

'I have great dependence on the calm pacific
disposition of the Duke of Devonshire.'

HORACE MANN in a letter to HORACE WALPOLE, 3 December 1756

BORN IN 1720, the eldest son of the third Duke, the Marquis of
Hartington was educated at home and then sent on a Grand Tour. In
1741 he was elected member for Derbyshire and remained in the
House of Commons for ten years.

In 1751 Hartington moved to the Lords, and in 1755 agreed to
become Lord Lieutenant of Ireland. Only a few months later he
became Duke of Devonshire on the death of his father. Newcastle's
ministry had by now collapsed; and the Duke of Devonshire on
account of his influence and integrity, was asked to become Prime
Minister. He was reluctant to accept office, agreeing to do so only
out of an honest desire to serve his country, and was eager to withdraw in July 1757. On his resignation he was appointed Lord Chamberlain, an office he retained until 1762 when the new King, eager to
display his dislike of the Whigs, refused even to see him. The Duke
instantly resigned from all his offices and from political life. Two
years later, at the age of forty-four, he died from dropsy.

In March 1748 he married Charlotte Boyle, Baroness Clifford,
who brought him estates in Yorkshire and in Ireland. They had four
children.

A Good and Honourable Man
No one managed to find anything unpleasant to say about the fourth
Duke. In 1748 Mary Wortley Montagu, on hearing of his marriage,
wrote:

'I do not know any man so fitted to make a wife happy: with so great a vocation for matrimony, that I verily believe, if it had not been established before his time, he would have had the glory of the invention.'

Lord Waldegrave, one of the King's own household, paid tribute to him as Prime Minister:

'. . . though he had been disgusted by faction and perplexed with difficulties, he lost no reputation – for great things had never been expected from him as a minister – and in the ordinary business of his office he had shown great punctuality and diligence, and no want of capacity.'

JOHN STUART
Third Earl of Bute (1713–1792)

'Bute, you are the very man to be envoy at some small
German court where there is nothing to do.'

Attributed to FREDERICK, PRINCE OF WALES (1707–51)

BORN ON 25 May 1713, the elder son of the second Earl of Bute and of
Lady Anne Campbell, John Stuart was educated at Eton and from
1737 to 1741 sat in the House of Lords as a Scottish representative
peer.

It was in 1747 that Bute first met Frederick Prince of Wales when
he was invited to play whist in the royal tent at Egham races.

Soon, he had become a favourite in the royal household, and after
the Prince of Wales's death in 1751 his influence grew over his
widow, the Princess Augusta. He was appointed Groom of the Stole
to the young Prince George, imbuing him over the next few years
with all his own political ideals. When George became King in 1760,
he at once made clear his allegiance: 'My Lord Bute is your good
Friend,' he remarked to the Duke of Newcastle, the then Prime
Minister, 'he will tell you my thoughts at large.'

Lord Bute replaced Newcastle as Prime Minister in May 1762, his
ministry lasting a brief eleven months. One of the most savagely
derided of all Britain's Prime Ministers, Bute was miserable in office.
For the next few years, the King continued to consult Bute privately
but by 1766 his influence had waned. He died, depressed and forgotten, in 1792.

At the age of twenty-three, Bute married Mary Montagu, the
daughter of Lady Mary Wortley Montagu. They had eleven children.

The Hermit of Bute

From 1741 to 1746, Bute spent much of his time as a recluse on the
Isle of Bute,

> 'with as much pomp and as much uncomfortableness in his
> little domestick circle as if he had been King of the Island,
> Lady Bute a forlorn queen, and his children slaves of a despo-
> tick tyrant.'

In his isolation, he spent much of his time reading 'out of the way
books of science', mostly concerned with agriculture, architecture
and botany.

The Man of Fashion

Far from being disconcerted by the demands of London society, Bute
emerged from his self-inflicted exile a sociable man with a particular
liking for masquerades and private theatricals, especially if they gave
him the opportunity to display 'the best leg in London'.

Princess Augusta

It is doubtful whether Bute was actually Princess Augusta's lover, but
at the time there is no doubt that everyone was quite sure he was.
Horace Walpole went so far as to declare that he was 'as convinced of
amorous relations as if I had seen them together.' When the Princess
herself commented on the immodest conduct of one of her more
glamorous maids of honour, Elizabeth Chudleigh, the latter replied
quickly: 'Votre Altesse Royale sait que chacune a son But.'

The Doubting Minister

Even at the start of his short political career, Bute revealed a few
self-doubts and reservations about politics in a letter to his King. He
was never concise.

> 'As I now launch out into a stormy sea in hopes that I may in
> some measure answer your expectations that I may do some
> little good, here suffer me, Sir, to desire in the most solemn
> manner that I may have your Royal promise to ensure me a
> safe retreat again near your person, in case I find myself
> unable to do what I wish, let it proceed from what honest
> cause it may; whether from the storm of faction bearing me

down, from my talents not being calculated for the business I
enter on, from the independency of my mind not being able to
undergo the drudgery of public business, or lastly from finding my health and constitution impaired by it, or events of
private life rendering it insupportable to me, in any of these
cases suffer me once more to entreat you Sir as my King, my
Master and my Friend, to retire again next your person, or if
that suit not your convenience, remember I this day enter my
protest that you must not be displeased if I at a sudden
warning retire from courts and business at one and the same
minute.'

Less than two years later, he was frank, at least to some, about his
distaste for office:

'such inveteracy in the enemy, such lukewarmness (to give it
no harsher name), such impracticability, such insatiable
dispositions appear in those soi-disant friends, that if I had
but £50 per annum I would retire on bread and water and
think it luxury compar'd with what I suffer.'

To another, he claimed that his resignation had resulted from ill
health caused by a 'great relaxation of my bowells of many years
standing.'

His Unpopularity

Given Bute's extreme unpopularity, it is not surprising that he
wanted to resign in 1763. When Prime Minister he could not appear
undisguised on the streets without risking attack. Chesterfield
claimed:

'He went about the streets timidly and disgracefully, attended
at a small distance by a gang of bruisers, the scoundrels and
ruffians that attend the Bear Gardens.'

A jackboot and a petticoat, the caricaturists' emblems for Bute and
Princess Augusta, were frequently burned by mobs. As late as 1769 a
rabble attacked his house in London, and in 1771 effigies of himself
and the Princess were beheaded and burned by chimney sweepers on
Tower Hill.

The Man of Learning

A later Prime Minister, Shelburne, did his best to belittle Bute's erudition, condemning it as:

> '...A great deal of superficial knowledge, such as is commonly to be met with in France and Scotland, chiefly upon matters of Natural Philosophy, Mines, Fossils, a smattering of mechanicks, a little Metaphysics, and a very false taste in everything.'

This was too harsh: Bute was well-read and knowledgeable on many subjects. At Luton Hoo, which he bought in 1763, he formed an enviable library, an impressive collection of astronomical and mathematical instruments, and a valuable collection of plants.

GEORGE GRENVILLE
(1712–1770)

'When he has wearied me for two hours,
he looks at his watch to see if he may not
tire me for an hour more.'

Attributed to GEORGE III (1760–1820)

BORN ON 14 October 1712, the second son of Richard and Hester Grenville of Wotton, Buckinghamshire, George Grenville was educated at Eton and Christ Church, Oxford, and was called to the Bar in 1735. He entered the House of Commons in 1741 and held minor office almost continuously from 1744 to 1761. Having always lived very much in the shadow of his elder brother Richard and of William Pitt, Grenville surprised everyone by agreeing to become Leader of the House after Pitt's resignation in October 1761.

Grenville became First Lord of the Treasury and Chancellor of the Exchequer on Bute's resignation in April 1763. Although he gradually won the confidence of the House, by his integrity, firmness and administrative ability, the King never found him other than extremely boring. Had George III been able to find anyone to replace him sooner, Grenville's ministry would have been even shorter than it was. He was dismissed in July 1765 and spent his last five years in opposition. Grenville is now chiefly remembered for his notorious 1765 Stamp Act, by which the American colonies were taxed.

In 1749 Grenville married Elizabeth, the daughter of Sir William Wyndham. They had five daughters and four sons, the third himself becoming Prime Minister in 1806.

Marriage
Elizabeth Wyndham was twenty-nine when she married George

Grenville in 1749. It was said at the time that she looked forty-nine, her face having been badly marked by smallpox. She was the grand-daughter of the Duke of Somerset, who, when he died in December 1748, had left her a bequest of only £100 a year, 'just such a legacy as you would give to a housekeeper to prevent her going into service again.'

Despite this disappointment, Elizabeth proved an excellent wife. They had nine children but she also showed such an astute interest in her husband's political career that a friend commented in 1765 that 'she was the first prize in the marriage lottery of our century.'

The Boring Politician

It is often said that Prime Ministers nowadays are not what they were. People who make that remark do not have George Grenville at the forefront of their minds. True, he was extremely worthy, winning for himself this eulogy from Edmund Burke, a political opponent:

> 'Undoubtedly Mr Grenville was a first-rate figure in this country. With a masculine understanding; and a stout and resolute heart, he had an application undissipated and unwearied. He took public business, not as a duty which he was to fulfil, but as a pleasure he was to enjoy; and he seemed to have no delight out of this House, except in such things as some way related to the business that was to be done within it. If he was ambitious, I will say this for him, his ambition was of a noble and generous strain. It was to raise himself not by the low, pimping politics of a court, but to win his way to power, through the laborious gradations of public service; and to secure to himself a well-earned rank in parliament by a thorough knowledge of its constitution, and a perfect practice in all its business.'

It was a friend and cousin, Thomas Pitt, who betrayed the real truth:

> 'He had nothing seducing in his manners. His countenance had rather the expression of peevishness and austerity . . . He was to a proverb tedious . . . He was diffuse and argumenta-tive, and never had done with a subject after he had con-vinced your judgement till he had wearied your attention.'

What was worse, it was simply impossible to divert his attentions away from the world of politics:

'He was a man born to public business, which was his luxury and amusement. An Act of Parliament was in itself entertaining to him, as was proved when he stole a turnpike bill out of somebody's pocket at a concert and read it in a corner in despite of all the efforts of the finest singers to attract his attention.'

CHARLES
WATSON-WENTWORTH

Second Marquess of Rockingham (1730–1782)

'I thought that I had not two men in my bedchamber
of less parts than Lord Rockingham.'

Attributed to GEORGE III, when Rockingham
was made leader of the Whigs.

HE WAS BORN on 13 March 1730, the fifth but eldest surviving son of
Thomas Watson-Wentworth by Lady Mary Finch, daughter of the
seventh Earl of Winchilsea. An adventurous boy, whilst still at Eton
he rode off accompanied by a single servant to join the Duke of
Cumberland's forces at Carlisle against the young Pretender. His
father died in 1750 and, as head of a prominent Whig family and
owner of Wentworth, Rockingham was appointed a lord-lieutenant,
a Lord of the Bedchamber, and, by the time he was thirty, a Knight of
the Garter.

On the death of the Duke of Devonshire in 1764 he was chosen
leader of the Whigs, and after the dismissal of George Grenville in
1765 became First Lord of the Treasury, his first and only political
office. Facing opposition both from the King and from within his
own Cabinet, the first Rockingham administration was doomed to
failure. He was dismissed in August 1766 but, despite ill health and
an apparent dislike for the cares of politics, he continued to rally
the Whigs until his return to office for a few brief months from
March 1782 until his death on 1 July. He and his wife Mary left no
children.

The Runaway Soldier

When Lord Higham, as he was known at the time, rushed off to join
the Duke of Cumberland's forces, like most fifteen-year-olds he gave

48

little thought to the worry this would cause his mother. Later, he was very repentant, writing apologetically to his mother:

'*Dear Madam*,
  When I think of the concern I have given you by my wild expedition, and how my whole life, quite from my infancy, has afforded you only a continued series of afflictions, it grieves me excessively that I did not think of the concern I was going to give you and my father before such an undertaking; but the desire I had of serving my King and country as much as lay in my power, did not give me the time to think of the undutifulness of the action. As my father has been so kind as entirely to forgive my breach of duty, I hope I may, and shall have your forgiveness, which will render me quite happy.
    I am, Madam,
      Your very dutiful son,
        HIGHAM'

The Gambler

It seems that Rockingham would bet on almost anything. According to Horace Walpole, when young he ran a match from Norwich to London between five geese and five turkeys.

The Improving Landlord

The writer Arthur Young paid tribute to Rockingham's achievements as a landlord:

'Every discovery of other counties – every successful experiment in agriculture – every new implement (and many of his Lordship's own invention) introduced at a great expense – Draining, the general management of grassland, and manure . . . are, at Wentworth, carried to the utmost perfection.'

Weaknesses

For the rest, Rockingham was hampered by constant poor health and by his own reticence and timidity. George III wrote to him on one occasion when he was Prime Minister, encouraging him to speak up for himself:

'I am much pleased that opposition has forced you to hear your own voice, which I hope will encourage you to stand forth in other debates.'

News Of His Death

Horace Walpole wrote an account of Rockingham's death in a letter to his friend Horace Mann. He also commented on his character and achievements:

'The death was not a sudden one. The Marquis has been ill above a week, and in danger for some days. At first Dr Warren thought it water in his stomach, then changed his opinion – Sir Noah Thomas doubted whether it was water. It signifies little now what it was. He was always of a very bad constitution. I remember an elder brother of his at Eton, who was subject to violent convulsions, and died of them. Lord Rockingham was extremely splenetic about his health (the consequence of bad) and some years ago wanted to have his side opened, believing he had an abscess there. Six weeks ago I heard that Dr Warren told him he could not live if he continued in business.

'Well! no man ever before attained twice the great object of his wishes, and enjoyed it both times for so short a season: the first time but a year – now, not four months. The death of the late Duke of Devonshire, and the want of a leader, set Lord Rockingham at the head of the Whigs, from his rank, great fortune, and fair character. Those were his pretensions and merit. His parts were by no means great; he was nervous, and mere necessity alone made him at all a speaker in Parliament, where, though he spoke good sense, neither flattery nor impartiality could admire or applaud. He was rather trifling and dilatory in business than indolent. Virtues and amiability he must have possessed, for his party esteemed him highly, and his friends loved him with unalterable attachment. In the excess of faction that we have seen, he was never abused, and no man in public life, I believe, had ever fewer enemies – His death may be more remembered than his actions would have been, and may have greater consequences than any plan of *his* would have had, for he countenanced a system rather than instigated it. Whoever is his successor, will not be of so negative a character.'

WILLIAM PITT
First Earl of Chatham 1708–1778

'In every station
Mr Pitt serv'd the nation
With a noble disdain of her pelf:
Then where's the great crime,
When he sees a fit time
If a man should for once serve himself?'

Anonymous contemporary ditty

BORN IN LONDON on 15 November 1708, the second son of Robert and Harriet Pitt, he was educated at Eton, at Trinity College, Oxford, which he left after one year, and at the University of Utrecht. In 1731 he joined the King's Own Regiment of Horse and in 1735 entered the House of Commons for the pocket borough of Old Sarum. His powerful oratory soon made him leader of the opposition to Walpole, whose dislike of his young opponent was so strong that he deprived him of his commission.

Left a substantial legacy by the Duchess of Marlborough in 1744, Pitt was finally admitted to office in 1746, only to be dismissed in 1755 after the death of his chief ally Pelham. By 1756, George II was obliged to call on Pitt to become Secretary of State in a ministry headed by the Duke of Devonshire. Without the support of the Duke of Newcastle, it was doomed to failure, and in 1757 Pitt finally agreed to take charge of the war and foreign affairs in a ministry theoretically headed by his old enemy Newcastle. Four years of glory followed with Pitt leading the country to tremendous victories against France. By 1761, however, the death of George II and emergence of Lord Bute had undermined Pitt's supremacy and he resigned. Although Pitt took no rewards himself his wife Lady Hester, whom he had married in 1754, was given a peerage and a pension.

In 1766 Pitt, ill and more difficult than ever, was sent for to head, as

Lord Privy Seal, a hand-picked ministry of his own adherents. At the same time he was created Earl of Chatham and given a large pension, but his removal to the Lords meant that much of his popularity evaporated. Suffering from depression verging on insanity, Chatham left the management of affairs to Grafton, finally resigning in 1769. During the 1770s, he made occasional dramatic appearances in the House of Lords and on 7 April 1778 collapsed in the House after opposing a motion for the withdrawal of our fleets and armies from the provinces of North America. He died one month later.

The Manic Depressive

Pitt, his brother Thomas, and four out of five of his sisters, were mentally unstable. Throughout his life, periods of strain and over-activity were followed by attacks of acute nervous depression. Fortunately, whilst managing the conduct of the Seven Years' War all was well, but in 1767, whilst theoretically Prime Minister, he was verging on insanity. Having from boyhood suffered acutely from gout, observers were used to seeing him look weak and ill, but by 1767 it was clear to many that this was not just gout. Thomas Whateley wrote to George Grenville:

> 'He sits most part of the day leaning his head down upon his hands, which are rested on the table. Lady Chatham does not continue generally in the room; if he wants anything he knocks with his stick; he says little even to her if she comes in; and is so averse to speaking, that he commonly intimates his desire to be left alone, by some signal rather than by any expression. The physicians, however, say there is nothing in his disorder which he may not recover, but do not pretend to say there is any prospect of its being soon.'

Grafton was even more alarmed:

> 'Though I expected to find Lord Chatham very ill indeed, his situation was different from what I had imagined; his nerves and spirit were affected to a dreadful degree, and the sight of his great mind bowed down, and thus weakened by disorder, would have filled me with grief and concern, even if I had not long borne a sincere attachment to his person and character ... The interview was truly painful.'

Spending much of his time in a small room at the top of his house at North End, Hampstead, he at one stage pleaded with his landlord to let him add thirty-four new bedrooms for his secretaries and his children. He also expressed the wish to buy a group of neighbouring houses because they were said to impede the view. Not always wanting to eat, when he was hungry he demanded immediate meals. The unfortunate household soon learned to keep a succession of chickens ready in case of need. These would then be put through a hatch in the wall of his room so that Chatham would have no need to face his servants. It was only after Chatham had persuaded the King in October 1768 that he could no longer continue in office that he began to make a steady recovery.

The Actor

As friends and foes alike admitted, Pitt was a tremendous actor. At Court, he was the perfect courtier, bowing so low, it was said, that the tip of his long nose could be seen between his legs; in the House of Commons, he was the incomparable orator. Sometimes, too, he was the brave invalid, wearing black velvet to accentuate his pallor or swathing his gouty leg in flannel. Horace Walpole found fault with one performance in 1756:

> 'The weather was unseasonably warm, yet he was dressed in an old coat and waistcoat of beaver laced with gold; over that, a red surtout, the right arm lined with fur, and appendent with many black ribands, to indicate his inability of drawing it over his right arm, which hung in a crape sling, but which, in the warmth of speaking, he drew out with unlucky activity and brandished as usual. On his legs were riding stockings. In short, no aspiring Cardinal ever coughed for the Tiara with more specious debility.'

There were none, though, to criticize the quality of his last public appearance when he dragged himself into the House of Lords leaning upon his son William and on Lord Mahon, and again wearing black velvet. When his turn to speak came, he raised one hand in the air and declared:

> 'I thank God that I have been enabled to come here this day –
> to perform my duty, and to speak on a subject which is so

deeply impressed on my mind. I am old and infirm – have one foot, more than one foot, in the grave. I have risen from my bed to stand up in the cause of my country – perhaps never again to speak in this House.'

Before the debate was over he had collapsed, caught in the arms of the Duke of Cumberland, Temple, and Lord Fitzwilliam.

Lady Hester

When Pitt married Lady Hester Grenville in 1754, she was thirty-three and he was already forty-six. She was an exemplary wife, nursing him through gout and depression with a good-natured devotion that never faltered. Thomas Coutts described her as 'the cleverest *man* of her time in politics and business' and from 1773 sent all his letters about the family's precarious finances to her rather than to her husband. After Chatham's death, she took over full control of the family estates, managing much more efficiently than ever her husband had and admitting in her Accounts:

> 'State of my affairs from May 1778: I had no money to set out with. The grant paid nothing to me till the year 1780 – I had Burton (Pynsent) – till 1780 it paid nothing (being let) beyond the annuitants and taxes . . . the Farms all out of condition . . . Hayes was an expense both to me and Lord Chatham very considerable . . . I kept Burton House in repair, finished the housekeeper's room and the rooms over: left the garden and plantations in order and have improved the farms.'

The Devoted Father

Pitt had five children, all of whom he loved dearly. He gave them as much of his time as he could, joining Hetty chasing butterflies on the lawn, and teaching the boys to ride. When separated from them, he begged Hester to send news:

> 'Send me, my sweetest life, a thousand particulars of those *little-great* things which, to those who are blessed as we, so far surpass in excellence and exceed in attraction, all the *great-little* things of the busy restless world.'

When he was left in charge on one occasion he passed on to Hester extraordinary details of their state of health:

'My account is happy, Dearest love. Our sweet little boy passed the night well, and is quite easy this morning, having had, before going to bed, a copious motion. The discreet Pam and I agreed to give but four grains of rhubarb this morning, with confection, which William took about the hour of six. As he is not yet out of bed, I can say nothing of looks, but I trust I shall find him well enough to take the air if the day proves fine. I have seen the maid who sat up in his room, she says his sleep was perfectly quiet.'

The worst letter writer of the age

Many of Pitt's letters were neither so frank nor so clearly expressed. With Hester, he sometimes tried just too hard, as when he asked:

'What Guardian angel of mine can have so blinded you, and poured into your noble Heart a tender delusion so infinitely flattering to my glory and partial to my Happiness or to draw from you so sweet an excess of everything that can exalt and bless me about the lot of mortals?'

When replying to a letter from Bute offering him a choice of various royal favours, he became excessively reverential:

'Penetrated with the bounteous favour of a most benign sovereign and Master, I am confounded with his condescension in deigning to bestow one thought about an inclination of his servant, with regard to the modes of extending to me the marks of his royal beneficence.'

The Haughty Politician

As Secretary of State, Pitt would not, according to Shelburne, allow his Under-Secretaries to sit in his presence. To those who dared cross him, he was contemptuous. When the Lord-Lieutenant of Rutland, the Earl of Exeter, wrote to argue about a militia matter, he must have been startled to receive the following reply:

'*My Lord,*
 The matter of your Lordship's letter surprises me as much as the style and manner of it. I never deceive, nor suffer any man to tell me I have deceived him. I declare upon my honour, I know nothing of the order to march the Rut-

landshire militia, if any such be given. I desire, therefore, to know what your Lordship means by presuming to use the expression of being deceived by me. I am your Lordship's humble servant.

W. Pitt

I delay going out of town till I hear from your Lordship.'

The Landscape Gardener

Pitt took a particular interest in landscape gardening, spending large sums of money planting trees at both Hayes and Burton Pynsent. When asked about his former employer the ninety-two-year-old coachman John Mumford commented in 1833 that Chatham's favourite pursuit had been 'taking up and re-planting trees'. There was something manic about it all: trees were, if necessary, planted by torchlight and at Burton Pynsent one hundred and fifty trees were ordered by sea from Halifax. They arrived at Plymouth and then had to be carted the whole way across Devon and Somerset.

The Poet

In 1772, hearing that David Garrick, the actor, was in the area, Chatham invited him to visit Burton Pynsent with the words:

> *Leave, Garrick, the rich landscape, proudly gay,*
> *Dock, forts, and navies bright'ning all the bay;*
> *To my plain roof repair, primaeval seat!*
> *Yet there no wonders your quick eye can meet,*
> *Save, should you deem it wonderful to find,*
> *Ambition cur'd, and an impassioned mind;*
> *A statesman without power and without gall,*
> *Hating no courtiers, happier than them all;*
> *Bow'd to no yoke, nor crouching for applause;*
> *Vot'ry alone to freedom and the laws.*
> *Herds, flocks, and smiling Ceres deck our plain.*
> *And, interspers'd, an heart-enlivening train*
> *Of sportive children frolic o'er the green;*
> *Meantime, pure love looks on, and consecrates the scene.*
> *Come, then immortal spirit of the stage,*
> *Great Nature's proxy, glass of ev'ry age!*
> *Come, taste the simple life of Patriarchs old,*
> *Who, rich in rural peace, ne'er thought of pomp or gold.*

AUGUSTUS HENRY FITZROY

Third Duke of Grafton (1735–1811)

'Like an apprentice, he thought the world should
be postponed to a whore and a horse race.'

Letters, HORACE WALPOLE (1717–97)

BORN IN September 1735, Augustus Henry Fitzroy was the son of
Lord Augustus Fitzroy, a naval officer who died from malaria when
he was only twenty-five. He went to Westminster and to Peterhouse,
Cambridge, and in 1756 entered the House of Commons as MP for
Bury St Edmunds. A few months later, on the death of his grand-
father he became Duke of Grafton and soon afterwards was appointed
Lord-Lieutenant of Suffolk.

At the age of thirty in 1765, Grafton took office as Secretary of
State in Rockingham's ministry. After nine months, and having failed
to bring Pitt into the ministry, he resigned. When Pitt (now Lord
Chatham) became Prime Minister and Lord Privy Seal in 1766,
Grafton, his devoted follower, was made first Lord of the Treasury.
By March 1767 Chatham's ill health meant that Grafton had in effect
replaced him as Prime Minister and after Chatham's resignation in
1768 Grafton, by now disillusioned with politics, reluctantly took his
place. He made way for Lord North in 1770 and in 1771 agreed to
become Lord Privy Seal. He resigned in 1775 over the government's
American policy, returning to the Privy Seal in 1782, first under
Rockingham and then again under Shelburne.

Although he continued occasionally to speak in the House of
Lords, Grafton gradually retired from the political scene. He died in
1811 at the age of 77.

Grafton was married first to Anne Liddell, by whom he had three
sons and one daughter. They drifted apart and Grafton divorced her

in 1769. Two months later he married Elizabeth Wrottesley, daughter of the Dean of Windsor. She bore him twelve children.

Marriage and Divorce

Although it was common in the eighteenth century for married men (and women) to have clandestine affairs, divorce was unusual. Grafton had married Anne Liddell when he was twenty-one, and after only a few years they separated. What offended society was that Grafton, whilst head of his ministry, flaunted his mistress at the Opera in the presence of the Queen, and even paraded her at his own house. The lady in question was Nancy Parsons, the daughter of a Bond Street tailor, who had lived in the West Indies with a merchant called Horton. She was the heroine of a contemporary rhyme:

> *From fourteen to forty, our provident Nan*
> *Has devoted herself to the study of man.*

Sometimes known as Mrs Horton, she was rather unfortunately described as 'the Duke of Grafton's Mrs Horton, the Duke of Dorset's Mrs Horton, everybody's Mrs Horton'.

Grafton came under strong attack, particularly in the letters of 'Junius', anonymous but venomous epistles appearing regularly in the *Public Advertiser*. Luckily for him, the deserted Duchess herself took a lover, and became pregnant by him, thus providing her husband with the opportunity of obtaining a divorce. Very soon afterwards Grafton abandoned his mistress, remarried, and became a pillar of respectability. Later in life, he became a regular worshipper at a Unitarian chapel in the Strand and published several works on religion and morality.

And Politics

Shy and sensitive, Grafton often appeared more interested in his estates and in horse-racing than in politics. Even in 1768, at the height of Grafton's power and influence, Grenville could write in a letter:

> 'The account of the Cabinet Council meeting being put off, first for a match at Newmarket, and secondly because the Duke of Grafton had company in his house, exhibits a lively picture of the present administration.'

FREDERICK NORTH
Second Earl of Guilford (1732–92)

'When Barré stern, with accents deep
Calls up Lord North and murders sleep
And if his Lordship rise to speak,
Then wit and argument awake.'

DAVID GARRICK (1717–79)

THE HON. Frederick North was born in April 1732, the eldest son of Francis North who, after 1729, was third Baron Guilford, and after 1734 was seventh Baron North. He was educated at Eton, where he was known as Blubbery North, and at Trinity College, Oxford, and in 1754 he entered the House of Commons.

At the age of twenty-three, North married a sixteen-year-old heiress, Anne Speke. From 1759 to 1765 he was Junior Lord of the Treasury and in 1766 was appointed Joint Paymaster by Chatham. At the end of 1767 he became Chancellor of the Exchequer and Leader of the House of Commons, and in 1770 George III, who had for a time been taught by North's father, persuaded him to become First Lord of the Treasury. For a time all went well, and in 1774 Chatham was forced to admit that 'North serves the crown more successfully and more sufficiently upon the whole than any other man now to be found could do'. However, the reverses of the American War undermined his authority and he urged the King for several years to let him retire before he was finally allowed to do so in 1782. He returned to power in coalition with Fox a year later but the King remained hostile to the alliance seizing the excuse of the defeat of Fox's India Bill in the Lords to dismiss his ministers. Always near-sighted, North went completely blind in his retirement. He died from dropsy at the age of sixty in August 1792.

Appearance

North was described by Horace Walpole in his memoirs of the reign of George III:

> 'two large prominent eyes that rolled about to no purpose (for he was utterly short-sighted), a wide mouth, thick lips, and inflated visage gave him the air of a blind trumpeter. A deep untuneable voice, which, instead of modulating, he enforced with unnecessary pomp, a total neglect of his person, and ignorance of every civil attention, disgusted all who judge by appearance.'

According to Lord Broughton, Heber heard that in Algiers North asked the Dey permission to see his women. After giving the matter some thought, the Dey decided, 'He is so ugly, let him see them all.'

The Family

At Covent Garden one night between acts, the man sitting next to Lord North asked him:

'Who is that plain-looking lady in the box opposite?'
'That is my wife.'
'Oh, I don't mean her, I mean the lady next to her.'
'That, sir, is my daughter: we are considered to be three of the ugliest people in London.'

Trouble with Dogs

Once, while he was in the middle of a speech, a dog found its way into the chamber and started to bark continuously. It was driven out but found its way back only to begin barking again. North paused, looked at it, and remarked 'Spoke once.'

Having been appointed Joint Paymaster with George Cooke, North was walking, for the first time, up the steps to the office he was to share with Cooke. Looking down, he saw on the steps a heap of dog mess so he turned to the messenger behind him and ordered: 'Take that away, and give his half of it to Mr Cooke.'

Help Cometh From . . .

A poor cousin of Lady North, the Reverend William Speke, was once invited to preach to North. He chose the text 'Help cometh not from the East, nor from the West, nor yet from the South.' Soon afterwards, Dr Speke was appointed to a better living near Ilminster.

Sleeping

North was often accused of being asleep on the Treasury Bench. On one occasion, an opponent, enraged at the sight of the slumbering North, exclaimed: 'Even now, when voices of warning and protestations are raised against him, the noble Lord is asleep,' to which North, without opening his eyes, retorted, 'I wish to God I was.'

In 1769, after he had presented the annual budget proposals, North was compelled to listen to an opposition attack led by George Grenville. Grenville embarked on what was evidently going to be a very lengthy history of past revenues and expenditures by the government, so North asked a neighbour to wake him up when Grenville reached modern times. After a while, the obliging neighbour prodded him. North listened to Grenville again for a few moments and then protested: 'Zounds! You have waked me a hundred years too soon.'

A Compromise

A member of the Opposition put forward what he claimed was a compromise but which, in fact, conceded nothing. 'The reciprocity is all on one side,' protested North.

Concerts

When George III scolded him for never going to concerts, arguing: 'Your brother, the Bishop, never misses them, my lord,' North had his reply ready:

'Sir, if I were as deaf as my brother, the Bishop, I would never miss them either.'

Billingsgate

When he was presented with a petition from constituents of Billingsgate by a man who found it necessary to add his own coarse arguments to their case, North remarked:

'I cannot deny that the Hon. Alderman speaks not only the sentiments, but the very language of his constituents.'

On His Resignation

North resigned on a bitterly cold and snowy day. As a result of the news of his resignation, the House rose much earlier than usual and many members had to wait for their carriages. North had his waiting at the door, got in with some friends, and said:

'Goodnight, gentlemen, it is the first time I have known the advantage of being in the secret.'

In Retirement

His happy domestic life was described by Horace Walpole who wrote that he found:

> 'the unremitting attention of Lady North and his children most touching. Mrs North leads him about, Miss North sits constantly by him, carves meat, watches his every motion, scarce puts a bit into her own lips; and if one cannot help commending her, she colours with modesty and sorrow till the tears gush from her eyes. If ever loss of sight could be compensated, it is by so affectionate a family.'

Meeting with Barré

Out walking in Tunbridge Wells, he was told he was being approached by his old political enemy, Colonel Barré, who was now also blind. Instead of slipping away, North stopped his old adversary and spoke to him:

> 'Though you and I have had our quarrels in the past, I wager there are no two men in England who would be happier to see one another today.'

A Tribute

In the preface to the fourth volume of the Bury edition of the *Decline and Fall*, Gibbon wrote:

> 'Were I ambitious of any other Patron than the Public, I would inscribe this work to a Statesman, who, in a long and stirring, and at length an unfortunate administration, had many political opponents, almost without a personal enemy; who has retained, in his fall from power many faithful and disinterested friends, and who, under the pressure of severe infirmity, enjoys the lively vigour of his mind, and the felicity of his incomparable temper. Lord North will permit me to express the feelings of friendship in the language of truth.'

WILLIAM PETTY[*]
Second Earl of Shelburne, First Marquess of Lansdowne (1737–1805)

'The Jesuit of Berkeley Square.'

Attributed to GEORGE III (1760–1820)

BORN IN Dublin on 20 May 1737, William was the son of the Hon. John Fitzmaurice and his wife, Mary. As a boy, he spent a lot of time with his grandparents at Kerry, where he learned little. After his father had been made an Earl, more attention was given to the education of the son and heir, and William was sent to Christ Church, Oxford.

During the Seven Years' War, Fitzmaurice fought in the Foot Guards, was made a colonel, and appointed aide-de-camp to George III. On his father's death in 1761, he entered the House of Lords and only two years later became President of the Board of Trade in Grenville's administration. After only five months he resigned, but was soon in office again, this time as Chatham's Secretary of State (1766–8). In 1782, he again became Secretary of State, and on Rockingham's death later that year the King asked him to form a ministry. Like quite a few other politicians in the first years of the reign of George III, Shelburne was mistrusted by the King. He was also disliked by many of his colleagues, and survived as First Lord of the Treasury for only a few months. By the end of February 1783 he had resigned and never held political office again. In 1784 Pitt made him a Marquess. He died in May 1805 at the age of sixty-eight.

Shelburne was married first to the Lady Sophia Carteret, by whom

---

[*]William's father assumed the name of Petty in 1751 when he inherited the fortunes of his mother's family.

he had two sons. She died in 1771 and in 1779 he married the Lady Louisa Fitzpatrick by whom he had a son and a daughter.

Unpopularity

Shelburne had the distinction of being the most unpopular politician of his age. Horace Walpole was particularly venomous:

> 'His falsehood was so constant and notorious that it was rather his profession than his instrument . . . A Cataline and a Borgia were his models in an age when half their wickedness would have suited his purposes better.'

Nathaniel Wraxall, a politician and author of historical memoirs, gave a more balanced judgement:

> 'In his person, manners and address, the Earl of Shelburne wanted no external quality requisite to captivate or conciliate mankind. Affable, polite, communicative, and courting popularity, he drew round him a number of followers or adherents. His personal courage was indisputable. Splendid and hospitable at his table, he delighted his guests by the charms of his conversation and society. In his magnificent library, one of the first of its kind in England, he could appear as a philosopher and a man of letters. With such various endowments of mind, sustained by rank and fortune, he necessarily excited universal consideration, and seemed to be pointed out by nature for the first Employments. But the confidence which his moral character inspired did not equal the reputation of his abilities. His adversaries accused him of systematic duplicity and insincerity.'

He was widely known as 'Malagrida', a name first given to him by the *Public Advertiser*. (Malagrida was a well-known Portuguese Jesuit.) It is said that Goldsmith once remarked:

> 'Do you know that I never could conceive the reason why they call you Malagrida, for Malagrida was a very good sort of man.'

Gainsborough, after failing miserably to achieve Shelburne's likeness, flung down his pencil and declared crossly:

> 'D—— it! I never could see through varnish, and there's an end.'

The reasons for his unpopularity are not hard to find. He appeared devious and affected: the Prince of Wales, the future George IV, described him advancing to receive the Garter 'bowing on every side, smiling and fawning like a courtier.' He was also tactless and arrogant, contemptuous of politicians and of political parties. He did not even inspire loyalty in some of the intellectuals he claimed as friends. Jeremy Bentham, who spent some time at Bowood, Shelburne's country house, later wrote:

> '. . . his manner was very imposing, very dignified, and he talked his vague generalities in the House of Lords in a very emphatic way, as if something grand were at the bottom of it all, when, in fact, there was nothing at all.'

The Intellectual Politician

Despite his early lack of formal education, Shelburne grew to be a man of culture and learning. Many of his political ideas were in advance of those of his contemporaries (e.g. on Catholic emancipation and parliamentary reform) and his houses at Bowood and Berkeley Square became refuges for the most liberal thinkers of the time – men like Benjamin Franklin, Samuel Johnson, Priestley, Mirabeau and Romilly. His enormous library was finally sold by Sotheby's. The sale lasted thirty-one days.

WILLIAM HENRY CAVENDISH-BENTINCK

Third Duke of Portland (1738–1809)

'He totters' [jibed the opposition] 'on a crutch,
His brain, by sickness long depressed
Has lost the sense it once possessed,
Though that's not saying much.'

Anonymous contemporary satire

BORN IN April 1738, the eldest son of the second Duke, Lord Titchfield, as he was known, was educated at Eton and at Christ Church, Oxford and in 1762 took his place in the House of Lords as his father's successor.

At first an enthusiastic Whig, Portland took office briefly as Lord Chamberlain in Rockingham's first ministry, and as Lord Lieutenant of Ireland in his second. He refused to take office under Shelburne but in 1783 agreed to become nominal head of the notorious Fox-North coalition. It was an uneasy alliance, distrusted by the King from the start, and when Fox's India Bill failed in the House of Lords, the ministry collapsed.

During the first years of opposition to Pitt, Portland continued through rank and influence to lead the Whigs. Disenchanted with Fox's support of the French Revolution, Portland gradually became a supporter of the ruling Tories and in 1794 accepted the Home Office. Under Addington he was Lord President of the Council, and remained in the Cabinet without a post in Pitt's second ministry. In 1807, on the fall of the coalition Ministry of All Talents, he was asked to form a government. He was now approaching seventy, weak and unfit for any sort of office, let alone that of Prime Minister. He tottered on for two and a half years, the nominal head of a government lacking almost any cohesion. Portland suffered a stroke in August 1809 and resigned. He died in October.

In 1766 Portland married Lady Dorothy Cavendish, the only daughter of the fourth Duke of Devonshire (see above). They had four sons and one daughter.

An Unfit Prime Minister

Portland is chiefly remembered for his total incapacity for office in his second ministry. He never spoke in Parliament, hardly ever attended Treasury meetings, and sometimes was not even told of planned Cabinet meetings. At least he recognized his own shortcomings, admitting before he accepted office:

> 'My fears are not that the attempt to perform this duty will shorten my life, but that I shall neither bodily nor mentally perform it as I ought.'

Patron of the Arts

His house at Wellbeck was filled with treasures. In 1784 he excelled himself buying from Sir William Hamilton the Roman glass known as the Barberini (or Portland) vase, which is now in the British Museum.

WILLIAM PITT
(1759–1806)

'A sight to make surrounding nations stare:
A Kingdom trusted to a schoolboy's care'

The Rolliad, 1784*

WILLIAM PITT was born in May 1759 at Hayes, the second son of William Pitt and of Lady Hester Grenville. Often ill as a boy, he was not sent away to school, but went at the precociously early age of fourteen to Pembroke Hall, Cambridge. He was called to the Bar in 1780 and entered the House of Commons in 1781 where he made an immediate impression. When Shelburne became Prime Minister in 1782, Pitt was appointed Chancellor of the Exchequer at the age of twenty-three. On Shelburne's fall, Pitt was himself twice within a month invited to become Prime Minister. He refused, recognizing that he would be dependent on North's support. Within less than a year, the Fox-North coalition had fallen, and Pitt had returned to office as First Lord of the Treasury and Chancellor of the Exchequer. He was twenty-four.

Few expected Pitt's administration to last longer than several weeks. In fact, he was in power continuously for the next seventeen years. A brilliantly successful peacetime administrator, serious problems began to emerge only after the outbreak of war with France. It was his desire to remove disabilities from the Irish Catholics that caused his resignation in 1801. In 1804 he returned but faced stronger opposition within the House of Commons. He was also by now a sick man. Defeats at Ulm and Austerlitz, as well as the death of Nelson, depressed him and he died on 23 January 1806 at the age of forty-six.

*A series of verses about MPs produced by members of the Whig opposition.

The Precocious Child

The ablest child of Lord Chatham, Pitt was groomed for stardom from an early age. Near the end of his life, Lord Chatham wrote a letter to his wife, addressing some lines 'to the *Hope* and *Comfort* of my Life, my dear William'.

By the age of thirteen, William had written a five-act tragedy in blank verse, called *Laurentius King of Clarinium*. He had been asked to read aloud from Shakespeare and from Milton, and, even more impressive, to translate passages from the classical authors as he read:

> 'When I was a lad, my father used every evening to make me translate freely before him and the rest of the family, those portions of Livy, Virgil and c. which I had read in the morning with my tutor, Mr Wilson.'

An Encounter with Gibbon

In 1780 Edward Gibbon the eminent historian, and Pitt were fellow-guests at a dinner given by members of Lincoln's Inn for officers of the militia who had protected the Inn during the Gordon riots. It seems that the author of *The Decline and Fall of the Roman Empire* expected to hold the stage, but the young William Pitt was not content to listen in silence. Gibbon's host described what happened:

> 'Mr Gibbon, nothing loath, took the conversation into his own hands, and very brilliant and pleasant he was during the dinner and for some time afterwards. He had just concluded, however, one of his best foreign anecdotes, in which he had introduced some of the fashionable levities of political doctrine then prevalent, and, with his customary tap on the lid of his snuff-box, was looking round to receive our tribute of applause, when a deep-toned but a clear voice was heard from the bottom of the table, very calmly and civilly impugning the correctness of the narrative and the propriety of the doctrine of which it had been made the vehicle. The historian, turning a disdainful glance towards the quarter whence the voice proceeded, saw, for the first time, a tall, thin, and rather ungainly-looking young man, who now sat quietly and silently eating some fruit. There was nothing very prepossessing or very formidable in his exterior, but, as the few words he had uttered appeared to have made a considerable impres-

sion on the company, Mr Gibbon, I suppose, thought himself bound to maintain his honour by suppressing such an attempt to dispute his supremacy. He accordingly undertook the defence of the propositions in question, and a very animated debate took place between him and his youthful antagonist, Mr Pitt, and for some time was conducted with great tact and brilliancy on both sides. At length the genius of the young man prevailed over that of his senior, who, finding himself driven into a corner from which there was no escape, made some excuse for rising from the table and walked out of the room. I followed him and, finding that he was looking for his hat, I tried to persuade him to return to his seat. "By no means," said he. "That young gentleman is, I have no doubt, extremely ingenious and agreeable, but I must acknowledge that his style of conversation is not exactly what I am accustomed to, so you must positively excuse me." And away he went in high dudgeon, notwithstanding that his friend had come to my assistance. When we returned to the dining room we found Mr Pitt proceeding very tranquilly with the illustration of the subject from which his opponent had fled, and which he discussed with such ability, strength of argument, and eloquence, that his hearers were filled with profound admiration.'

The Aloof Politician

Although it was always said that Pitt was warm and gay with his friends, he did not make friends easily, and to the rest of the world he presented a chilling exterior. Sir Nathaniel Wraxall, an MP and author of historical memoirs, noticed how, when he went into the House of Commons, he paid no attention at all to his backbenchers:

'From the instant that Pitt entered the doorway ... he advanced up the floor with a quick and firm step, his head erect and thrown back, looking neither to the right nor to the left, nor favouring with a nod or a glance any of the individuals seated on either side, among whom many who possessed five thousand pounds a year would have been gratified even by so slight a mark of attention.'

The Bachelor

Pitt was renowned for his indifference to women. There were probably many mothers who longed for him as a son-in-law. Probably the best known was Madame Necker, the wife of the French finance minister, who asked Horace Walpole to raise with Pitt the suggestion that he should marry Madame Necker's daughter. Nothing came of the suggestion and the daughter went on to become Madame de Staël.

It was not that Pitt did not occasionally enjoy the company of women. For a while the imperious Jane, Duchess of Gordon was his favourite hostess, and she could hardly be said to have been shy and retiring:

> *The Duchess triumphs in a manly mien;*
> *Loud is her accent, and her phrase obscene.*

When they met again after a long spell of not seeing each other she challenged him with the words: 'Well, Mr Pitt, do you talk as much nonsense now as you used to do when you lived with me?'

'I do not know, madam, whether I talk so much nonsense,' he replied, 'I certainly do not *hear* so much.'

For a very short while at the end of 1796 and the beginning of 1797 it seemed that his friendship with Lord Auckland's daughter, the young Eleanor Eden, might end in marriage. It seems that he loved her, and she certainly loved him. Why the match should have failed, then, remains a mystery. Pitt wrote to her of 'decisive and insurmountable obstacles' to the match. He can hardly have thought that his position was too insecure to take a wife. It has been suggested that Pitt was afraid of the streak of insanity in his family but in a letter to his friend Addington (the future Prime Minister) there is no hint that this was the reason for his withdrawal:

> 'The first answer indeed [from the Edens] . . . tho' thoroughly kind, was the most embarrassing possible, as it stated that the sentiments entertained [by Pitt] to be mutual and pressed for explanation and discussion, proposing at the same time any interval of delay in order to take the chance of overcoming the difficulties and desiring me to continue coming in the interval as if nothing had happened. I had then nothing left but to convey in my answer quite explicitly tho' with as much tenderness as I could, that the decision I had felt myself obliged to take was final and that further discussion could only produce increased anxiety and could lead to no good.

This was understood and received as I meant it should; and the answer I received last night, considers the thing as over, and proposes to contradict the reports gradually, and with the delicacy which the subject requires. I hope I may collect from the manner in which it is written that the shock has been as little distressful in its consequences to any part of the family, as I could flatter myself. If that hope should be well-founded, I think I can command my feelings enough to bear the rest and not be wanting either to the calls of public duty or to what remains to me of the private relations of my life . . .'

The truth is probably that Pitt, a long-standing bachelor, had thoroughly cold feet about going through with the match and had extricated himself as quickly and as painlessly as possible.

The Heavy Drinker

It was probably when he was at Oxford that Pitt was given the advice to drink a bottle of port a day for the sake of his health. The advice proved disastrous, Pitt becoming a very heavy drinker, particularly during the years when he was running the war against Napoleon. By 1800 he was forced to live with the Addingtons for ten days 'for the sake of his health'. Joseph Farrington wrote in his diary:

> 'Sir Walter Farquhar has been down to see him and allows him and the Speaker to drink a bottle between them after dinner but none after supper. Mr Pitt one night pressed for some, but the Speaker was rigid.'

It was years of drink and overwork that together undermined his health and caused his early death at the age of only forty-six. According to his niece, Lady Hester Stanhope, the life he led would have ruined even the healthiest constitution, and Pitt was never strong:

> 'Oh, doctor, what a life was his! Roused from sleep (for he was a good sleeper) with a despatch from Lord Melville; then down to Windsor; then, if he had half an hour to spare, trying to swallow something; Mr Adams with a paper, Mr Long with another, then Mr Rose, then with a little bottle of cordial confection in his pocket off to the House until three or four in the morning; then home to a hot supper for two or three hours

more, to talk over what was to be done the next day: – and wine, and wine. Scarcely up next morning when "rat-a-tat" twenty or thirty people one after another, and the horses walking before the door from two till sunset, waiting for him. It was enough to kill a man – it was murder.'

The Stoical Patient

In 1786 one of Pitt's cheeks swelled, and a tumour was removed by John Hunter at Downing Street. Pitt would not let the surgeon tie down his hands and asked how long the operation would take. He was told six minutes and remained absolutely motionless throughout that time even though he must have been in excruciating pain. When his ordeal was over, his only comment was: 'You have exceeded your time by half a minute.'

The Unmethodical Administrator

A brilliant administrator, Pitt was surprisingly unmethodical. Papers were never neatly filed away in his desk but instead were stuffed in drawers and often forgotten. Replies were never written immediately: the British Ambassador in France wrote asking for the Garter and had to wait a full year for a reply.

Like his father, he was equally bad at managing his personal finances. He seldom looked at his accounts and was seldom out of debt. Unfortunately, unlike his father, he did not have a wife to sort out the financial mess for him. When he died, he was £40,000 in debt even though his friends had raised £12,000 for him as recently as 1801. Wilberforce was convinced he had been cheated:

'This must have been roguery, for he really has not for many years lived at a rate of more than £5 or £6,000 per annum.'

Love of Children

Even when weighed down with the cares of office, Pitt always enjoyed playing with children. In 1804 he joined his niece and three small boys in a game which involved Pitt trying to fight the others off with a cushion whilst they all tried to blacken his face with burnt cork. When the game was at its height, Lord Castlereagh and Lord Liverpool were announced. One of the small boys later recalled how Pitt had washed his face, interviewed his colleagues as quickly as he possibly could, and then returned to the game with undisguised relish.

HENRY ADDINGTON
First Viscount Sidmouth (1757–1844)

'As London is to Paddington
So Pitt is to Addington'

GEORGE CANNING (1770–1827)

'Thank God for a government without one of these damned men of genius in it.'

Anonymous Tory squire

BORN ON 30 May 1757, the eldest son of a middle-class doctor, Addington was educated at Cheam, Winchester, and Brasenose College, Oxford. He read for the Bar, but in 1784, encouraged by the spectacular success of his childhood friend William Pitt, entered the House of Commons as MP for Devizes. Pitt in 1789 chose Addington as Speaker, a position he held with great success until 1801 when he became Prime Minister on Pitt's resignation.

As Prime Minister, Addington was at first successful enough. George III liked and trusted him; Pitt gave him his support; and the country as a whole reacted favourably to a man who made peace and reduced taxation. Soon, though, it became clear that the peace would not last. Addington was not a man to inspire confidence, and it became only a matter of time before Pitt was returned to office.

Addington's political career was by no means over in 1804. Created Viscount Sidmouth in 1805, he was Lord Privy Seal in the Ministry of All Talents, and a reactionary Home Secretary under Liverpool. Finally retiring from the Cabinet in 1824, Sidmouth still had another twenty years ahead of him. He died on 15 February 1844.

Addington was married first to Ursula Mary Hammond, by whom he had two sons and four daughters. She died in 1811 and in 1823 he married Maria Anne Townsend, the widowed daughter of Lord Stowell.

The Doctor

One of the few really interesting things about Addington was that he was so solidly middle class. His father Anthony had begun practising medicine in Reading but, with an astuteness that came from ambition, had chosen to specialize in mental illness. Soon he had moved to London and had become a fashionable physician, daily consulted by the likes of Lord Chatham.

Henry Addington was not ashamed of his background, even though it was frowned on by many. Lord Holland was at least honest when he confessed:

> 'The hostility he met with from the upper classes of society proceeded, I fear, more from his want of birth than his other manifold deficiencies.'

It was rather endearing then that Addington should have so enjoyed parading his smattering of medical knowledge. He told everyone he met how the King's physician had been in despair in 1801 because his royal master could not sleep. 'Hops!' Addington had instantly suggested, a hop pillow had been brought and the King had slept. Even his own brother did not escape from unwanted advice: being told that 'nothing is so effectual in cleansing the kidney and in bringing off nebulous matter from the bladder as a teaspoonful of brandy in soda water'.

It was no surprise that Addington was dubbed 'the Doctor' and ridiculed mercilessly in rhymes and caricatures.

The Poor Speaker

As an orator, Addington was never better than mediocre. He sat in the House of Commons for two years before he dared speak and was appointed Speaker before he ever had chance to master the art of parliamentary debate. When Prime Minister, his efforts were feeble. Harriet Lady Bessborough wrote in a letter:

> 'Hare says he heard but one sentence in Mr Addington's speech the other night. He woke from his sleep and heard: "For as this is that which was said to . . ." Hare was quite satisfied and turned to sleep out the rest.'

The Drinker

Addington, usually a sober, cautious figure, liked wine. He and Pitt once got drunk at a banquet at Canterbury and were booed by a mob:

> 'A pretty story will this make in the papers. The Minister and the Speaker dined with the corporation of Canterbury, got very drunk and were hissed out of the town.'

He was at his worst when Prime Minister. Joseph Farington recorded in his diary:

> 'He wants spirits and courage for his situation and though a temperate man, now drinks perhaps 20 glasses of wine at his dinner before he goes into the House of Commons to invigorate himself.'

The Writing Table

Addington was neither very funny nor very interesting. One of the few humorous stories about him concerns an incident in 1812 soon after Spencer Perceval had been assassinated. Lords Hertford and Cholmondely were leaning on a writing table when it broke. Addington (by now Lord Sidmouth), considerate as always, caught at it to break their fall and covered himself with ink. 'Well, I did hope to have gone out of office with clean hands,' he declared.

On the Reform Bill

As he grew older, Sidmouth became implacably reactionary, attacking Grey for his Reform Bill:

> 'I hope God will forgive you on account of this bill: I don't think I can.'

On Old Age

'In youth, the absence of pleasure is pain, in old age, the absence of pain is pleasure.'

WILLIAM WYNDHAM
Baron Grenville (1759–1834)

'I am not competent to the management of men. I never was so naturally, and toil and anxiety more and more unfit me for it.'

Memoirs, DUKE OF BUCKINGHAM (1753–1813)

BORN IN October 1759, the youngest son of George Grenville (Prime Minister 1763–5) he was educated at Eton and at Christ Church, Oxford. Despite literary leanings, Grenville gravitated towards politics and in 1782 entered the House of Commons. Lord Shelburne made him Chief Secretary for Ireland and when William Pitt, his first cousin, became Prime Minister, Grenville was appointed Paymaster-General. In 1786 he became Vice-President of the Board of Trade, in 1789 Secretary of State, and in 1790, by now elevated to the peerage, he was made Foreign Secretary and Leader of the House of Lords.

When Pitt returned to office in 1804 Grenville refused to serve unless Fox was included. On Pitt's death he was asked to form a government, including in it all the notable men of all parties. After only fourteen months, the Ministry of All Talents, as it was known, collapsed over George III's refusal to accept Roman Catholic emancipation.

Grenville's political career was over. He was still only forty-eight and lived on, mostly in the country, until January 1834 when he died at the age of seventy-four.

In 1792, Grenville married Anne Pitt, the daughter of Lord Camelford and a relative of William Pitt. They had no children.

The Scholar
A distinguished classical scholar at Oxford, in retirement Grenville printed an annotated Homer, and wrote *Nugae Metricae*, a volume

of translations into Latin from Greek, Italian and English. He also edited the letters of his uncle, Lord Chatham (Prime Minister 1766–8).

The Reluctant Politician

Grenville breathed a secret sigh of relief when his political life was over in 1807, admitting in a letter to his brother, Lord Buckingham:

> 'The deed is done and I am again a free man, and to you may I express what it would seem like affectation to say to others, the infinite pleasure I derive from my emancipation.'

Unpopularity

An apparently austere and unsympathetic manner meant that Grenville was disliked by many. The old Lord Liverpool (the father of the future Prime Minister) wrote of him in 1807:

> 'Lord Grenville is the most extraordinary character I ever knew. He has talents of uncommon industry, but he never sees a subject with all its bearings, and consequently his judgment can never be right. He is not an ill-tempered man, but he has no feelings for anyone, not even for those to whom they are most due. He is in his outward manner offensive to the last degree. He is rapacious with respect to himself, and his family, but a great economist with respect to everyone and to everything else.'

The Warm-Hearted Husband

Towards his wife Anne, Grenville was warm and loving. Some of his friends noticed that marriage had improved him in several ways. Lord Mornington wrote to him in October 1792:

> 'I cannot tell you with how much pleasure I saw your menage. I told Pitt that matrimony had made three very important changes in you which could not but affect your old friends – (1) a brown lapelled coat instead of the eternal blue single breasted, (2) strings in your shoes, (3) very good perfume in your hair powder.'

He and his wife lived at Dropmore, a small estate he had bought in Buckinghamshire. There he collected books, china, prints and pictures, and created a beautiful garden.

THE HON. SPENCER PERCEVAL

(1762–1812)

'Perhaps the most straightforward man I have ever known'

GEORGE III (1760–1820)

'Such was his private, such his public life,
That all who differ'd in polemic strife,
Or varied in opinion with his plan,
Agreed with one accord to love the man.'

Anonymous contemporary epitaph

THE HON. Spencer Perceval was born in London on 1 November 1762, the second son of John, Earl of Egmont, and his wife Catherine, a great-niece of Spencer Compton (Prime Minister 1742–3). He was educated at Harrow and at Trinity College, Cambridge, before deciding as an impoverished younger son, to head for a career at the Bar. In 1790 he married, after a good deal of parental opposition the pretty daughter of Sir James Wilson of Charlton, near Woolwich. They first lived in lodgings over a carpet shop in Bedford Row, their poverty exacerbated by the birth of five children in the first six years of marriage. Fortunately, Perceval's legal career was a success, and in 1796 he was confident enough to broaden his horizons and to enter the House of Commons.

In 1798 Perceval became Solicitor-General, and in 1802 he was promoted to Attorney-General. On the death of Pitt, and his replacement by the Ministry of All Talents, Perceval became the leader of the Opposition. In 1807, in the Portland administration, he was appointed Chancellor of the Exchequer and Chancellor of Duchy of Lancaster, and won widespread admiration of his abilities. On the resignation of Portland in 1809 he became Prime Minister but on 11 May 1812 he was shot by John Bellingham in the lobby of the House of Commons, the only Prime Minister of England ever to be assassinated.

An Evangelical Anglican

Perceval, his wife Jane, and their brood of twelve children, were all staunch Anglicans. Family prayers were said every day, and, once Prime Minister, Perceval wrote a special prayer for Divine Guidance.

When he practised at the Bar, Perceval went to great lengths to avoid seeing his clients on a Sunday. On the rare occasions when he was forced to agree to a Sunday consultation, he always delayed them until after the evening church service. Later, he once put off the re-assembly of parliament so that members would not have to travel on a Sunday.

A Philanthropist

Despite being far from rich, Perceval always gave away as much as he could to help the poor. When he moved from Bedford Row to Lincoln's Inn Fields he told the parish clerk to help what poor people he thought fit and then to send him the bill.

When Pitt died, his friend Wilberforce tried – with little success – to raise a fund to pay off his debts. Perceval was alone in immediately offering £1000, a sum he could little afford.

Life at Downing Street

Although a man who loved nothing better than the company of his wife and children, while at 10 Downing Street Perceval lived an almost separate existence. He ate both breakfast and dinner alone, seeing his family really only on Sunday when he and his wife led a procession of their children 'their faces washed and their hair pleasingly combed' to St Margaret's, Westminster or, if they were in the country, to Ealing Parish Church.

Portents of Doom

When Jane Perceval sorted through her husband's papers after his death she found part of his last message to his eldest son where he wrote of his life 'with a sense of the improbability of its long continuance'. Later Lord Arden claimed to have found a copy of the *Rambler* with a note in the margin written by Perceval.

> *'I do not weep, the springs of tears are dry,*
> *And of a sudden I am calm, as if*
> *All things were well, and yet my husband's murdered.'*

Assassination

John Bellingham, 'a tall, large-boned man, about forty years of age, with a long thin visage and aquiline nose' was a man with a carefully nurtured grievance. When young, he had been a merchant's clerk and at one stage had represented a Liverpool firm in Archangel in Russia where he had been imprisoned for five years after falling into debt. After his release and return to England, he had become obsessed with obtaining compensation from the British government, approaching the Foreign Office, members of parliament, the Treasury, and the Prime Minister himself. By May 1812 all his efforts had failed to bear fruit, and he began sitting in the public gallery of the House of Commons returning to his lodgings to get in some daily shooting practice on Primrose Hill.

After lunch on 11 May, Perceval became so absorbed in his work at No. 10 that he was late setting off for the House of Commons. Wilberforce, at a meeting in another house in Downing Street, noticed Perceval rushing past the window and interrupted the discussion to praise the integrity and worth of the Prime Minister.

Just after five, Perceval left his cloak and stick with an attendant at the St Stephen's entrance and entered the crowded lobby of the House of Commons. There his assassin raised his pistol to the Prime Minister's chest, shot him, and then sat down with remarkable calmness on a bench by the wall. Perceval died immediately, his body being taken to the Speaker's picture room where, according to one newspaper, one of his young sons saw it by chance before he had been properly informed of his father's death. His youngest daughter Frederica kept until her death in 1900 various relics of her father, including the blood-stained rug on which he died. Jane Perceval rejected the idea of a burial in Westminister Abbey and buried her husband at St Luke's, Charlton, close to the house where he was born.

Bellingham was tried at the Old Bailey on Friday, 15 May. He was unrepentant and noticeably sane, announcing:

> 'If I am destined to sacrifice my life, I shall meet my doom with conscious tranquility; I shall look forward to it as the weary traveller looks for the promised inn, where he may repose his weary frame, after enduring the pelting of the pitiless storm. Gentlemen, it now remains between God and your consciences as to what your verdict will be.'

The jury needed only ten minutes to examine their consciences before deciding that he was guilty. Two days later he was executed at Newgate in front of a cheering mob who auctioned his clothes as souvenirs.

ROBERT BANKS JENKINSON
Second Earl of Liverpool (1770–1828)

'He was a very honest, upright man and deserves a higher character as a statesman than I dare say History will grant to him.'

Journal: 1820–32, MRS ARBUTHNOT

JENKINSON WAS born on 7 June 1770, the eldest son of Charles Jenkinson, MP, (later Lord Hawkesbury and Earl of Liverpool) by his first wife Amelia, who died before her baby was a month old. He was educated at Charterhouse and at Christ Church, Oxford, where he founded a debating society with George Canning. After a European Tour, he entered the House of Commons as a follower of Pitt, and an active supporter of the war against France, even becoming colonel of a regiment of yeomanry. On Pitt's resignation in 1801 he was appointed Foreign Secretary, moving over to be Home Secretary on Pitt's return to power in 1804, and continuing in the same office under Portland. Under Perceval, Liverpool was Secretary of War and the Colonies. He became First Lord of the Treasury in May 1812 at the age of forty-two after Perceval's assassination.

For the next fifteen years, Liverpool headed a ministry strong enough to deal successfully with the outbursts of disorders occurring in the aftermath of the Napoleonic Wars. In February 1827 he was found unconscious from a stroke on the floor of his study and resigned two months later. He lived on, a pathetic invalid nursed by his second wife, finally dying in December 1828.

Liverpool was married first to Lady Louisa Hervey, the third daughter of the eccentric fourth Earl of Bristol, Bishop of Derry. After her death in 1821 he married Mary Chester. There were no children from either marriage.

Mr Jenkinson as an Undergraduate

Although praised by many as a young man, the young Jenkinson did not please everyone. Lady Strafford met him when staying at Addiscombe, and viewed him critically:

> 'Mr Jenkinson was at Home, from Oxford – he is well educated, well informed, and sensible . . . if he had been my son, I should have wished him to be more inclined to listen to what the Chancellor and Mr Pitt said, than to express his own ideas on Politicks, Government, and Commerce . . . but he spoke well, and his Language was good, and it was obvious that he had really a great Deal of Knowledge. I have a Notion that at Oxford, if they are good Scholars, they contract High Ideas of themselves, which wear off when they come to live with the rest of the world.'

Appearance

It was not meant as a compliment when it was remarked by contemporaries that he had the longest neck in England. His expression too came in for some criticism. James Hare pointed out that he looked 'as if he had been on the rack three times, and saw the wheel preparing for a fourth'.

Liverpool later managed to look distinguished but unkempt. Mrs Arbuthnot described her reaction to Lawrence's portrait of him, on show in London in 1821.

> 'It is impossible to conceive anything more exquisitely like or where the character and the *manière d être* of the individual is more perfectly caught. It has exactly his *untidy* look and slouching way of standing; it has, too, all the profound and penetrating expression of countenance which marks this distinguished statesman.'

The Militia

George Canning, an Oxford friend, took a cynical view of Jenkinson's zeal for service with the militia. Jenkinson made the mistake of showing Canning one of his recruiting sergeant's posters. The temptation was too much for Canning, who immediately secretly produced a long parody on the following lines:

Tight lads, who would wish for a fair opportunity,
Of defying the Frenchmen, with perfect impunity . . .
'Tis the bold Colonel Jenkinson calls you to arm,
And solemnly swears you shall come to no harm.

The parody was printed in the form of a poster, and a whole packet of them was produced at a dinner-party organized by a mutual friend. The packet was addressed to Jenkinson, with a covering note claiming that many copies of the poster had already been pinned up in the streets. The joke was not a success. Jenkinson burst into tears of mortification and had to be comforted for two hours by Lady Malmesbury, a fellow-guest, before he was in a fit state to leave.

The joke did nothing to lessen Jenkinson's devotion to the militia and even after his marriage he used to spend most of the summer with his militia unit.

Marriage

Lord Hawkesbury was not pleased when he learned that his son wished to marry the dowryless daughter of a notorious eccentric. Both the King and the Prime Minister had to intervene on Jenkinson's behalf before his father reluctantly allowed the match to proceed. It was an extremely happy marriage, despite the absence of children, and the couple were rarely separated. When Louisa died in June 1821 Liverpool was so overwhelmed with grief that he refused to see anyone for several days. According to one report, Louisa had left instructions that no one was to touch her body apart from her husband and that when he had finally lifted her into her coffin he had almost fainted.

A Quiet Life

Both Liverpool's wives encouraged him in his quest for a quiet domestic life. Some thought it too quiet, one guest describing a visit to Coombe in 1824 with the words:

> 'This is unquestionably the dullest house in which I ever passed a day.'

There was sometimes some fun. In June 1820 Princess Lieven went to dinner with the Liverpools in London and described how her host had the notion 'of jumping over the back of a big sofa on which I was seated, and establishing himself on a little footstool hovered and then settled on the ground, looking very comic.'

Signs of a Temper

Described by a friend as 'one of the best tempered men living', Liverpool was nevertheless highly strung. As his health gradually deteriorated his temper also worsened and his unfortunate tendency to burst into tears when upset resurfaced. When told that Lord George Cavendish was not going to vote with his Government on one particular issue, Liverpool stamped out of the house and into his waiting carriage muttering all the way 'Damn the Cavendishes'.

The Stroke

On the morning of Saturday 17 February 1827 the Prime Minister suffered a serious stroke. After a few days he was still paralysed on his right side and unable to talk but there was no immediate demand for his resignation. In early March, George IV wrote politely to the Prime Minister's wife to say that her husband was not to be upset by any talk of resignation and it was not until the end of March that it was decided a replacement would have to be found.

GEORGE CANNING

(1770–1827)

'Mr Canning's death will not do all the good it might have done
at a later period. But it is still a great public advantage.'

ARTHUR WELLESLEY, DUKE OF WELLINGTON (1769–1852)

GEORGE CANNING was born in London in April 1770, the son of
George and Mary Ann Canning, a disinherited Irish couple trying to
manage on an annual allowance of £150. Within a year of his birth,
his father had died, and his mother took to the stage in order to
provide for herself and her infant son. When he was eight, Canning
was removed from his mother's care, and brought up by his uncle,
Stratford Canning, a prosperous merchant. He distinguished himself
both at Eton and at Christ Church, Oxford, and was called to the Bar
in 1791.

Canning came into the House of Commons under Pitt's patronage
at the age of twenty-three, and by the end of 1795 had been appointed
Under Secretary at the Foreign Office. In 1800 he married Joan Scott,
an heiress, and was made Joint Paymaster General only to resign with
Pitt a few months later. He consistently opposed Addington's
ministry, but when Pitt returned to power achieved no more than the
minor post of Treasurer of the Navy.

After Pitt's death in 1806 Canning was again in opposition but he
returned to office in 1807 as Foreign Secretary under Portland.
Castlereagh was Secretary for War and the two men soon found
working harmoniously together impossible, eventually fighting a
duel. In 1814 Canning went to Portugal as Ambassador, from 1816 to
1820 he was President of the Board of Control, and in 1822 he again
became Foreign Secretary after the suicide of Castlereagh. Abroad,
his efforts were in favour of popular freedom whilst at home he
advocated Roman Catholic emancipation and reform of the Corn

Laws. Canning at last became Prime Minister after Lord Liverpool had suffered a stroke in 1827 but died after only a few short months in office.

His Mother, the Actress

Not only did Canning's mother become an actress, and a bad one, but she made matters worse by living openly with a dissolute actor, Samuel Reddish, by whom she had several children. In 1783 she decided to marry Richard Hunn, a Plymouth silk mercer, but instead of settling down to a respectable middle age, the couple decided to try their hand at acting together. By the time Canning had got through Oxford he had learned to be critical of his mother's chosen profession. In a letter attempting to show how it could only harm his legal career if it were known that his mother was an actress, he argued:

> '. . . everything is surely to be considered, not so much as what it really is, as what the world *thinks* it to be. When I say everything, I mean only such things as concern neither religion nor morality (where all is fixed and settled beyond the wavering of wordly opinion) – such things as are in themselves indifferent or variable, and therefore take their colour from the light in which the world may please to view them. Among these are professions; and there is perhaps no subject on which public opinion decides more positively than on the respectability or *dis*respectability of different pursuits and occupations.'

Later, Mary Ann's marriage to Hunn broke down and she retired from the stage to try and make her fortune from an eye ointment she had invented. Canning was persuaded to test the ointment and his eye immediately became sore and inflamed.

Canning remained loyal to his mother, but not to the extent of wanting her near him. In 1795 he turned down an invitation to stay with a friend near Plymouth in case his mother decided to visit, which 'would be rather inconvenient and distressing' and he firmly resisted all her demands to be allowed to live near him in London. Even so, he wrote to her weekly, made sure she had enough money, and was painstakingly helpful to all his Reddish and Hunn half-brothers and sisters.

Canning and the Princess

It is likely that Canning had some sort of affair with the notorious Caroline Princess of Wales in the summer of 1799. At that date, she was still a respectable figure, living at Montague House, Blackheath, and being consoled in her seclusion by the company of such pillars of the establishment as Pitt and Eldon. Canning became a regular visitor, and it seems likely that it was a visit to the Princess that Canning was describing to his friend Granville Leveson-Gower when he wrote:

> 'The keeper left us for a few minutes and the thing is too clear to be doubted. What am I to do? I am perfectly bewildered.'

His dilemma was solved for him by his introduction to Joan Scott, with whom he immediately fell in love. It does seem that there probably was something between Canning and the Princess. How else can one explain his evident relief at the Princess's reaction to being informed about Miss Scott? He was received, he said:

> '... it is impossible to say *how* kindly! Never, never shall I forget or cease to be grateful for the generous, amiable, disinterested affection, which was shown on that occasion.'

The Princess became godchild to the Cannings' eldest son, and in 1820 Canning felt honour bound to resign from a Cabinet bent on putting her on trial in order to secure a divorce for her husband, now King George IV.

Duel with Castlereagh

On 19 September 1809 Castlereagh challenged Canning to a duel, the latter having demanded Castlereagh's dismissal from the War Office. Canning took the danger extremely seriously, making his Will, and taking his leave of Joan:

> 'There would be no end to taking leave and of saying how dearly I have loved you. I hope I have made you sensible of this, dearest, dearest, Joan. I hope I have been kind and good and affectionate towards you. I hope I have made you happy. If you have been a happy wife – and if I leave you a happy mother and a proud widow, I am content. Adieu, Adieu.'

The two men accompanied by their seconds met at 6 pm on Putney Heath. Canning's second loaded his gun for him, explaining:

> 'I must cock it for him for I cannot trust him to do it himself. He has never fired a pistol in his life.'

Not surprisingly, the duellists missed each other at the first attempt. Canning fired again and missed, but the second time Castlereagh fired he shot through the flesh of Canning's left thigh. He was immediately helped to a nearby house where a surgeon was already waiting, but he soon returned home where he was well enough to write several letters, including one in which he made light of his wound:

> 'You can hardly conceive how slight a matter it is – provided (that is) that it passes through quite clean, carrying only a little bit of your nankeen breeches so big ⬭ with it – and comes out on the other side, without turning to the right or the left to any of the arteries and bones, etc the which lie thereabouts. If you have a mind to try the experiment, I would recommend Lord Castlereagh as the operator.'

The Bishop's Sermon

After Legg was appointed Bishop of Oxford, he made the mistake of asking Canning to be present at his first sermon:

> 'Well', asked the new incumbent, 'how did you like it?'
> 'Why,' replied Canning, 'I thought it rather – short.'
> 'Oh, yes, I am aware that it was short; but I was afraid of being tedious.'
> 'You *were* tedious.'

Narrow Gates

Lady: 'Why have they made the spaces in the iron gate at Spring Gardens so narrow?'
Canning: 'Oh, ma'am, because such very fat people used to go through.'

On Phillimore and Wynn

According to Benjamin Haydon, the painter, Canning wrote the following rhyme about two of his contemporaries, Phillimore and Wynn:

> *'Oh, Phillimore*
> *Is such a bore,*
> *He makes me cry*
> *But tho' a bore*
> *Is Phillimore*
> *He don't spit in my eye.'*

(which, apparently, Wynn always did)!

The Rhyming Despatch

Canning sent Charles Bagot, Ambassador in The Hague, a despatch in a cipher he did not possess. He immediately confessed that he was unable to decipher it and hoped this would 'not be productive of any public inconvenience.' When the despatch was finally deciphered, it was found to contain the following rhyme:

> *In matters of commerce the fault of the Dutch*
> *Is giving too little and asking too much;*
> *With equal protection the French are content:*
> *So we'll lay on Dutch bottoms just twenty per cent.*
> Chorus of officers – *We'll lay on Dutch bottoms just twenty per cent.*
> Chorus of douaniers – *Nous frapperons Falck avec twenty per cent.*

Bagot was not amused, writing crossly to Canning:

> 'You have fretted me to fiddlesticks, and I have a great mind not to give you the satisfaction of ever knowing how completely your mystification of me has succeeded.'

FREDERICK JOHN ROBINSON

First Viscount Goderich. First Earl of Ripon
(1782–1859)

'In a very short time, I came to form a low estimate
of the knowledge and information of Lord Ripon.'

WILLIAM GLADSTONE (1809–98)

THE HON. FREDERICK JOHN ROBINSON was born on 1 November 1782, the second son of Lord and Lady Grantham. He went to Harrow and to St John's College, Cambridge, and for two years acted as private secretary to his cousin Lord Hardwicke who was Lord Lieutenant of Ireland.

In 1806 he entered the House of Commons, attaching himself not so much to any political party as to a succession of individuals – Lord Hardwicke, Charles Yorke, Lord Castlereagh, George Canning, Robert Peel. Liverpool was confident enough of him to make him President of the Board of Trade in 1818, remarking to Peel 'Upon Robinson's claims, his Talents and his Character, it is unnecessary for me to say anything to you.'

He was made Chancellor of the Exchequer in 1823, and, under Canning, was created Viscount Goderich and appointed Colonial Secretary and leader of the House of Lords. On Canning's death, it was to Goderich that George IV turned to form an administration. It lasted only five months: a competent administrator, Goderich totally lacked any qualities of leadership, and failed to unite any sort of following behind him. Forced into resignation, Goderich did not take office under Wellington, but returned as Colonial Secretary under Grey and then as President of the Board of Trade (1841–3) and as President of the Board of Control (1843–6) under Peel. Little is known of his life in retirement after 1848. His health gradually deteriorated, and he died after a bout of influenza on 28 January 1859.

In 1814 Robinson married Lady Sarah Hobart, daughter of the fourth Earl of Buckinghamshire.

The Promising Harrovian

Although he never really shone in later life, Robinson was outstandingly successful at school:

> 'He was an excellent scholar for his age, and shone: particularly in composition, his exercises being not less remarkable for the ease with which he despatched them, than for their brilliancy. The pride and favourite of the masters, he had likewise the singular good fortune to be popular among his school fellows, with whom his gaiety served as an antidote to the jealousy which, even at schools, often attaches to superior merit. Without being at all handsome, his countenance had an ingenious and pleasing expression, his blue eyes beaming with intelligence and good humour. His future attainment of very high distinction in public life was confidently predicted by the general voice of the school.'

The Duke of Phussandbussle

During Robinson's spell in Europe with Castlereagh in 1813 he was nicknamed the Grand Duke of Phussandbussle by his companions. One of the other members of the mission left a letter addressed to Robinson in this way on his desk. From then on, Robinson often referred to himself as the Grand Duke.

Robinson's fussings were well described by Croker in a letter to Peel:

> 'Imagine Robinson's fuss – about to be married – the Lady very tender; her father very jocose; the writings very long; the lawyers very dilatory; the board of trade very exigent; Castlereagh's movements very doubtful and the thermometer at 84 in the shade.'

The Difficult Wife

Not a great deal has been written about Sarah Hobart, and what has is not in her favour. Robinson may have married her for her money, since she was due to inherit all the unentailed estates of the Hobart family, but there is no doubt that after their marriage he became an exemplary husband. She, in her turn, was an extremely difficult wife. Part of the trouble no doubt stemmed from the tragedy of their first two children – a son who died when he was two days old, and a daughter, Elinor, who died in 1826 when she was only ten. The horror of her daughter's death for a while made Lady Sarah forget her own problems, but by the end of 1826 she had lapsed into a state verging on madness. Emily Eden, a not-very-loyal-friend, described how she was:

> '. . . as she knows that her mind is beyond her own control, the provoking thing is that from the moment she begins to be ungovernable, she refuses to see anybody except servants who cannot contradict her. As long as Mr Robinson is forthcoming that does not signify, as to a certain degree he prevents her from doing anything outrageously foolish . . . She very seldom speaks at all, unless she is excited to defend some religious point.'

Sometimes, if her husband was away, she would send messages that she was dying in order to get him to return. Once, it was his own health that concerned her: he told her that he had a headache, took some medicine, and retired to bed; his wife sent for three doctors who all had to be sent back when Robinson emerged from his room fit and well. Not surprisingly, Robinson found the worry about his wife and the cares of office all too much for him and began to hint to Liverpool that he would like to be relieved of the Exchequer.

Lady Sarah was no better a year later, when her husband was Prime Minister. Pregnant again, she was extremely demanding, causing Emily Eden to declare:

> 'All the poor little children who read History a hundred years hence will come to the Goderich administration and . . . they will not have any idea what a poor creature he is.'

Even the birth of a son and heir did not improve her temper:

> 'Such a mess! She is crosser than ever, now she has all her wishes gratified. In short, all the stories that we have all known of her are nothing compared to what we might know now.

> 'Sister will not hear of her being crazy, though I have
> proved to her now advantageous it would be to Sarah's char-
> acter . . . it is extraordinary the number of good stories the
> Opposition letters bring of Lord and Lady Goderich.
> However, all those of her meddling in Politics are perfectly
> unfounded. Her attention to her own self is never disturbed
> for a moment, and she does not ever ask for any public
> information. Gooch is appointed her third physician in ordi-
> nary and she was unusually cross on Friday because he had
> not called before two. She had had Clarke and Pennington,
> but as she observed with the sweetest resignation, "Physi-
> cians I believe, always neglect their dying patients."'

According to the diarist Charles Greville, even the King did not
escape hearing about the health of his Prime Minister's wife:

> '. . . in the midst of all the squabbles which preceded the
> breaking up of his administration [Goderich] went whining
> to the King and said "Your Majesty don't know what vexation
> I have at home, with my wife's ill health, etc." The King telling
> the story said "G. . d. . . . the fellow, what did he bother me
> about his wife for? I didn't want to hear all his stories about
> her health."'

Significantly, her health improved a lot once her husband was no
longer Prime Minister. Lord Morley noted in a letter to Lord
Granville:

> 'He and Lady Goderich, having shut their doors and been
> invisible for years, are both recovered and apparently in the
> highest spirits.'

By the 1830s she had recovered enough to form an elementary
school at their country house, Nocton Hall, where children were
educated for one penny a week.

The Chancery Case

Robinson once sat next to Lord Lyndhurst in Chancery Court whilst
two lawyers argued over a complicated case. Before he left, Robinson
whispered to Lord Lyndhurst:
'Will, I don't know how the case may be decided; but, in my

opinion, Mr Hart has so completely answered Mr Bell that he has not a leg to stand on.'

Lord Lyndhurst whispered back: 'I am sorry I cannot agree with you, for – they are both on the same side.'

An Unfortunate Joke

Croker recorded one of Robinson's less successful dinner-party stories:

> 'Everyone knows the story of a gentleman's asking Lord North who "that frightful woman was?" and his lordship's answering, that is my wife. The other, to repair the blunder, said I do not mean *her* but that monster next to her. "Oh!" said Lord North, "that monster is my daughter." With this story Fred Robinson, in his usual absent enthusiastic way, was one day entertaining a lady who he sat next to at dinner, and lo! the lady was Lady Charlotte Lindsay – the monster in question.'

ARTHUR WELLESLEY
First Duke of Wellington (1769–1852)

'Proud Wellington, with eagle beak so called,
That nose, the hook where he suspends the world.'

Age of Bronze, LORD BYRON (1788–1824)

THE HON. ARTHUR WESLEY (the family reverted to the name of Wellesley in 1797) was born in Dublin, the third surviving son of Garret, first Earl of Mornington, by Anne Hill, daughter of Arthur, first Viscount Dungannon. His father, who had been appointed Professor of Music at Trinity College Dublin in 1764, died in 1781, leaving a family of six sons.

Arthur was first sent to Brown's preparatory school in Chelsea, where he later described himself as a 'dreamy, idle and shy lad' who loved to play the violin. He then went to Eton with his younger brother Gerald, but left after only three years so that the money could be spent on his more academic younger brothers. When he was seventeen he received his first commission in the 73rd Regiment, the first step in a brilliant military career which took him through the Flanders campaign to India, the Spanish Peninsula, and culminated in his great victory over Napoleon at Waterloo in 1815.

Wellington's career as a politician had begun before his military career was over. In 1790 he was elected member of the Irish Parliament for Trim, a pocket borough under the control of his eldest brother, and for a while was aide-de-camp to the Lord-Lieutenant of Ireland. In 1807, on the Duke of Portland's coming into power, he was appointed Chief Secretary for Ireland, though he insisted that this office should 'not impede nor interfere with his military promotion or pursuits'. Meanwhile, he had the previous year married Kitty Pakenham whom he had not seen since leaving for India, eleven years previously.

After Waterloo, Wellington remained in France until the Bourbon government had been successfully established, returning to London in 1818 to become a Cabinet member and Master General of the Ordnance in Lord Liverpool's administration. When Canning became Prime Minister in 1827, Wellington resigned his place in the Cabinet, as well as the position of Commander-in-Chief to which he had only recently been appointed.

In January 1828, on the resignation of Goderich, Wellington became Prime Minister. He faced a difficult task: he lacked the support of the Canningites, and his measures to remove disabilities from both dissenters and Roman Catholics led to opposition from ultra-Tories. Wellington remained deaf to what by now were clamorous demands for parliamentary reform, confidently asserting that the 'legislature and system of representation deservedly possessed the full and active confidence of the country'. By November 1829 he was forced to resign and his attempt to form a government in 1832 after the Lords had defeated the Reform Bill, was again a failure. During Peel's first administration (1834/5) he held the post of Foreign Secretary, and on Peel's return to office in 1841 he became the leader in the House of Lords, though without taking control of any department. In 1846, on Peel's leaving office, he finally retired though he remained Commander-in-Chief until he died suddenly in 1852 at the age of eighty-three.

Entry Into the Army

Lady Mornington did not consider the army an obvious choice of career for Arthur. She wrote despairingly to her daughter-in-law: 'I vow to God I don't know what I shall do with my awkward son Arthur,' and in 1787 commented to a friend: 'Arthur has put on his red coat for the first time today. Anyone can see he has not the cut of a soldier.'

Marriage to Kitty

In 1805, on his return from India, Wellesley wrote proposing to Kitty Pakenham – whom he had not seen for eleven years. When he went to Ireland to marry her, he was shocked at the appearance of his thirty-four-year-old bride. 'She has grown ugly, by Jove!' he whispered to his brother Gerald. Many years later he confessed to Harriet Arbuthnot:

'I married her because they asked me to do it and I did not know myself. I thought I should never care for anybody again and that I shd. be with my army and, in short, I was a fool. I will tell you the whole story if you like.'

The marriage was not harmonious. Throughout it, one of the chief sources of annoyance to her husband was that Kitty, through simple-minded generosity, distributed to family servants and hangers-on quite large sums of money. Little more than a year after their marriage, the rift was already apparent in a letter he wrote to Kitty:

'. . . I am much concerned that you should have thought of concealing from me any want of money which you might have experienced. I don't understand now how this want occurred, or why it was concealed; and the less there is said or written upon the subject, the better; for I acknowledge that the conclusion I draw from your conduct upon the occasion is that you must be mad, or you must be a Brute, and most particularly fond and avaricious of money. Once for all your require no permission to talk to me upon any subject you please; all that I request is that a piece of work may not be made about trifles . . . and that you may not go into tears because I don't think them deserving of an uncommon degree of attention.'

Kitty died in April 1831, leaving debts she had hidden from her husband totalling £10,000.

Women

Wellington enjoyed the close companionship of a number of women, the most important being Harriet Arbuthnot, whose husband 'Gosh' remained a devoted friend to Wellington after her death in 1834. Later, Wellington found consolation with two successive Lady Salisburys, and with Angela Burdett-Coutts – whose proposal of marriage he gently turned down at the age of seventy-seven. His oddest relationship was with Maria Jenkins, a beautiful young evangelist who had decided it was her mission in life to save the soul of the Duke of Wellington. The Duke first visited her in 1834 and at their second meeting in December was quite carried away at the sight of the lovely, pure creature in front of him:

'This must be for life! This must be for life! . . . Do you feel sufficiently for me to be with me a whole life?'

His ardour soon cooled but his pleasure in female society, his loneliness, and his military zeal in dealing with correspondence led to a total of 390 letters being written to Miss Jenkins in the last eighteen years of his life. When she heard of his death, Maria Jenkins' first thought was of her own failure – he had died without being 'born again'.

An Erratic Shot

Shooting at the Shelleys in Sussex in 1819 Wellington managed to pepper a dog and a keeper's gaiters, before going on to injure the arms of a cottager unsuspectingly hanging out her washing at an open window.

> 'I'm wounded, Milady.'
> 'My good woman, this ought to be the proudest moment of your life. You have the distinction of being shot by the great Duke of Wellington.'

Wellington himself admitted his singular want of accuracy. On 13 January 1823 he wrote to Mrs Arbuthnot:

> 'I want consolation . . . having had the misfortune of shooting Lord Granville this day. I have put nine shots in his face; luckily his eyes escaped unhurt, and he feels no inconvenience but the smarting pain . . . Lady Granville was very good-humoured about it.'

Deafness

Wellington was always slightly deaf, the result of a family weakness, but the affliction became much worse in 1822 when he allowed a quack doctor, John Stevenson, to treat his left ear with a strong caustic solution. The effect was devastating and he was to remain stone-deaf in that ear for the rest of his life. Wellington confessed:

> 'Indeed, I never was so unwell, as I do not remember before in my life having passed a day in bed. All my efforts to bully and bluster failed for the first time; and strange to say! I was near fainting in the effort to dress myself, and was obliged to give it up. We are sad Creatures after all!'

He still managed to be painstakingly polite to his torturer when he
came to apologize:

> 'Don't say a word about it; you acted for the best: it has been
> unfortunate no doubt for both of us, but you are not at all to
> blame.'

On Being a Politician

Wellington entered politics out of a fervent desire to serve his
country. He detested the world of politics. On becoming Prime
Minister he pointed to a pile of red boxes and green bags in his room
and complained to his friend John Croker:

> 'There, there is the business of the country, which I have not
> time to look at – all my time being employed in assuaging
> what gentlemen call their *feelings*.'

He was unhappy to find out that matters could not be settled as
simply as they were in the army:

> 'One man wants one thing and one another; they agree to
> what I say in the morning, and then in the evening they start
> with some crotchet with deranges the whole plan. I have been
> accustomed to carry on things in quite a different manner: I
> assembled my officers and laid down my plan, and it was
> carried into effect without any more words.'

He never felt the need to be polite to politicians. A baronet once
asked him at Apsley House:

> '. . . I have a question to put. I wish to ascertain whether, if
> your Grace were to return to office you would support prin-
> ciples of moderate reform.'
> 'That is your question, is it?'
> 'Yes, my Lord.'
> 'Then allow me to put a question in return: What right have
> you to ask me?'

Duel

Whilst actually in office, Wellington fought a duel with Lord
Winchilsea over a letter the latter had written in the *Standard* about

Wellington's acceptance of Catholic Emancipation. The duel took place at Battersea Fields on 21 March 1829, the Duke firing wide and Winchilsea shooting into the air. Wellington then rather coldly accepted a written apology from Lord Winchilsea, touched his hat with two fingers, and rode off.

George IV

The King had a fantasy that he had led the German charge at Salamanca, disguised as General Bock. 'Was not that so?' he bellowed down the dinner table.

'I have often heard your Majesty say so,' replied Wellington tactfully.

On Paying for a Picture

When Sir William Allan came to him for £1260 for his painting of Waterloo, Wellington began counting out banknotes.

> ' "Your Grace might prefer to draw a cheque on your bank to save time and trouble?" suggested Sir William.
> "Do you suppose I would let the clerk in Coutt's know what a fool I've been?" '

A Mannerism

Tom Moore was sitting for his portrait to Sir Thomas Lawrence when he noticed:

> '. . . his portrait of the Duke of Wellington scratching his elbow. Mentioned it once to the Duke: "Me!" he exclaimed, "me have such a trick! I'm sure I haven't": and all the while he was speaking his fingers were unconsciously at work at the elbow.'

Generosity

When General Alava was driven from Spain by reactionaries he was given a house on Wellington's estate and introduced to Coutts's:

> 'This is my friend, and as long as I have any money at your house, let him have it to any amount that he thinks proper to draw for.'

A Waterloo veteran, Sergeant Townsend, came to his door at Stratfield Saye.

> 'Do you know anything about gardening?'
> 'No, your Grace.'
> 'Then *learn – learn* and return this day fortnight at the same hour. Take the place of gardener at Walmer Castle.'
> 'But I know nothing of gardening.'
> 'Neither do I, neither do I.'

Mr Jones

A minor official went up to the Great Duke in Pall Mall, mistaking him for the secretary of the Royal Academy.

> 'Mr Jones, I believe.'
> 'If you believe that, you'll believe anything.'

An Admirer

A man helped him across Hyde Park Corner, taking the opportunity to state:

> 'My Lord, I have passed a long and not uneventful life, but never did I hope to reach the day when I might be of assistance to the greatest man that ever lived.'
> 'Don't be a damned fool.'

Sang Froid

At the height of his unpopularity in 1831, he sat at his desk in Apsley House as the mob stoned the windows. One stone narrowly missed him, breaking a glass-fronted bookcase behind him. He wrote to Mrs Arbuthnot:

> 'It is now five o'clock and beginning to rain a little, and I conclude that the Gentlemen will now go to their Dinners!'

The Reformed House of Commons

Asked what he thought of the composition of the new House of Commons as he surveyed its members from the Peers' Gallery:

> 'I have never seen so many bad hats in my life!'

Woburn

In 1834 the Duke of Bedford commented that the nation's choice
was between anarchy and despotism and that he preferred anarchy:

> 'I can tell Johny Bedford, if we have anarchy, I'll have
> Woburn.'

A Present for Lady Jersey

There was a story in the Jersey family of how he went to Lady Jersey's
birthday party, and on discovering that he had no present for her he
picked up a Meissen figure:

> 'My dear Duke, how charming! Exactly matches one I've got
> in the outer drawing room.'

Original Papers

In order to deal with the vast quantities of original family documents
and stories, etc. sent to him he had a supply of return slips printed:

> 'Avoid to impose upon others the care of original papers
> which you wish to preserve.'

Love of Children

Wellington was extremely good at playing with children, especially
other people's. When his butler caught a gang of small boys robbing
fruit trees, their leader comforted the others: 'Never mind, let's go to
the Duke; he allows everything and gives you what you like directly.'

Benjamin Haydon, the painter, described one morning at Walmer
Castle:

> 'In the midst, six dear noisy children were brought to the
> windows. "Let them in," said the Duke, and in they came and
> rushed over to him, saying "How d'ye do, Duke? how do d'ye
> do Duke?" One boy, young Grey, roared, "I want some tea,
> Duke." "You shall have it, if you promise not to slop it over
> me, as you did yesterday." Toast and tea were then in demand.
> Three got on one side, and three on the other, and he hugged
> them all. Tea was poured out, and I saw little Grey try to slop it
> over the Duke's frock-coat. Sir Astley [Cooper, a fellow guest]
> said, "You did not effect this." They then rushed out on the

leads, and after breakfast I saw the Duke romping with the whole of them, and one of them gave his Grace a devil of a thump. I went round to my bedroom. The children came to the window, and a dear little black-eyed girl began romping. I put my hand out, and said "I'll catch you!" Just as I did this, the Duke, who did not see me, put his head out at the door, close to my room, No. 10, which leads to the leads, and said "I'll catch ye! – ha, ha, I've got ye!" at which they all ran away. He looked at them, and laughed, and went in.'

Sparrow Hawks
The Queen asked him earnestly how to get rid of the sparrows from inside the Crystal Palace: Try sparrow hawks, Ma'am.'

CHARLES GREY
Second Earl Grey (1764–1845)

'That Earl who forced his compeers to be just
And wrought in brave old age what youth had planned.'

Anonymous contemporary couplet

THE ELDEST surviving son of Colonel Charles Grey and his wife Elizabeth, Charles Grey was born in Northumberland on 13 March 1764. He received a traditional English education at Eton and at Trinity College, Cambridge before going on an equally traditional Grand Tour. In 1786 he entered the House of Commons where he soon became well known for his attacks on Pitt and for his support of parliamentary reform. He held office briefly in the Ministry of All Talents, first as First Lord of the Admiralty and then as Foreign Secretary. This was followed by a period of twenty-four years in opposition until 1830 when he returned to office as First Lord of the Treasury at the age of sixty-six. In 1834, after his Great Reform Bill had safely become law, extending political power to some of the new middle classes, he resigned in favour of Melbourne.

In 1794 he married Mary Ponsonby, daughter of the first Lord Ponsonby. They had fifteen children, ten of whom survived.

Schools
At the age of six, Charles Grey was sent on a four-day journey down to London to start school at Marylebone. He quickly fell ill and was dispatched to the care of a nurse who happened to live at Tyburn where, as soon as he was well enough to go out, he was taken to see some Jews being hanged. Over fifty years later he still used sometimes to wake sweating from a nightmare recollection of this sight.

Grey did not see the need to send his own sons to public school. A series of governesses and tutors were imported to Howick, their house in Northumberland where the numerous Grey off-spring lived an idyllic life, even, to the astonishment of observers, calling their parents 'Charles' and 'Mary'.

Grey and Georgiana

As a young man, Grey fell for the charms of the beautiful Georgiana Duchess of Devonshire, whose marriage to the ineffectual fifth Duke, devastatingly described by Fanny Burney as 'looking like a very mean shopkeeper's journeyman', was little more than a sham. Seven years older than Grey, she was at the height of her beauty and popularity when she met the young politician in 1785. At first, there was token resistance. She revealed in a letter to her confidante Lady Elizabeth Foster:

> 'Lord Henry Fitzgerald told me that the handsomest man and woman in England should be together, but I will not be childish enough to let anything so foolish as my liking to talk to so young a man be thought of.'

Soon, however, Georgiana was for the first and only time in her life passionately in love. It was even said that when the Prince of Wales himself called one day at Devonshire House he was refused admittance, but that when he drove away he caught sight of Charles Grey looking out of a window.

The affair ended dramatically in 1791 when the Duke discovered that his wife was expecting Charles Grey's child. Georgiana was banished abroad, and in February 1792 gave birth at Aix-en-Provence to a daughter who was given the name of Eliza Courtney. The heart-broken Georgiana wrote a stream of letters to her former lover via Lady Melbourne, addressing him throughout, in the interests of discretion, as 'Mr Black'. Grey, it seems, was less inconsolable, shying away from an entanglement that had already become an embarrassment.

'He is a brute, a beast,' denounced Lady Elizabeth Foster, 'and I have no patience with him. There is a want of feeling and consideration that makes me quite mad with him.'

Even Georgiana was forced to admit to Lady Melbourne that her former lover's attitude towards her was not all that might be wished:

'Black has been again very cruel, and my letters from him yesterday have given me a headache.'

As the years passed, relations between the two grew easier:

'. . . he is now very good natured to me, but I do not see him often and I do not believe anybody knows I ever do see him.'

Meanwhile, Eliza Courtney was brought up by Grey's parents as their own daughter, later marrying a general and having two children. Not entirely appropriately, Grey gave a gold pendant to Georgiana containing their own hair, and that of Eliza, intertwined with the inscription '*Il m'est fidèle.*'

It is doubtful whether Mary Ponsonby knew of the affair when she married Grey. There is certainly no reason to believe the family tradition that the Duke of Devonshire presented Eliza Courtney to the new Mrs Grey on her wedding day.

Howick

Once married, Grey became the most domestic of men, devoted to wife, fifteen children and to the family home, and notoriously unwilling to leave the pleasures of Howick for the turmoil of London politics. So many ingenious excuses were used to explain his absence from London that his colleagues lost patience. By 1808, an exasperated Turney was writing to him:

'Have you a reason which you can publicly assign for staying away? The death of your uncle has removed the old one, a scanty income. What new one have you got which you can state? You must show yourself in the field as the leader of a party, or you must cease to be so.'

The surprising thing is that Grey lasted the course as a political leader as long as he did. As early as 1804 he had protested to his wife:

'I feel more and more convinced of my unfitness for a pursuit which I detest, which interferes with all my private comfort, and which I only sigh for an opportunity of abandoning decidedly and for ever. Do not think this is the language of momentary low spirits: it really is the settled conviction of my mind.'

Yet, twenty-six years later when he finally became Prime Minister, all the letters and diaries of the period observed that he actually appeared to be enjoying himself. His friend Creevey noticed his new high spirits:

> 'March 14th 1831. At Lord Grey's. Grey was all alive O! quite overflowing, never ceasing in his little civilities to myself, wanting me to eat this or drink that: – "Do Creevey, I assure you it's damned good; I know you'll like it." Can't you see him? It was not amiss for a Prime Minister to call out at dinner: "Do you think, Creevey, we shall carry our Reform Bill in the Lords?"'

and again:

> May 27. While I was riding in the Park yesterday I received rather a smartish pat on my shoulder from an unseen stick. When I turned round and saw my assailant in quite an ultra fit of laughing, who do you suppose it could be? No other than our Prime Minister. When I praised his royal Master [Grey had just been given the Garter], he said: "He *is* a prime fellow, is he not?"'

The Duke of Northumberland's Gates

In 1807, Grey lost his seat owing to the influence of the Duke of Northumberland, whom he never quite forgave. One of Grey's grandsons later recalled:

> 'Lord Grey was very kind to his grandchildren. His son, Uncle Francis, asked him to let the boys come to Alnwick. They were given ten shillings, which they spent on a hatchet each, and as they walked home they cut notches in all the Duke of Northumberland's gates. They were dragged up to Grand-papa by Uncle Francis, and he told him they had spoilt all the Duke of Northumberland's gates. "No, boys, did you really?" answered Lord Grey. "Here is ten shillings more, and if there are any gates that are not notched, go and cut them."'

Retirement at Howick

Despite the death of his wife, Grey's decade of retirement at Howick

was peaceful and happy. Again, Creevey painted the scene for
posterity:

> 'Just as I was in the midst of writing the last sentence, Lord
> Grey stalked into the great library, his spectacles aloft upon
> his forehead, and I saw at once he was for *jaw* so I abandoned
> my letter for you and joined him . . . It would do you good to
> see me send him to bed every night at half after eleven o'clock,
> which is half an hour beyond his usual time. This I do
> regularly, and it amuses him much. He looks about for his
> book, calls his dog, Viper, and out they go, he having been all
> day as gay as possible, and not an atom of that *gall* he was
> subject to in earlier life . . . The same tranquillity and cheerful-
> ness, amounting almost to playfulness, instead of subsiding
> have rather increased during my stay, and have never been
> interrupted by a single moment of thoughtfulness or gloom.
> He could not have felt more pleasure from carrying the
> Reform Bill, than he does apparently when he picks up half-a-
> crown from me at cribbage. A curious stranger would
> discover no out-of-the-way talent in him, no powers of con-
> versation; a clever man in *discussion* certainly, but with no
> fancy, and no judgement (or very little) in works either of
> fancy or art. A most natural, unaffected, upright man, hospit-
> able and domestic; far surpassing any man one knows in his
> noble appearance and beautiful simplicity of manners, and
> equally surpassing all his contemporaries as a splendid public
> speaker. Take him all in all, I never saw his fellow; nor can I
> see any imitation of him on the stocks.'

WILLIAM LAMB
Second Viscount Melbourne (1779–1848)

'Lord Melbourne sees [the Queen] every day for a couple of hours, and his situation is certainly the most dictatorial, the most despotic, that the world has ever seen. Wolsey and Walpole were in strait waistcoats compared to him.'

Letter to Sir Robert Peel of 15 August 1837,
JOHN WILSON CROKER (1780–1857)

THE SECOND son of Peniston Lamb, a nondescript landowner married to a brilliant, dominating wife, William Lamb's prospects in life were transformed when his elder brother died in 1805, making him heir to the peerage, the family estates, and a vast fortune. This enabled him to give up the Bar for politics, and also to marry Lady Caroline Ponsonby, only daughter of the third Earl of Bessborough, a match which had previously been thought impossible.

William Lamb entered the House of Commons in the year of his marriage but it was not until Canning became Prime Minister in 1827 that he took government office as Irish Secretary, only to resign under Wellington the following year.

In February 1829 he inherited his father's seat in the House of Lords, and when Grey became Prime Minister, Melbourne was appointed Home Secretary. Though nominally a Whig, he was by temperament conservative and could muster only lukewarm support for the 1832 Reform Bill. In 1834, on the resignation of Grey, he was summoned by William IV to form a ministry but his cabinet was too divided to form a stable administration and by November he had been dismissed. He returned again in April 1835 supported only by a small majority in the Commons and opposed by most of the House of Lords and by the King, to head a ministry which, at the kindest interpretation, provided a period of consolidation following the passing of the 1832 Reform Act. Melbourne's role as Prime Minister became immeasurably easier and pleasanter with the accession of the eighteen-year-old Queen Victoria in 1837. His divided and largely discredited ministry lurched on until 1839 and was dislodged by Peel only because of the Queen's over-zealous support. He was finally forced to resign in August 1841, and after his stroke in 1842 the leadership of the Whigs passed to Lansdowne. Melbourne still clung to the hope of returning to office almost until the time he died in 1848.

His Parentage

Peniston Lamb's marriage to Elizabeth Milbanke soon lapsed on both sides into open adultery. One rumour was that William was the son of Lord Egremont, Lady Melbourne's lover at the time of his birth. When the painter Landseer was being shown the pictures at the family home at Brocket by Melbourne he paused in front of one of Lord Egremont. William broke in at once:

> 'Aye, you have heard that story, have you? It's all a damned lie, for all that! But who the devil can tell who's anybody's father?'

Marriage with Caroline

Although Caroline Ponsonby was well-connected and attractive it was clear almost before she married William Lamb that she was a liability. A nervous, almost hysterical temperament together with an indulged upbringing had combined to make her quite impossible. Very soon after her marriage, she was behaving as oddly as ever. When her grandmother, Lady Spencer, first went to see her at Brocket she was kept waiting for an hour whilst Caroline tried to calm herself down and then 'when she did at last come in she desired to see me alone and began panting and throwing herself in a chair.'

As early as 1809 she was admitting her shortcomings in a letter to her husband:

> 'I think lately my dearest William we have been troublesome to each other which I take by wholesale to my own account and mean to correct. . . . I will be silent of a morning, entertaining after dinner, docile, fearless as a heroine in the last volume of her troubles, strong as a mountain tiger.'

Melbourne was not the man to control her. Infuriated by his restraint and by his apparent lack of concern she flaunted her lovers, most notably Byron, in his face. In 1822 Caroline's French maid indiscreetly revealed a bed-time conversation between husband and wife.

> *Caroline (drunkenly banging on her husband's door)*: 'I must and will come into your room. I am your lawful wife. Why am I to sleep alone?'
> *William*: 'I'll be hang'd if you come into my room, Caroline, so you may as well go quietly into your room. Get along, you little drunken . . .!'

The charade finally came to an end in 1825 when relatives negotiated a formal separation. Caroline withdrew to Brocket, her health broken and her feeble grip on reality shattered. The tragedy of their marriage was compounded by the fact that their only child, Augustus, was an epileptic who never advanced beyond a mental age of eight or nine. He died in 1836 at the age of 29.

Vanity

Melbourne was proud of his good looks. Caroline Lamb's caustic cousin, Harriet Cavendish, once observed him engrossed in amateur theatricals. Her verdict was that he was:

> '. . . too much occupied with his beauty and expression of countenance and makes crooked smiles to the audience when he ought to be attending to his companions.'

In his late thirties, his hair began to grow grey. He later admitted to Queen Victoria that at first:

> 'I had all the grey hairs pulled out. I had three women at it and in a week's times there were just as many, and you have no idea how painful it is, when you go on doing it for an hour together.'

Divorce Suits

Melbourne has the unique record among prime ministers of being directly involved in two court actions brought by enraged husbands. Soon after he arrived in Dublin in 1828 he met Lady Branden, the beautiful, entertaining wife of a gout-ridden clergyman, considerably

older than herself who conveniently spent most of the year out of
Ireland. It was not long before the husband brought an action against
Melbourne, alleging the seduction of his wife. Fortunately for Mel-
bourne, the plaintiff's case was so weak that the case was dismissed.
Having learned nothing from one indiscretion, Melbourne pro-
ceeded in the 1830s to become very friendly with Caroline Norton,
Sheridan's grand-daughter and the wife of an unsuccessful barrister.
Melbourne protested the innocence of their friendship but their
indiscretion shocked London society. Lord Howick wrote in his
diary in 1835:

> 'It is not very right that Mrs Norton should be asked every-
> where to meet Lord M. I think even *he* must be shocked at it.'

The same year, Lord Malmesbury reported:

> 'Met Mrs Norton at the French Ambassador's. She talked in a
> most extraordinary manner and kicked Lord Melbourne's hat
> over her head. The whole *corps diplomatique* were amazed.'

Again an aggrieved husband brought a civil suit for damages against
Lord Melbourne, and again the suit failed dismally. This time the
case reached court, where the only documentary evidence that could
be produced against Melbourne proved laughable. It consisted of
three notes written by Melbourne:

> 'I will call about half past four or five o'clock. Yours,
> Melbourne.'

> 'How are you? I shall not be able to call today, but probably
> shall tomorrow. Yours, Melbourne.'

and finally:

> 'There is no house today. I shall call after the levée about four
> or half past. If you wish it later let me know. I shall then
> explain to you about going to Vauxhall. Yours, Melbourne.'

Flagellation
Philip Ziegler is the first biographer of Melbourne to draw attention

to his curious interest in beatings. He made a survey of a series of forty letters between Lady Branden and Lord Melbourne to discover that only four contain no reference to beatings. In one letter he remarked with obvious relish:

> 'If I did not think that you were too angry to be jested with, I should say that I would certainly get a rod for you and apply it smartly the first time that I see you.'

Another time he actually cut from a book a print showing a woman beating a naked child, wrote her a lengthy account of the subject, and praised the woman's 'great heartiness and grace'. Nor were these inclinations confined to his relationship with Lady Branden alone. Many years later, Mrs Norton wrote him a letter from Italy in which she described an inlaid box she had seen in an antique shop and had nearly bought because the design was of 'your favourite subject of a woman whipping a child'.

Handwriting

Melbourne's handwriting became almost completely illegible. He admitted as much to Queen Victoria:

> 'I used to write a very ugly hand, but it used to be a very legible hand, and now I've got to write a hand that almost nobody can read; what I judge from is, that when I've read it over myself I can't read it, and so I think if I can't read it nobody else can.'

On Honours

Melbourne retained a healthy disrespect for honours, himself refusing the Garter four times. He once vetoed the Order of the Thistle for a Scottish nobleman on the grounds that he would eat it. When a marquis pleaded for another honour he was unmoved: 'God, does he want a Garter for the other leg?'

Food and Drink

He continually ate and drank too much, once returning from the House of Lords at four in the morning to eat his way through a four-course meal and drink a whole bottle of Madeira.

Old Age

Melbourne's idiosyncrasies became more disturbing as he grew older. He slept at the wrong times, once falling asleep three times during a conversation with the Queen, and frequently talked to himself. He was heard on one occasion to say to himself at Brook's, 'I'll be hanged if I do it for you, my lord,' and when he sat with the Queen in the royal box at the opera and the audience demanded an encore – 'That is too bad, rather a bore.' At dinner at Holland House he can hardly have put the shy young man sitting opposite him at his ease when he suddenly asked him during a lull in the conversation:

> 'Do you not consider that it was a most damnable act of Henry IV to change his religion with a view to securing the Crown?'

Queen Victoria's Coronation

His appearance was described by Disraeli:

> 'Melbourne looked very awkward and uncouth, with his coronet cocked over his nose, his robes under his feet, and holding the great sword of state like a butcher.'

There was good reason for his discomfiture, seeing he had had violent diarrhoea the previous day which he had tried to suppress with massive doses of laudanum and brandy. After the coronation, he did not attend Cabinet meetings for a week.

With Queen Victoria

For the first few years of her reign the young and impressionable Queen faithfully recorded in her journals many of the conversations between herself and Melbourne. The relationship between them was complex: Melbourne was at various times father, tutor, lover and statesman. For a time she swallowed (and recorded) all his pearls of wisdom:

On Resting

'For recruiting the spirits there is nothing like lying a good deal in bed.'

On Fires

'I always have a fire when I am worried or annoyed, it's astonishing how it dissipates trouble!'

On Wife-Beating

'Why, it is almost worthwhile for a woman to be beat, considering the exceeding pity she excites.'

On Euthanasia

'If they get the habit of doing such a thing when a person is in a hopeless state, why, they may do it when a person is *not* in a hopeless state.'

On Doctors

'English physicians kill you, the French let you die.'

On Prisons

When the Duke of Richmond remarked to the Queen and her Prime Minister how disgraceful it was that people often came out of prison worse than they went in, Melbourne interjected: 'I am afraid there are many places one comes out of worse than one went in; one often comes out worse of a ballroom than one went in.'

It was only when Melbourne's levity passed to the subject of Prince Albert that the Queen was not amused. Clarendon recorded that when the Queen stated that one of the things she liked most about Albert was the way he paid no attention to other women, Melbourne's unguarded reply was unfortunate: 'No, that sort of thing is apt to come later.'

The Queen's reaction was frigid: 'I shan't forgive you for that.'

SIR ROBERT PEEL

(1788–1850)

'I never knew a man in whose truth and
justice I had a more lively confidence.'

DUKE OF WELLINGTON (1769–1852)

ROBERT PEEL WAS born near Bury in Lancashire on 5 February 1788,
the eldest son of a wealthy cotton manufacturer and calico printer.
He was sent to Harrow and then to Christ Church, Oxford, where he
achieved a double first in classics and mathematics.

Peel entered Parliament in 1809 and was given his first post by
Perceval a year later, when he was appointed Under-Secretary for the
Colonies and War. From 1812 to 1818 he was Chief Secretary for
Ireland, where he met Julia Floyd, the daughter of the second-in-
command of the Irish military forces, whom he married in 1820. In
1822 he accepted the post of Home Secretary, an office he held with
great distinction. He resigned when Canning became Prime Minister
but returned as Home Secretary and Leader of the House of
Commons under Wellington.

Peel succeeded to his father's baronetcy and large income in 1830
but his interest in politics remained as strong as ever. In the reformed
House of Commons he rallied the Conservatives and revived their
fortunes to such an extent that he led them back into office from 1834
to 1835, and again from 1841 to 1846 when he headed a strong
reforming Cabinet. As Prime Minister, he encouraged free trade,
reorganized the banking system, and grappled with the Corn Laws,
which he finally succeeded in repealing in June 1846 to the consternation of many die-hard Tories. The Repeal cost him his office: he
was defeated on an Irish Coercion Bill in the Commons the night that
the Lords passed the Repeal of the Corn Laws, and resigned four days
later, refusing any honours. In June 1850 he was thrown from his
horse on Constitution Hill and died a few days later.

Apparent Coldness

Peel often appeared to be cold and aloof, especially at large gatherings. A radical MP, who was Chairman of a House of Commons Committee, once went to Peel with a request from his Committee. Peel listened to him politely enough, but when the MP had finished speaking Peel continued to gaze silently at him until he rather nervously picked up his hat and said: 'I beg your pardon, Sir Robert, I see you think I have been taking too great a liberty in coming to you as I have done. I wish you good morning.'

Peel's reaction was immediate. 'Good gracious, you are quite mistaken. I was only thinking how best I could comply with your request,' and he went on to apologize for his unfortunate manner, which he said often led him into trouble.

Kindness

Peel was extremely kind to young MPs at the start of their parliamentary careers. He introduced William Gregory, the grandson of one of his Irish colleagues, to the Speaker and gave him an open invitation to his house in Whitehall Gardens. Gregory often went there, and if Peel was too busy to leave his desk to chat, he would be entertained by other members of the family. When Gregory tactlessly waved his hat in the air with delight on the day Ashley defeated the government on the factory question, Peel remained as amiable as ever.

> 'My good fellow, I shall give you a scolding if you wave your hat over my head whenever you beat me; and the Speaker will give you a scolding if you wave it at all.'

Honours

When Wellington wrote in 1842 asking Peel to allow him to propose to the Queen that he should be given the Garter, Peel wrote back:

> 'So far as private feelings are concerned, I do not desire the Garter. I might indeed say, with perfect truth, I would rather not have it.'

He was equally hostile to other honours:

> 'It seems to me that the distinction of the Peerage, and every

other distinction, has been degraded by the profuse and incautious use which has been made of them.'

Books and Paintings

A wealthy man, Peel could afford to indulge in his passion for books and pictures. He had special collections of books on Ireland and on the French Revolution, and over a period of years built up an impressive collection of paintings, mostly of the Dutch and Flemish schools and including works by Rubens, Ruysdael, Rembrandt, Jan Steen, Wouwerman, and Hobbema. The best of these were displayed in a gallery, sixty-four feet long, on the first floor of his London house at Whitehall Gardens.

Partridges at Drayton

Charles Adderley, the Conservative MP for North Staffordshire, sat one summer morning with Peel after breakfast at Drayton Manor, the house Peel's father had built in Staffordshire. Peel asked him if he would like to see some partridges, took some corn from a basket in the corner of the room, and then stood near some open French windows with his hand held out full of corn. He called to the partridges and, after a moment or two, several began to appear, then a few more, and soon a whole covey was feeding inside the room.

A Wager

In December 1823 Peel spent a week-end at Sudbourne, Lord Hertford's house in Suffolk. Lord Hertford and Henry Baring entered into a bet that Peel could not kill in one day a pheasant, a woodcock, a wild duck, a rabbit and a hare. Peel backed himself for 300 guineas, began shooting at ten, and had won his money by 1 o'clock.

A Card Sharper

Lady Dorothy Nevill recorded a story about Peel in her book, *Reminiscences*.

'A few years before his death, Sir Robert with one or two friends, happened to be going to the Alexandra Park to witness a balloon ascent, or something of that sort (as a matter of fact, I believe it was a parachute descent by the well-known Professor Baldwin), when, making his way to the grounds, he found himself in close proximity to a man who was doing the three-card trick. Drawing himself up, as he used to do, he said to his companions, "I thought this old swindle was extinct; however (with a wink) as we have come across it, I shall expose the rascal." He at once proceeded to push himself to the front of the little crowd which stood round the illicit operator, but as soon as he got there his expression softened, and relenting, he whispered "The poor man is a sad bungler, he cannot do the trick at all." Soon, however, Sir Robert yielded to the blandishments of the sharper whilst his friends were present (and no money was on), proving completely successful in spotting the court card, which he did almost every time. The rest of the party, having applauded his skill, said they would walk slowly on to the Palace, which they did; but finding some time later that no Sir Robert appeared, someone went back to look for him, and to his *great* astonishment, discovered the missing Baronet still in close proximity to the card-sharper, but now in a furious rage, all his money being lost. "I ought to convict you," he was saying. "I am a magistrate, and you sir, (this in his grandest manner, his hat fiercely cocked, and one hand in a Napoleonic pose just inside his coat) – you sir, are a rogue, a thief, and a vagabond.'''

The Fatal Fall

On Saturday, 29 June 1850 Peel went out about five o'clock for a ride, promising Julia that he would not be late back as they were to dine that evening with the Jerseys. He had bought his eight-year-old horse only a couple of months previously after one of his friends had tested it for him, even in London traffic. In fact, it turned out later that the horse had been rejected by Sir Henry Peyton, one of the best riders of the day, because it tended to kick and buck, and even Peel's own coachman had advised his master not to ride it.

Near the top of Constitution Hill, Peel met two ladies he knew accompanied by a groom on a lively, nervous horse. Almost immediately, Peel's horse began to buck, threw Peel over its head, and then stumbled on top of the prostrate Peel, hitting his back with its knees. Two doctors rushed to the spot from nearby St George's Hospital, and he was gently lifted into a carriage to be driven home to Whitehall Gardens. He died on Tuesday, 2 July.

JOHN
First Earl Russell (1792–1878)

'Next, cool and all unconscious of reproach
Comes the calm "Johny, who upset the coach."
How formed to lead, if not too proud to please –
His fame would fire you, but his manners freeze.
Like or dislike, he does not care a jot:
He wants your vote, but your affections not;
Yet human hearts need sun, as well as oats,
So cold a climate plays the deuce with votes:
And, while his doctrines ripen day by day,
His frost-nipped party pines itself away.'

The New Timon, LORD LYTTON (1803–73)

JOHN RUSSELL, BORN in London in August 1792, was the second son of another John Russell who became the sixth Duke of Bedford. A sickly child, he was sent from Woburn first to Westminster and then to a private tutor before proceeding to Edinburgh University.

As early as 1813 he took his place among the Whigs as member for Tavistock, but spent his first seventeen years in the House of Commons in opposition. His favourite causes were parliamentary reform and Catholic emancipation, and when the Whigs at last returned to power he was made Paymaster General, and asked to pilot the Electoral Reform Bill through the House of Commons.

In Melbourne's second administration, Russell became Home Secretary and Leader of the House of Commons, moving to the Colonial Office in 1839. In 1835 he married Adelaide, widow of the second Lord Ribblesdale, but she died three years later, leaving him the care of two daughters and several step-children. In 1841, he married again, this time Lady Fanny Elliott, Lord Minto's daughter.

Russell finally became Prime Minister in 1846 on the defeat of Peel but he was very much overshadowed by his Foreign Secretary, Palmerston, and survived only two months after Palmerston had been dismissed. He agreed to be Leader of the House of Commons in the coalition government led by Lord Aberdeen from 1852 to 1855, and in 1860 joined Palmerston's second administration as Foreign

Secretary. In 1861 he accepted an earldom, and became Prime Minister for a final eight months on the death of Palmerston in 1865. Ill health and diminished capacity for leadership led to his resignation in June 1866, and he retired from active politics in 1868 after a career as a reformer spanning fifty-five years. He died from a fever in May 1878.

Frailty

John Russell was born two months prematurely. He grew to a height of just under five foot five and weighed only eight stones, a disproportionately large head topping the skinny frame. Throughout his long life he remained frail. In 1825 Hobhouse recorded one day that Lord John:

> 'Fell down in a sort of fit; his face was a little distorted, but he recovered immediately. His brother did not show any great anxiety and he told us that Lord John did not like to have these attacks noticed.'

During the 1831 election campaign in Devonshire, Sydney Smith came down to support Russell's campaign. He found that the locals for some reason could not believe that the architect of the Reform Bill should be so small. Smith took the opportunity of indulging in whimsy:

> 'My dear friends, before this Reform agitation commenced Lord John was over six feet high. But, engaged in looking after your interests, fighting the peers, the landlords, and the rest of your natural enemies, he has been so constantly kept in hot water that he is boiled down to the proportions in which you now behold him.'

Mother

It was a tragedy that Georgiana Russell died when her youngest son, John, had just gone to his first school. She had already sent him his first letter addressed 'To the best of all good little boys J.R., I miss your dear voice when I wake, and I regret you every moment of the day.'

A Whig Boyhood

As a boy, Russell was once instructed to crawl across the floor of the

Long Gallery at Woburn until he came to the chair in which Charles James Fox was sitting, and to 'tickle the silk-clad legs until the sleeper woke up and stopped snoring.'

Manner

Russell had an unfortunate offhand manner, sometimes failing to recognize people he knew well. On one occasion at Buckingham Palace:

> '... he was seen to get up suddenly, turn his back on the Duchess of Sutherland, by whom he had been sitting, walk to the remotest part of the room, and sit down by the Duchess of Inverness. When questioned afterwards ... he said, "I could not have sate any longer by that great fire; I should have fainted," "Oh, that was a very good reason for moving, but I hope you told the Duchess of Sutherland why you left her?" "Well no. I don't think I did that. But I told the Duchess of Inverness why I came and sate by her!"'

His cool exterior had both its strengths and its weaknesses, as was recognized by Sydney Smith:

> 'There is not a better man in England than Lord John Russell, but he is utterly ignorant of moral fear; there is nothing he would not undertake. I believe he would perform the operation for the stone; build St Peter's – or assume ... the command of the Channel Fleet; and no one would discover by his manner that the patient had died, the church tumbled down, and the Channel Fleet been knocked to atoms.'

Wives

As a young man, Russell was determined to marry – although he did not manage it until he was over forty. In 1817 he proposed to Elizabeth Rawdon and was rejected, not surprisingly since she had only two hours earlier accepted John's brother, William. Years later, he fell in love with Lady Emily Cowper, who married Lord Ashley instead. Next he liked the look of two daughters of Sir Thomas Hardy, first proposing to Emily, only to be refused again. Losing confidence, poor Russell asked his brother to propose to Emily's sister Louisa for him. The scheme did not come off, and it was not until 1835 that he met and married the tiny young widow of Lord Ribblesdale.

Russell's second wife, Fanny, was twenty-four when she agreed to marry the forty-eight-year-old widower with two children and four step-children. She hesitated a while before accepting him and told her mother that 'she was too old to think it necessary to be what is called desperately in love.'

The second Lady John Russell was not a great social asset to her husband. She produced four children with some difficulty and a great deal of noise, and suffered a series of miscarriages. On 23 November 1848 she wrote to her sister-in-law Lady Minto:

> 'We must buy every great blessing at a great price, that of children perhaps at the greatest, and you and I have often lamented together over the loss of our *careless* days – in short we wished to shake ourselves free of husbands and children . . .'

Queen Victoria strongly disapproved of Fanny, finding her interfering as well as troublesome. She wrote in her Journal (16 October 1853) that 'the quiet passing off of the late Cabinet was mainly owing to *her* not having come up to town with Lord John.' Antagonism between the two women was never far from the surface. In 1853, when the Russells were summoned to Windsor, Fanny was anticipating trouble even before they arrived. She claimed to her sister-in-law:

> 'Stand I will *not*, even at the risk of her think me lazy or affected, one of which epithets . . . she applies to every woman less strong than herself.'

The same year, Lord John refused to attend the Queen at Balmoral, but the Queen got her own back in October when, invited to Windsor again, the Russells asked if they might take their new baby with them and had got into their carriage ready for departure before a message came that there would be no room for the baby.

Daily Bath

Russell's salary as Paymaster of the Forces enabled him to get a house and install a bath. He was one of the first Englishmen known to bathe every day.

Chequers

It was unheard of for the Prime Minister not to have a house in the country. Sir George Russell, who was no relation, actually drove over to Woburn to tell the duke that he would like to offer Chequers to the Prime Minister, but the duke was so offhand that Russell left without making his offer. Subsequently, Lord John used to say he had lost Chequers 'for want of a glass of sherry and a biscuit'. In the end, the Queen provided the Russells with Pembroke Lodge in Richmond Park.

Dealing with Victoria and Albert

Russell did not believe in winning over the Queen by flattery. Both Victoria and Albert found him brusque, and for his part, he clearly found explaining political events to the Queen tedious. On 23 June 1849 he wrote to her that:

> 'The Transportation Bill was then committed, and the usual nonsense was spoken upon it till past one in the morning.'

On 11 January 1852 Prince Albert found him very inattentive and:

> 'almost unwilling to listen to me, breaking off the conference in the midst of the most important subject by looking at his watch and expressing his fears that he would be late for the train.'

Inefficiency

As Prime Minister, Russell had no governmental department to check his muddles. Consequently, papers got mislaid, enclosures left out of letters, and whole sheets left out of envelopes. Once, a letter to Lord Erroll was addressed just to Paris. Another time, Baron Brunnow opened an envelope addressed to him and delivered by special messenger to find it contained a letter to Mme de Lieven.

EDWARD GEORGE GEOFFREY STANLEY

Fourteenth Earl of Derby (1799–1869)

'The brilliant chief, irregularly great,
Frank, haughty, rash, the Rupert of debate
Nor gout, nor toil, his freshness can destroy
And time still leaves all Eton in the boy,
First in the class and keenest in the ring,
He saps like Gladstone and he fights like Spring'.

The New Timon, LORD LYTTON (1803–73)

STANLEY WAS born at Knowsley, Lancashire, on 29 March 1799, the eldest son of one of the richest and most distinguished Whig families. Like many of his class he was educated at Eton and at Christ Church, Oxford, before entering the House of Commons in 1820. Under Canning and then Goderich he was Under-Secretary for the Colonies, but refused office under Wellington. Grey appointed him Chief Secretary for Ireland, and then in 1833 Colonial Secretary, where he was responsible for the abolition of slavery. During Melbourne's second administration, he formally joined the Tories, and was appointed Peel's Colonial Secretary in 1841. He differed from Peel over the question of the Corn Laws and resigned in 1845.

Derby finally became Prime Minister in 1852 after the defeat of Russell. His ministry was in a minority in the House of Commons, and by December he had resigned. His second administration began in February 1858 after the resignation of Palmerston and lasted for over a year until June 1859. He became Prime Minister for the third and last time in June 1866 but by now, old and gout-ridden, allowed Disraeli to emerge as the real force behind the administration. Once the Household Suffrage Reform Bill had been safely piloted through all its stages he resigned, and died in the autumn of 1869 at the age of seventy leaving a widow (to whom he had been married forty-four years), two sons and a daughter. Disraeli best summed up his political achievements: 'He abolished slavery, he educated Ireland, and he reformed Parliament.'

The Grand Tour

Like most young Whig grandees, Stanley went on a Grand Tour. His, though, had the distinction of including a two-week stay in a Neapolitan gaol after he had knocked down an officer, who had used violent language in front of him.

Stanley went on to visit the United States in 1824. Exploring the country near the Mississippi, he and a travelling companion came upon a shanty where three small children were living entirely alone, their parents having gone away three days earlier:

> 'They showed us their bed with two deerskins thrown on it, and requested our assistance in carrying it into a log hut, as they said it was very cold in the shanty; we afterwards cut up a large tree at their request for firewood and left these young children of independence.'

The Happy Family Man

Stanley was happiest at home at Knowsley with his wife, whose parties were described as 'of a dullness as depressing as a London fog.'

Charles Greville observed him there in July 1837:

> 'It is a strange thing to see Stanley (at Knowsley); he is certainly the most natural character I ever saw; never seems to think of throwing a veil over any part of himself: it is the straightforward energy which is the cause of this, that makes him so comfortable as he is. In London he is one of the great political leaders, and the second orator in the House of Commons, and here he is a lively rattling Sportsman, apparently devoted to racing and rabbit-shooting, gay, boisterous, almost clownish in his manners, without a particle of refinement.'

The Turf-Loving Scholar

An accomplished scholar who translated the *Iliad* into blank verse, Stanley was equally at home at Newmarket:

> 'If any of his vociferous disciples and admirers, if some grave

members of either House of Parliament, or any distinguished foreigner who knew nothing of Lord Stanley but what he saw, heard or read of him, could have suddenly found themselves in the betting room at Newmarket on Tuesday evening and seen Stanley there, I think they would have been in a pretty state of astonishment. There he was in the midst of a crowd of blacklegs, betting men, and loose characters of every description, in uproarious spirits, chaffing, rowing, and shouting with laughter and joking. His amusement was to lay Lord Glasgow a wager that he did not sneeze in a given time, for which purpose he took pinch after pinch of snuff, while Stanley jeered him and quizzed him with such noise that he drew the whole mob around him to partake of the coarse merriment he excited.'

The Arrogant Politician

Stanley's charms were marred by an arrogance that made him disregard the feelings of others. As early as 1834, Ronayne was complaining in the House of Commons of Stanley's habit of propping his legs 'upon the table like a man in a North American coffee house'. Later, members of the House of Lords reacted badly when Lord Derby corrected their English for them during debates:

> 'Lord Derby would insolently correct Lord Granville across the House of Lords. Lord Granville always said "wropped up". "Wrapped" Lord Derby would say in a tone clear to the reporters.'

The Cure for Gout

A wine merchant tried to persuade Derby to drink his sherry as a cure for gout. Derby is said to have replied: 'I have tasted your sherry and prefer my gout.'

The Ailing Prime Minister

During his last ministry, the gout-ridden Lord Derby admitted to Disraeli that he was 'everything that a Prime Minister ought not to be'. The Queen of Holland visited him at Knowsley in September 1867. She did not find a very dynamic Prime Minister.

'. . . he was carried up and downstairs, not from *pain*, but from *weakness*, and it was positive *exertion* to lead me from the drawing room to the dining room. At dinner his colour would get ghastly white, like a corpse . . . he seemed like a candle burning out. His feverish eyes, his ghastly paleness, were at times quite frightful.'

GEORGE HAMILTON GORDON

Fourth Earl of Aberdeen (1784–1860)

'You complain'd of Lord Aberdeen's unceasing
conversation, but with his knowledge and cleverness
it was not such a bad substitute for a book.'

Letter of November 1812 to Lord Granville Leveson-Gower,
LADY BESSBOROUGH

BORN IN Edinburgh on 28 January 1784, the eldest son of Lord and
Lady Haddo, George Gordon was an orphan by the age of eleven. He
was educated at Harrow where he was a contemporary of three other
future Prime Ministers, Goderich, Peel and Palmerston, and then at
St John's College, Cambridge. A Grand Tour completed his education, and sparked off a lifelong interest in archaeology. In 1805 he
married Catherine Hamilton, the daughter of the first Marquess of
Abercorn and in 1806 began his political career with his election as a
Scottish representative peer.

For the next few years, Aberdeen's main interests were his wife and
family, his Scottish estates, and his studies of architecture. With the
death of Catherine in 1812 he sought consolation in work and agreed
to go on a special mission to Austria. Soon he was appointed Ambassador at Vienna and assisted Castlereagh at the Congress of Chatillon
and then at Paris. On his return to England, he was created an
English peer, and in 1815 took as his second wife Harriet, the widow
of his first wife's brother.

It was not until Wellington became Prime Minister that Aberdeen
first took ministerial office. He was first appointed Chancellor of the
Duchy of Lancaster and then Foreign Secretary, a post he held again
under Peel. The death of Peel made him head of the Peelites, and in
1852 he at last became Prime Minister at the head of a coalition of

Whigs, including Russell and Palmerston, and Peelites, including Gladstone. The onset and conduct of the Crimean War overshadowed the Coalition's domestic achievements and led to its downfall in 1855. Plagued by headaches for a number of years, Aberdeen's health failed in 1859 and he died, weary and depressed on 14 December 1860.

The Blacksmith's Daughter

Not all Aberdeen's forebears were Scottish aristocrats. As a young man, his grandfather (the third Earl) visited Hatfield Hall, Stanley, and on his way stayed the night at the Strafford Arms, Wakefield. He found the mutton chops provided for his supper there so delicious that he asked to see the cook, and was entranced to meet Catharine Hanson, the daughter of the local blacksmith. What followed is not quite clear, but when Lord Aberdeen reappeared at the Strafford Arms at the end of his visit, Catharine followed him to his room with a loaded shotgun and threatened to shoot him if he did not marry her. They did marry and had two sons and four daughters.

Appearance

Not many people thought Aberdeen handsome. An exception was Lord Melbourne, as Queen Victoria reported in her Journal (8 February 1839):

> 'We had grcat fun about Lord Aberdeen, who Lord M(elbourne) would have was very handsome, and asked several of the ladies if they didn't think Lord A was very handsome, and nobody did; "Oh! he has a beautiful magnificent expression; a sweet expression," said Lord M.'

A commoner view was that of Lady Lyttelton expressed in 1846 – 'more of a scarecrow than ever and quite as stiff as timber.'

Tragedies

Aberdeen's first wife died of tuberculosis after only six years of marriage. He tried to explain his anguish to a friend, writing that only 'he who beholds the object of his admiration and love, gradually wasting before him, who thinks he hears for the last time sentiments of wisdom and virtue, and the exercise of innocent gaiety who knows that even the kisses which she lavishes on her children are numbered' could possibly understand. After she had died, he wore mourning for the rest of his life, and consoled himself with his three young daughters, Jane, Alice and Frances. Before he was fifty he had seen all three daughters die of the same disease after nursing them with a devotion unusual in a nineteenth century father. By the time his last daughter had died he found it impossible to speak of his losses but, according to his son, he shut himself up at the Foreign Office for several days, completely alone.

There was no sign of bitterness in Aberdeen until the very last year of his life when he refused to rebuild a local parish church in Scotland. At the time no one could understand his refusal, but after his death several scraps of paper were found, on each of which he had written a text from Chronicles:

> 'And David said to Solomon, My son, as for me, it was in my mind to build an house unto the name of the Lord, my God: but the word of the Lord came to me saying: Thou hast shed blood abundantly, and hast made great wars; thou shalt not build an house unto my name, because thou hast shed much blood upon the earth in my sight.'

No one can say whether this was Aberdeen's final judgement on his own role in the Crimean War or no more than a reflection on the tragedies of his life.

A Second Wife

Aberdeen soon set about the task of finding a second wife to be a mother to his daughters and to provide him with a son. He made the mistake of pursuing two women at once, Susan Ryder and Anne Cavendish, without being in love with either. He wrote to his brother Robert in June 1814:

> 'I do not know what to do – but in the meantime I shall take Lady Georgiana's advice and do nothing hastily. Without making myself particular with either, I shall go on with both as I see them, and then decide on the best view I can take of the whole affair.'

In the end, he chose neither, but married instead Harriet, the widow of his first wife's brother, Lord Hamilton, and who he himself had earlier described as 'certainly one of the most stupid persons I ever met with.'

Although happy at first, the two quickly drifted apart. Harriet disliked Haddo, the family home, and refused to go, so that from about 1819 they began regularly to spend time apart. Unlike his first wife who had always made light of her sufferings, Harriet liked to let people know when she was feeling ill. Her husband's reaction was brisk:

> 'I hope you feel comfortable today', he wrote in July 1819, 'as I do not like the thought of your being low and nervous, especially as you have no good reason.'

Harriet's reasons may have been better than Aberdeen supposed, since she too died of tuberculosis in 1833.

Hunting Otters

Aberdeen soon progressed from a youthful condemnation of Scotland – 'what a country where murder is the only amusement' to a great love of his inherited estates. One of his chief interests there was otter-hunting, and his hounds were painted by Landseer in 'The Otter Speared'. Lord Stanley once turned down an invitation to stay, but confessed that he might have changed his mind if he could have been guaranteed a sight of Aberdeen in a kilt, up to his waist in water, hunting otters.

The Man from the Russian Embassy

In 1829, Aberdeen accompanied the Russian ambassador, Prince Lieven, and his family on a visit to see Bridge House, Lord Abergavenny's home. The invitation had only been to the Russian embassy, so during their two-hour visit Aberdeen throughout masqueraded as a Russian diplomat.

The Sea-Sick Minister

Aberdeen, very much against his will, once had to attend Queen Victoria while she was cruising aboard her yacht. The Queen, who had grown to like Aberdeen, tried to cheer him up:

> 'I believe, my lord, you are not often sea-sick.'
> 'Always, Madam.'
> 'But, not *very* sea-sick.'
> '*Very*, Madam.'

HENRY JOHN TEMPLE
Third Viscount Palmerston (1784–1865)

'If the devil has a son, his name is surely Palmerston'

Translation of a contemporary German rhyme

PALMERSTON WAS born at the family home, Broadlands in Hampshire, on 20 October 1784. Superfically his father appeared a typically dull Tory landowner, but a keen interest in literature, art and science revealed his real qualities. His mother, Mary Mee, was the daughter of a wealthy Dublin merchant into whose house Lord Palmerston had been carried after falling from his horse one day in the streets of Dublin.

Harry, as he was known in the family, spent much of his early childhood in Italy before being sent to Harrow and then in 1800, to Edinburgh University, where he studied political economy. As a young man, he seemed to everyone to be a paragon of good behaviour. Lord Minto, who visited Harry and his own son in 1802, reported to Lord and Lady Palmerston:

> 'Diligence, capacity, total freedom from vice of every sort, gentle and kind disposition, cheerfulness, pleasantness and perfect sweetness are in the catalogue of properties by which we may advertise him if he should be lost.'

In 1802, at the age of seventeen, Harry inherited his father's Irish viscountcy, and the next year proceeded to St John's College, Cambridge. His political career began in 1807 when he was appointed a Junior Lord of the Admiralty by Lord Portland, and in 1809, aged 25, he became Secretary of War, having actually turned down the Exchequer on the grounds that he lacked experience. He was content to remain at the War Office for the next nineteen years, resigning in 1828 when Wellington was Prime Minister.

It was in Lord Grey's administration of 1830 that he first became Foreign Secretary, a post he held again with great distinction under Melbourne. In the Whig administration of 1846–51, Russell was forced by popular demand to return him to the same post despite the vehement opposition of Queen Victoria who considered that he was dangerous and uncontrollable. During this period he was the most popular statesman in the country with his policy of protecting and strengthening British interests throughout the world, by force if necessary. His policy was carried to an extreme in the Don Pacifico incident when a British squadron was despatched to recover the losses of a Portuguese Jew with a British passport whose house had been plundered by an Athenian mob. His action then had been opposed even by some members of his own party but it still proved popular in the country. A celebration dinner was organized for him by 250 members of the Reform Club at which a nine-course dinner was consumed and the national anthem enthusiastically sung.

The Queen, unmoved by this display of national sentiment, in 1851 managed to force Russell to remove him from office. His career, however, was far from over. In 1855 it was widely thought that only he could prevent further disaster in the Crimean War, and at the age of seventy he was appointed Prime Minister:

'I am for the moment, *l'inévitable*', he reported in triumph to his brother.

During his first ministry (1855–8) he was preoccupied with the Crimean War, and then with troubles in India. He returned in 1859 for a more tranquil term of office at the head of a strong ministry including both Russell, at the Foreign Office and Gladstone, at the Exchequer. At home, though nominally a Whig he remained at heart conservative, doing his best to thwart further plans for electoral reform. As the Grand Old Man of British politics he had finally won acceptance, even admiration, from his monarch, and when he died in office in October 1865 he was widely regretted.

First Seat

Palmerston first entered parliament as member for Newport (Isle of Wight). This was a pocket borough presented to Palmerston by Sir Leonard Holmes who, concerned lest the new MP should erode his own influence, stipulated that Palmerston should never visit the constituency, even at election times.

Women

Although Palmerston did not marry until he was fifty-five, he and his wife had been lovers for years. She was Emily Cowper, Melbourne's sister, and one of Society's leading hostesses. There had been plenty of other mistresses too. When he became a member of Almack's, the exclusive gambling club, it was generally thought that at least three of the seven Lady Patronesses, in whose hands the final decision on membership rested, were his lovers. In 1839, only a few months before his marriage to Lady Cowper, who was by now a widow, he committed one of his worst indiscretions. The diarist Charles Greville relished the incident:

> 'Palmerston, always enterprising and audacious with women, took a fancy to Mrs Brand (now Lady Dacre), and at Windsor Castle, where she was in waiting, and he was a guest, he marched into her room one night. His tender temerity met with an invincible resistance. The lady did not conceal the attempt, and it came to the Queen's ears. Her indignation was somehow pacified by Melbourne, then all-powerful and who on every account would have abhorred an *escalandre* in which his colleague and brother-in-law would have so discreditably figured. Palmerston got out of the scrape with his usual luck, but the Queen has never forgotten and will never forgive it.'

Prince Albert used the incident in 1850 to try and turn the Prime Minister, Lord Russell, against Palmerston:

> 'How could the Queen consent to take a man as her chief adviser and confidential counsellor in all matters of State, religion, society, Court, etc. he who as her Secretary of State, and while under her roof at Windsor Castle, had committed a brutal attack upon one of her ladies? Had at night by stealth, introduced himself into her apartment, barricaded the door, and would have consummated his fiendish scheme by violence had not the miraculous efforts of his victim and such assistance attracted by her screams, saved her.'

Palmerston would probably have been even more irritated if he had heard Russell's reply to the effect that as Palmerston was now sixty-five he was unlikely to cause much trouble in that direction in the future.

Unpunctuality

The Palmerstons were famously unpunctual. As Foreign Secretary, Palmerston regularly kept foreign ambassadors waiting – the Belgian Minister, van de Weyer, claimed to have read his way through the whole of Richardon's *Clarissa* in Palmerston's ante-room. A Saxon diplomat, Count Vitzthum, reported that he once arrived at 94 Piccadilly, Palmerston's London home, for a large diplomatic dinner just in time to see his host disappearing on his horse for a little exercise in Rotten Row before the rigours of the evening. At Queen Victoria's first state banquet he managed to arrive after all the guests had sat down. Marriage did not make him any better. When Queen Victoria visited them at Brocket, which Emily had inherited from her brother, Lord Melbourne, Lady Lyttleton wrote that they 'make the poor Queen wait for dinner and drives till anybody but herself would be furious.' There was a saying at the time that 'the Palmerstons always miss the soup'. Before they visited Paris in 1846 Brougham took Lady Palmerston on one side to tell her that when they dined at the Tuileries she would see a large deep bowl with a ladle in it which would be of immense interest to her. It was a silver soup tureen.

Health

Palmerston was always remarkably healthy and amazed contemporaries with his stamina. He rose at seven, whatever time he had gone to bed the previous night, and rode or swam before breakfast every day. At the end of the day he worked at home at a special desk at which he stood so that he would not fall asleep. From Broadlands he used to ride so fast over to Stockbridge to see his racehorses that when he arrived he had to go round the yard several times in order to slow down. In his seventies he continued to shoot as much as ever, and when hunting stags in France refused to wear anything over his pink coat, protesting 'rien ne perce un habit rouge'. At the age of seventy-nine, he rode to Harrow for the annual speech day, covering the twelve miles in less than an hour, and he celebrated his eightieth birthday by covering quite large distances of the south coast on horseback to inspect fortifications. Less than a month before he died his wife told her son that she had seen him jump over some railings at Brocket when he thought no one was looking.

As an old man, Speaker Denison warned him to take good care of his health and not to catch cold by walking home late at night. Palmerston replied:

> 'Oh, I do indeed. I very often take a cab at night, and if you have both windows open it is almost as good as walking home.'

There were, in the last few years of his life occasional lapses of memory. In August 1864 he wrote to Russell about the American Civil War only to follow it with a second hurried letter in which he was forced to admit that he had in the first letter throughout written Bucharest instead of Richmond. The following year he disconcerted Russell by asking him if France had been a party to the treaty establishing the independence of Belgium in 1831.

Appetite

Although Palmerston was to some extent careful about his diet, often only eating an orange for his lunch even if he had invited guests, he was still capable of eating his way through what to us would appear to be an inordinate amount. Speaker Denison was so impressed by the Prime Minister's appetite that he recorded in his journal exactly what he ate at the traditional Speaker's Dinner at the start of the 1865 parliamentary session. Palmerston, he wrote:

> '. . . ate for dinner two plates of turtle soup; he was then served very amply to a plate of cod and oyster sauce, he then took a pâté: afterwards he was helped to two very greasy-looking entrées; he then despatched a plate of roast mutton; there then appeared before him the largest, and to my mind the hardest, slice of ham that ever figured on the table of a nobleman, yet it disappeared just in time to answer the inquiry of his butler: "Snipe, my Lord, or pheasant?" He instantly replied "Pheasant" this completing his ninth dish of meat at that meal.'

He then went on to down a pudding, a jelly, some dressed oranges and half a large pear.

Only a few days before his death he appeared to be recovering from the chill he had caught and managed to eat a mutton chop washed down with port for breakfast.

Race-Horses

From the time he was a very young man, Palmerston kept race-horses. In 1841 his horse Illiona won the Cesarewitch and in 1853 he won the Ascot stakes with Buckthorn. Even when he became Prime Minister his horses remained dear to his heart. In 1859 his trainer, Day, managed to slip his way into the House of Commons and get a message through to Palmerston. As soon as he received it Palmerston left the Irish debate going on in the Chamber to talk to Day about horses. Day congratulated his employer on becoming Prime Minister:

'Oh, thanks John, I have won my Derby.'

Creditors

Always a philanthropic landlord both in Hampshire and in Ireland, Palmerston's attitude towards his creditors was less praiseworthy. He had to be sued by anxious creditors nineteen times in thirty years. A butcher who had tired of waiting for payment from Palmerston's agents once forced his way into Palmerston's presence demanding immediate payment. Palmerston wrote out a cheque but then spoiled the effect by ungraciously throwing the pen he had used out of the window. In May 1835 his landlord in Piccadilly sent in the bailiffs for the year's rent owing to him. The bailiffs had to wait in the house three days before they were paid.

BENJAMIN DISRAELI
First Earl of Beaconsfield (1804–1881)

'The present man will do well, and will be particularly loyal and anxious to please me in every way. He is vy. peculiar, but vy. clever and sensible and vy. conciliatory.'

Letter of 29 February 1868 to Crown Princess of Russia,
QUEEN VICTORIA (1837–1901)

DISRAELI WAS born on 21 December 1804 near Gray's Inn, London. He was the eldest son of middle-class Jews of Italian origin, Isaac and Marian Disraeli, but he and his brothers and sisters were brought up as Anglicans. He was educated at private schools at Islington, Blackheath and Epping, and then trained as a solicitor, a profession he soon found he disliked.

In 1826 Disraeli published his first novel, *Vivian Grey*, but it did not bring him the instant social celebrity that has often been claimed. Other novels and a nervous breakdown followed and it was not until 1837 that he succeeded in entering the House of Commons as Conservative member for Maidstone. Two years later he married Mary Anne Wyndham Lewis, a rich widow, twelve years older than himself. The marriage was happy and Disraeli was devastated by her death in 1869.

The success of Peel in 1841 did not bring Disraeli into office, and during the 1840s he gravitated towards the young rebellious section of the Tory party known as Young England. During Derby's administrations of 1852, 1858 and 1866 he was Chancellor of the Exchequer, and finally became Prime Minister on Derby's resignation in February 1868. His first ministry lasted less than a year, but he returned to power in February 1874 with a large majority. Active chiefly in the field of foreign affairs, he dealt with troubles in eastern Europe, Afghanistan and South Africa. After the triumphs of the Treaty of Berlin in 1878 (when he was widely praised for having brought back 'Peace with Honour' and for having enforced a firm policy against Russia) his fortunes began to fail, and industrial and agricultural depression combined with divisions over foreign policy to cause his defeat at the 1880 election. He continued to lead the Conservatives in opposition and also published his last novel, *Endymion*. He died childless in 1881 and the title 'Earl of Beaconsfield', conferred on him in 1876, died with him.

On His Youth

Disraeli once took Lady Derby on a walk from Hughenden, his country home, to Bradenham, the house his father owned:

> Disraeli: 'It was there that I passed my miserable youth.'
> Lady Derby: 'Why miserable?'
> Disraeli: 'I was devoured by ambition I did not see any means of gratifying.'

The Dandy

The clothes Disraeli wore when he first met Henry Bulwer so impressed the latter that he could remember them in detail many years later:

> '. . . green velvet trousers, a canary coloured waistcoat, low shoes, silver buckles, lace at his wrists, and his hair in ringlets.'

In 1830 one outfit particularly delighted Disraeli: 'blue surtout, a pair of military light blue trousers, black stockings with red stripes, and shoes.' He claimed to his friend Meredith that he 'caused a sensation in Regent Street' and that:

> 'the people quite made way for me as I passed! It was like the parting of the Red Sea, which I now perfectly believe from experience.'

Affectation

In Malta on his Grand Tour, Disraeli wrote:

> 'To govern men you must either excel them in their accom-

plishments, or despise them ... Affectation tells here even better than wit. Yesterday at the racket court sitting in the gallery among strangers, the ball entered and lightly struck me, and fell at my feet. I picked it up, and observing a young rifleman excessively stiff, I humbly requested him to forward its passage into the court as I really had never thrown a ball in my life. This incident has been the general subject of conversation at all the messes today!'

Henrietta Sykes

In 1833 Disraeli met Henrietta Sykes, the beautiful but mercurical wife of Sir Francis Sykes, owner of Basildon in Berkshire. They soon became lovers and until he broke the affair three years later she dominated his life. The first surviving letter from Henrietta illustrates the nature of their relationship:

'12 o'clock Thursday night.
It is the night Dearest the night that we used to pass so happily together. I cannot sleep and the sad reality that we are parted presses heavily upon me—very, very heavily. I love you indeed I do, and I am thankful that you cannot quite share my sorrowfulness of feeling. The returning to *our* House and seeing the solitary chair and knife and fork and the bright fire blazing as if from cheerfulness spoke more forcibly to me than any language could do ...

The dear head is it better? That it were pillowed on my bosom for ever. I would be such an affectionate old nurse to my child and kiss and soothe every pain. You are in bed my love asleep from being tired and worn out. It is a comfort I know your room and the white couch and that when you write and say "I have been walking on the Terrace or the Common", all will be present to my imagination. I am blinded—Good Angels guard my dearest. A thousand and a thousand kisses. Good night. Sleep and dream of—your Mother.'

Unfortunately for Disraeli, Lady Sykes was not always so selflessly maternal. A later letter betrays an almost manic possessiveness:

'1 o'clock in bed.
Has he thought of his Henrietta this morning and wished her

to be snugly placed by him in that comfortable couch sipping coffee and kisses at the same time ... I love you even to madness, and do not suppose that I set [out] to show the power I have over you. I swear I suffer the torments of the damned when you are away and although there is nothing I would not sacrifice to give you a moments enjoyment I cannot bear that your amusement should spring from any other source than myself. Are you angry, love, at my selfishness. You never answer questions and I sometimes think I bore you by writing ... It appears an age since we parted and I would that we were never separated a moment. Is it vain to suppose you would love one better and better the longer we were together. I feel I am not the vain frivolous being I am set down to be and with you for my guiding star what would I not do to retain and cherish the love I've gained ...'

It was probably with some relief that Disraeli discovered during 1836 that Henrietta was also having an affair with Daniel Maclise, the Irish painter. Disraeli broke off his affair with Henrietta that autumn.

Marriage
On 22 May 1833 Disraeli wrote to his sister Sarah:

'Bye the bye, would you like Lady Z____* for a sister-in-law, very clever, 25000*l* and domestic? As for "love" all my friends who married for love and beauty either beat their wives or live apart from them. This is literally the case. I may commit many follies in life, but I never intend to marry for "love" which I am sure is a guarantee of infelicity.'

His scheme did not succeed, but in 1839 he married Mary Anne Wyndham Lewis, the rich widow of his senior colleague at Maidstone. She was twelve years older than Disraeli and when he had first met her as his colleague's wife, he had disliked her. When Mrs Bulwer wanted him to take Mrs Wyndham Lewis into dinner, he had protested: 'Oh, anything rather than that insufferable woman,' adding, as he often did, 'but Allah is great.'

He admitted candidly in a letter to Mary Anne of 7 February 1839:

*Lady Charlotte Bertie who later married Josiah Guest, MP.

> 'I avow, when I first made advances to you I was influenced by
> no romantic feelings.'

But he had already come to love her deeply. On 30 December 1838
he had written to her:

> 'I pass my nights and days in scenes of strange and fascinating
> rapture. Till I embrace you I shall not know what calmness is.
> I write this to beg you to have your hand *ungloved* when you
> arrive, so that you may stand by me, and I may hold and clasp
> and feel your soft delicious hand as I help your mother out of
> the carriage ... A thousand and 1000 kisses. More, more,
> come, come, come.'

Mary Anne in turn, warm-hearted, impulsive, scatterbrain that she
was, was devoted to her husband. She once wrote a list of their
contrasting qualities, his on the left, hers on the right:

> *'His eyes they are as black as Sloes,*
> *But oh! so beautiful his nose.*

Very calm	Very effervescent
Manners grave and almost sad	Gay and happy looking when speaking
Never irritable	Very irritable
Bad-humoured	Good-humoured
Warm in love but cold in friendship	Cold in love but warm in friendship
Very patient	No patience
Very studious	Very idle
Very generous	Only generous to those she loves
Often says what he does not think	Never says anything she does not think
It is impossible to find out who he likes or dislikes from his manner. He does not show his feelings	Her manner is quite different, and to those she likes she shows her feelings
No vanity	Much vanity
Conceited	No conceit
No self-love	Much self-love
He is seldom amused	Everything amuses her
He is a genius	She is a dunce
He is to be depended on to a certain degree	She is not to be depended upon
His whole soul is devoted to ambition	She has no ambition and hates politics

So it is evident they sympathize only on one subject: Maidstone, like most husbands and wives about their children.'

She once crushed her hand in a carriage door but suffered the pain in
silence so that Disraeli would not be upset before a speech.

Disraeli himself admitted her idiosyncrasies. He once said she
could never remember who came first, Greeks or Romans, but when
George Smythe spoke disrespectfully of her in Disraeli's presence he
crushed him immediately:

> 'George, there is one word in the English Language of which
> you are ignorant.'
> 'What is that?'
> 'Gratitude, George.'

Mrs Disraeli's Parsimony

Sir Henry Lucy recorded in his diary that when the Prince and
Princess of Teck came to stay at Hughenden, Mary Anne bought only
six rolls for breakfast. He also noted that she once ordered a quarter
of cheese, but sent it back because Disraeli had to return to London
at short notice.

A Legacy

In 1851 Mrs Brydges Williams, an elderly widow of Jewish origin
living in Torquay, wrote to Disraeli out of the blue inviting him to
become one of her executors, adding that 'whoever are my executors
will also be my residuary legatees.' After hesitating judiciously for
about six weeks, Disraeli conditionally accepted her offer. He and
Mary Anne visited their benefactress fairly soon afterwards and from
that time until her death in 1863, they remained good friends. From
1858 he wrote to her about thirty times a year, visited her annually,
and sent presents of game given to him by owners of country estates.
In return, she sent the Disraelis local fish—'gigantic soles and
colossal prawns', as he described them with a flourish. The residue of
her estate amounted to over £30,000, and Disraeli's lawyer, Sir Philip
Rose, thought it might be worthwhile making knowledge of the
bequest public:

> 'I wish you would consider whether some paragraph might

not be advantageously put in the newspapers alluding to the
bequest and the grounds for it. These things are catching and
the great probability is that the examples would be followed if
properly made known.'

Queen Victoria

The Queen loved Disraeli's peculiar brand of charm and flattery
which he himself had described as 'laying it on with a trowel'. When
he was first appointed Prime Minister, Victoria commented in a letter
to her eldest daughter Vicky:

> 'He is full of poetry, romance and chivalry. When he knelt
> down to kiss my hand wh. he took in both his – he said: "In
> loving loyalty and faith.".'

The same month, Disraeli wrote to the Queen suggesting a name for
the vacant Thistle:

> 'Yr Majesty is a much better judge of these matters than
> himself; and indeed there are few public matters on wh., he
> feels more and more every day, yr. Majesty is not much more
> competent to advise than be advised.'

Their mutual devotion deepened; Victoria sent him bunches of prim-
roses (his favourite flowers) and, finally in 1880, a valentine.

Meeting with Melbourne

Even before he entered the House of Commons Disraeli met Lord
Melbourne at a dinner party given by the Nortons (see Melbourne).
Melbourne was intrigued by the rather extraordinary young man
before him and asked:

> 'Well now, tell me, what do you want to be?'
> Disraeli: I want to be Prime Minister.
> Melbourne: No chance of that in our time. It is all arranged
> and settled. Nobody can compete with Stanley . . . If you are
> going to enter politics and mean to stick to it, I dare say you
> will do very well, for you have ability and enterprise; and if
> you are careful how you steer, no doubt you will get into some
> post at last. But you must put all these foolish notions out of

your head; they won't do at all. Stanley will be the next PM you
will see.'

Maiden Speech

Disraeli's maiden speech in the House of Commons on the subject of
Irish elections was a failure. Towards the end he had great difficulty
in making himself heard, but he did not give up until he had shouted
in a voice that could be heard above the uproar:

> 'I will sit down now, but the time will come when you will
> hear me.'

Physical Courage

Mrs Disraeli once admitted:

> 'Dizzy has the most wonderful moral courage in the world but
> no physical courage. When he uses his showerbath, I always
> have to pull the string.'

On Becoming Prime Minister

When congratulated by friends, Disraeli replied:

> 'Yes, I have climbed to the top of the greasy pole.'

On Becoming Lord Beaconsfield

When a friend asked how he liked being in the House of Lords he
said:

> 'I am dead; dead but in the Elysian fields.'

Wit

Disraeli hated the cold and particularly disliked this aspect of life in
English country houses. He described Windsor as 'that castle of the
winds' and once remarked on being given a glass of champagne:

> 'Thank God for something warm.'

During his last illness he was offered an air cushion to lie on:

> 'Take away that emblem of mortality,' he ordered.

The Peaks of New Guinea

Far from the world of Downing Street, Captain John Moresby was exploring the depths of New Guinea. He later wrote about two peaks he had discovered:

> 'Their relative position and the greatness suggested irresistibly the names I gave them. Mounts Gladstone and Disraeli. In connection with this, I wrote to each of those eminent men for permission to confirm my action, and, in due course I received the following replies. . .'

From Gladstone:

> 'Sir, I have the honour to acknowledge the receipt of your letter of June 24, and to return my best thanks for the compliment you have paid me, little deserved as it is, in naming after me the highest peak of the Finisterre Range in New Guinea.'

and from Disraeli:

> 'Allow me to acknowledge the compliment you have paid me by planting my name on the north-east coast of New Guinea, and in selecting a godfather so distinguished for the peak which faces Mount Disraeli'.

Disraeli is also said to have remarked:

> 'I hope we shall agree better in New Guinea than we do in the House of Commons.'

On His Last Speech

On 31 March 1881 he corrected his last speech for Hansard, declaring: 'I will not go down to posterity talking bad language.'

WILLIAM EWART GLADSTONE
(1809–1898)

'Oxford on the surface: Liverpool underneath.'

Anonymous contemporary saying

THE FOURTH son of John Gladstone, a wealthy corn merchant and ship-owner who later became an MP, Gladstone was born in Liverpool on 29 December 1809. He was sent to Eton, described by him as 'a very good place for those who liked boating and Latin verse,' and then to Christ Church, Oxford, where he was President of the Oxford Union and also took a double First in Classics and Mathematics. After six months travelling in France and Italy, he entered the House of Commons as Tory MP for Newark in 1832.

Gladstone's great abilities were quickly recognized by Peel who gave him a minor office in his 1835 administration and then appointed him to the Board of Trade in 1841. He was a notable Chancellor of the Exchequer under Aberdeen (1853–5), Palmerston (1855 and 1859–65) and Russell (1865–6). On Russell's resignation he became Leader of the Liberals and held office as Prime Minister four times (1868–74; 1880–85; 1886 and 1892–4) for a total of thirteen years. His first ministry was the greatest reforming administration of the nineteenth century, producing measures to disestablish the Irish church, to deal with the grievances of the Irish peasantry, to reform the army, and to improve education.

Later his achievements were limited by failing physical powers, by troubles abroad and by dissension within his own party, and above all, by his overwhelming concern for Ireland and its problems. He finally retired, to the evident relief of Queen Victoria, in March 1894 at the age of eighty-four, and died four years later on 19 May 1898.

Gladstone married Catherine, the daughter of Sir Stephen Glynne of Hawarden, in 1839. They had eight children. In addition to a busy political career lasting over sixty years, Gladstone published a number of books, on religion, classics, theology, and foreign affairs.

Proposals

In the spring of 1835, Gladstone met Caroline Farquhar, the sister of one of his Eton contemporaries. She was tall and beautiful, and Gladstone speedily made up his mind to propose to her. Instead of approaching the lady herself he wrote her father, Sir Thomas Farquhar, a long and tortuous letter:

> 'I scarcely dare to conjecture with what feelings you and Lady Farquhar will receive the request I am about to proffer to you . . . My father's liberality enables me, his fourth and youngest son, to contemplate a change of state, I trust, and believe, without impropriety, though I would guard myself against appearing to imply that any great advantages of fortune are ever likely to be within my reach. Neither would my inclinations, so far as I am acquainted with them, be such as to render acquisitions of this kind more probable . . . In my own person I have been blessed by Providence with what, though anything but great in itself, may nevertheless be deemed so when viewed in relation to either my expectations or deserts. But no one is more conscious than myself that the uncertainty of all things earthly has perhaps, in the present day, a peculiarly forcible application to one whose destinies have like mine early been committed upon the perilous contingencies of political life, and who is therefore especially bound to live with reference to those permanent and exalted objects which belong to our condition as human beings.'

The Farquhars' response was not encouraging but Gladstone continued to hope. By December Caroline's brother was forced to be blunt, confessing to his old friend: 'The barrier you have to overcome is the obtaining of my sister's affections.'

Less than two years later, Gladstone again attempted to find a bride, proposing to Lady Frances Douglas, the eldest daughter of the Earl and Countess of Morton. Again he was rejected. A mutual friend, the Dean of Edinburgh's wife, was both bold and kind enough to offer advice:

'Another time, dear Mr Gladstone, be more guarded of yourself . . . A young mind is startled by a proposal of this kind, when she has not had an opportunity even to suspect preference.'

So, in 1838 when Gladstone fell in love yet again, this time with Catherine Glynne, some of his old confidence had been eroded. He travelled with her family to Italy in January 1839 but, together at the Colosseum in moonlight, he could not find the courage to speak, and resorted to another of his circuitous letters, the second paragraph probably containing the longest sentence ever to be written in a love letter:

'I address you, my dear Miss Glynne, in terms below my desires, yet perhaps beyond my right to say in the simple words which I believe will in any event be most acceptable to you, and which no occasion has offered to address to you otherwise than by letter. My heart and hand are at your disposal.

'I seek much in a wife in gifts better than those of our human pride, and am also sensible that she can find little in me: sensible that, were you to treat this note as the offspring of utter presumption, I must not be surprised: sensible that the lot I invite you to share, even if it be not attended, as I trust it is not, with peculiar disadvantages of an outward kind, is one, I do not say unequal in your deserts, for that were saying little, but liable at the best to changes and perplexities and pains which, for myself, I contemplate without apprehension, but to which it is perhaps selfishness in the main with the sense of inward dependence counteracting an opposite sense of my too real unworthiness, which would make me contribute to explore another – and that other!

'For the substance of what I write I have no apology to offer which can be effectual. As respects its time, my own mind required no postponement, and I could not presume that it would give me any more reasonable hope of success to your affections. I wait your Command with the humility which I owe to a being so far purer and better than my own, and with other feelings which I have not the right to describe in the colours of truth. And, indeed, they are chequered with the consciousnesss that I ought to wish you a more blessed portion in life than that which alone it is in my power to tender. For pardon, for indulgence, I do not ask.

'Your own nature will yield me, unsolicited, much more than I desire. But I must cease. May you live, and die, it is not less my anticipation than my desire, from day to day more possessed of the peace which passeth understanding, and of the holiness which is its fountain.

'With esteem, with gratitude, suffer me by one more act of boldness to add, with warm and true affection,

I am Yours,

W. E. GLADSTONE'

The beautiful twenty-seven-year-old woman, who finally accepted Gladstone's hand six months later, was an ideal choice for him. Well-connected and devoutly religious without a hint of priggishness, she brought a much-needed breath of fresh air into Gladstone's life. Forty-seven years later her letter to her husband on their wedding anniversary was as fresh and devoted as ever:

'*My own own,*
We are away from one another, but not in spirit. My mind travels back to the 47 years of blessed memory with a thankful heart. Thank you for all you have done, for all you are, and for the lovely example you have been to me, in sorrow, or in joy! And Almighty God strengthen and help you more and more, and lift you up *continually* so that if further work and further toil and anxiety be yours, the same Hand which has so mercifully sustained you, may still lead you along the earthly path, until it leads to the Heavenly Habitation of rest and bliss, to the shadowless light of the full day.

'Darling old thing, I long to give you such a kiss. We are first going to church, and the best thing of all will be to pray for you, and to thank God for the extraordinary mercies which for 47 years have been given to us.

Till tomorrow,

Your loving

Wifie.'

She herself recognized that it was good for her husband that his wife was untidy, protesting unrepentantly:

'What a bore you would have been if you had married someone as tidy as yourself.'

She did not improve when she was the wife of the Prime Minister.
Their own daughter Mary was shocked to arrive at Carlton House
Terrace one day to find:

> '. . . all the fires out, the drawing [room] in a despairing state
> of disorder, and a heap of flowers to arrange with nought to
> put them in, and a dinner party impending in half-an-hour.'

It was the same daughter, Mary, who remembered them standing
together on the hearthrug with their arms around each other swaying
and singing:

> *A ragamuffin husband and a rantipoling wife,*
> *We'll fiddle it and scrape it through the ups and downs of*
> *life.*

Catherine and her sister, Lady Lyttelton, and their families invented
a kind of language for themselves known as Glynnese. Gladstone
himself did not use it much but delighted in hearing Catherine use it,
as she did on every possible occasion. She once walked into the
Cabinet Room at Number 10 as a meeting was breaking up and
announced that she had pulled a muscle in her leg:

> 'Such a quiz, William, I've sprouted a lameness.'

As an old lady, Catherine was more disorganized than ever. One
story was told by Henry Ponsonby to Campbell-Bannerman:

> 'She wrote this year to Borthwick, who is at Birkhall "Dear
> Lord Borthwick, will you let my son-in-law Mr Drew fish in
> your waters at Invercauld?" To which the answer had to be,
> "Dear Mrs G. I am not a Lord, I do not live at Invercauld, and
> I have no fishing." '

Rescuing Prostitutes

One of the most attractive things about the Gladstones was their
complete unworldliness. Determined to do good and to save souls,
they expended a tremendous amount of time, trouble, and money on

charitable works. During the cotton famine, for example, Hawarden was teeming with out-of-work Lancashire cotton workers being trained by Catherine to become domestic servants. Their chief charitable work, though, was the rescue of prostitutes and it is a tribute to Gladstone's glaring integrity that this work did not land him in more difficulties and embarrassments than it did. In retrospect, he was amazingly rash: walking the streets by night alone, one or two evenings a week, accosting prostitutes, even suggesting that they accompany him home to meet his wife and to be given food and shelter. His aim was to enable these women to escape from prostitution and be given a chance in life. His motives have been challenged, both at the time and almost ever since, but were probably impeccable. His achievements were manifold: in 1848 he helped to found the Church Penitentiary Association for the Reclamation of Fallen Women; in 1854 he and his wife founded the Clewer Home of Mercy; he was on the Management Committee of the Millbank Penitentiary; and in 1863 he helped found the St Mary Magdalen Home of Refuge at Paddington. Even so, his closest advisers were appalled by the obvious dangers involved in this sort of work. On 10 February 1882, Lord Granville and Lord Rosebery spun a coin to decide which of them should have the unenviable task of tackling Gladstone about his prostitutes. Rosebery lost, Gladstone listened, but his work went on. What made matters worse was the fact that Gladstone was undoubtedly susceptible to a pretty face. Lily Langtry was one of his favourites; he visited her occasionally and even included her in the privileged number invited to send their letters to him in double envelopes so that they would not be opened by his private secretaries.

Sometimes the threat of scandal almost surfaced but was stopped by Gladstone himself as in 1882 when a Colonel Tottenham, an MP, saw the Prime Minister talking to a prostitute on the Duke of York's steps and dined out on the story. One of the ladies who heard the story wrote to Sir Edward Hamilton (one of Gladstone's secretaries) who reported it to the Prime Minister. Gladstone promptly replied to the lady on a postcard:

> 'It may be true that the gentleman saw me in such conversation, but the object was not what he assumed, or, as I am afraid, hoped.
>
> W.E.G.'

Years after Gladstone's death, Peter Wright, a journalist, wrote that Gladstone had 'in private pursued and possessed every sort of woman.' Enraged at this attack on the reputation of a dead man, Gladstone's two surviving sons forced Captain Wright to sue them for libel. During the five-day trial in 1927, more attention was paid to Peter Wright's integrity as a serious author than to Gladstone's pursuit of prostitutes. After Captain Wright had left the witness box, the trial turned into a rout. The verdict for the defendants was greeted with loud applause, and the foreman of the jury saw fit to add:

> 'We are of the unanimous opinion that the evidence which has been placed before us has completely vindicated the high moral character of the late Mr W. E. Gladstone.'

The Stern Brother

Gladstone's only surviving sister, Helen, was at various times a sore trial to him. His forbearance was considerable when she took opium or became engaged to a Polish count whose family wanted her to live in Russia and become a member of the Russian Orthodox Church. What he absolutely could not tolerate though was that after her final conversion to Roman Catholicism she should have torn up the works of Protestant theologians to use as lavatory paper. He wrote to her on the subject on 24 November 1848:

> 'I write to you with the greatest reluctance on a most painful subject. I have lately been engaged in arranging the books in my father's library. . .
>
> 'I have this morning seen with my own eyes that which, without seeing, I would never have believed: a number of books upon religious subjects in the two *closets* attached to your sleeping apartments, some entire, some torn up, the borders or out coverings of some, remaining – under circum- stances which admit of no doubt as to the shameful use to which they were put.
>
> 'I do not enter into any discussion. The subject does not bear it . . . You have no right to perpetrate these indignities against any religion sincerely held.'

Gladstone and his Queen

'He speaks to me as if I was a public meeting.'

QUEEN VICTORIA

When they first met, Queen Victoria and Gladstone were perfectly friendly. In 1845, he first stayed at Windsor, carefully locking away his purse before going down to dinner and then worrying all evening how he would pay if he lost at cards. Luckily, he won two shillings and sixpence, but his worrying was not over. As he left to go to bed, the Groom of the Chamber told him the knee of his Court suit had split and Gladstone fretted over whether it had been like that all evening.

As the years passed, the Queen's cordiality noticeably lessened. Unlike Disraeli, Gladstone was incapable of flattering her. He was rash enough to suggest to her that she should fulfil more public duties, that she should not always cling rigidly to her dead husband's view of things, and that she should give the Prince of Wales more to do. In her turn, the Queen disliked Gladstone's popularity with the masses, his growing Radicalism, and his views on Ireland. By the 1870s she was calling him 'that madman, Gladstone', and by 1892, 'that dangerous old fanatic'.

After one audience with her in 1892 Gladstone made a note of the topics:

1. Inquiry for the Queen's health
2. The fogs of London and Windsor
3. The Laureateship. W. Watson
4. The Dowager Duchess of Sutherland . . .
5. The Roumanian Marriage . . .
6. Lord Acton: not yet personally known to the Queen
7. Condition of Lady Kimberley
8. Has Mrs Gladstone still a nephew who is a master at Eton
9. Dean Wellesley . . .
10. The Dean of Peterborough
11. Health of the Bp. of Rochester
12. Agricultural distress (HM seemed half inclined to lay it upon ("large importations")
13. Commission thereupon (not desired)

These are all or nearly all the topics of conversation introduced at the audience tonight. From them may be gathered in some degree the terms of confidence between H.M. and her Prime Minister. Not perhaps with perfect exactitude, as she instinctively avoids points of possible difference. But then it seems that such are now all points.'

A Visitors' Book

When visitors stayed at Raby Castle, the home of the Clevelands, they were asked to put their profession into the Visitors' Book. Disraeli put 'patriotism': Gladstone wrote 'apprentice'.

On Being Made Prime Minister

On 1 December 1868 Gladstone was, as he often did, cutting down a tree in the park at Hawarden. A telegram arrived telling him that the Queen's private secretary would be arriving from Windsor that evening. 'Very significant' remarked Gladstone having read it. Then he resumed work on the tree for a few minutes, put down his axe again, and announced to his guest who had been watching the whole operation: 'My mission is to pacify Ireland.'

The G.O.M.

From the early 1880s Gladstone was widely known as the Grand Old Man. To the Cecils, however, the initials stood for God's Only Mistake. During the Sudanese crisis, the initials were reversed to read M.O.G. – Murderer of Gordon. There was a song in the music halls at the time:

> *The M.O.G., when his life ebbs out,*
> *Will ride in a fiery chariot,*
> *And sit in state,*
> *On a red-hot plate*
> *Between Pilate and Judas Iscariot.*

Gladstone at the Theatre

Gladstone loved going to the theatre, especially to the Lyceum, where by 1892 his special chair had been upholstered and moved, and a velvet curtain put round it to protect him from draughts. The same year, when he was eighty-two, his daughter Mary saw him watching a performance from up in the 'flys'.

During one performance of *The Corsican Brothers* in 1880 Gladstone was backstage. He asked if he could be an extra in the Opera House scene, so was put behind one of the flats which represented the opera boxes and given strict instructions to remain hidden from view. Much excited, Gladstone forgot his orders and at one moment peered out too far. Instantly, he was recognized by the Lyceum audience who called out 'Bravo Gladstone'.

The Welsh Cow

In August 1892 a Welsh cow which had escaped from the woods at Harwarden rushed at him, threw him on his back and stood over him. The cow was shot and Gladstone returned home, not even telling his wife of the incident until dinner-time when she noticed he was looking rather unwell. The next day an enormous wreath arrived at Hawarden with a card attached. On the card was written:

> 'To the memory of the patriotic cow which sacrificed its life in the attempt to save Ireland from Home Rule.'

. . . And Margot Tennant

As an old man, Gladstone was one of the many conquests of the young vivacious Margot Tennant, who later married Asquith (see below). After one visit to Hawardcn, he sent her one of his better poems:

MARGOT

When Parliament ceases, and comes the Recess,
And we seek, in the country, rest after distress,
As a rule upon visitors, place an embargo
But make an exception in favour of Margot.

For she brings such a treasure of movement and life
Fun, spirit, and stir, to folk weary with strife.
Though young, and though fair, who can hold such a cargo
Of all the good qualities going as Margot.

She also claimed that, during the Committee Stage of the Home Rule Bill in 1893, he had the following conversation with Asquith:

Gladstone: Have you ever considered who is the ugliest man in the party opposite?

Asquith: Certainly, it is without doubt X.

Gladstone: You are wrong. X is no doubt an ugly fellow, but a much uglier is Y.

Asquith: Why?

Gladstone: Apply a very simple test. Imagine them both magnified on a colossal scale. X's ugliness would then begin to look dignified and even impressive, while the more you enlarged Y, the meaner he would become.

ROBERT ARTHUR TALBOT GASCOYNE CECIL
Third Marquess of Salisbury (1830–1903)

'I am always very glad when Lord Salisbury makes a
great speech . . . It is sure to contain at least one
blazing indiscretion which it is a delight to remember.'

Speech of 25 November 1887 at Hull by A.E. PARKER,
LORD MORLEY

THE SECOND son of the second Marquess, Robert Cecil was educated at Eton and at Christ Church, Oxford where he took a fourth in Mathematics. Uncertain what career to follow, he took a two-year trip to South Africa, Australia and New Zealand before entering the House of Commons and becoming a Fellow of All Souls, both in 1853.

In 1857, Lord Robert married Georgina Alderson, the daughter of one of the Barons of the Exchequer. For the first few years of their marriage, he eked out their small income by contributing a large number of articles to various reviews, but in 1865 his prospects were transformed by the death of his elder brother.

As Lord Cranborne, he held office briefly (1866–7) in Lord Derby's ministry, and in 1878, by now Lord Salisbury, he was appointed Foreign Secretary accompanying Disraeli to the Congress of Berlin. After Disraeli's death, he held office as Prime Minister three times: from June 1885 to January 1886, from July 1886 to August 1892, and from June 1895 to July 1902, and during most of this period was also Foreign Secretary. His wife died after a stroke in 1899 leaving him five sons and two daughters. Salisbury himself died at Hatfield on 22 August 1903 and was buried in the churchyard there, his family having turned down the offer of a grave in Westminster Abbey.

Childhood

Cecil was deeply unhappy both at his first school to which he was sent at the age of six and at Eton. Cleverer than the others boys, he was bullied mercilessly, writing to his father pathetically:

> 'I am bullied from morning to night without ceasing . . . I am obliged to hide myself all the evening in some corner to prevent being bullied . . . When I come into dinner they kick and shin me and I am obliged to go out of dinner without eating anything.'

Even during the holidays, horror of his school-fellows never left him, and if he was in London he kept away from the main streets for fear of bumping into a fellow Etonian. Cecil at last managed to persuade his father to take him away from Eton when he was fifteen. Yet, even though he kept his own sons at home until they were almost twelve, he then had them educated at Eton, giving them these few words of comfort. 'If you should ever be in danger of a flogging, take the train home immediately.' Salisbury had conquered his loathing for the place enough to accompany his two elder sons to the school for the first time but was afterwards so overcome by depression that when the time came for his two younger sons to go, he left it to his wife to deliver them safely.

Australian gold camps

Cecil's visit to Australia coincided with the gold rush of 1851. Still in a frock coat and white top hat, he visited some of the gold diggings in Victoria, recording in his journal the fairly primitive lifestyle with a surprising but obvious enjoyment:

> 'It was a solid meal, consisting of damper, mutton and potatoes – the two latter half-cooked in the embers of the camp-fire. We ate these provisions in a species of widened pannikin, something between a wash-hand basin and a soup plate, ingeniously constructed so as to be inconvenient in either capacity. Such a conventionality as a tablecloth was, of course, not to be expected. But I pitied the poor Commissioner, who, being deprived of his only pair of knives and forks by his guests, was reduced to the tantalizing expedient of carving with his penknife. I was honoured by the only chair in the place . . . Mr Cockburn (the Commissioner) sat in a

corner upon an inverted bucket . . . our beverage was tea, with a strong lash of stringy bark. Afterwards brandy made its appearance – good fiery stuff and no mistake. We sat up some time drinking grog.'

Middlesex Militia

The second Marquess was disappointed that his second son was not an energetic outdoor man, and that he showed no interest in the army. As Lord Lieutenant of Middlesex, he controlled the appointment of colonel of the county Militia and in 1855 attempted to confer the honour on Robert. His son was appalled, writing back immediately:

> 'Your proposition gave me a stomach-ache all this morning . . . I detest all soldiering beyond measure. As far as taste goes I would rather be at the treadmill.'

Marriage

Cecil's father at first forbade the marriage of his son to Georgina Alderson. Robert was uncompromising, arguing:

> 'Your objections to my marriage rested mainly on the "privations" it would entail. "Privation" means the loss of something I enjoy now. If the privation in question is the want of food, warmth, clothing, I am not prepared to face it. But I cannot lose anything else I now enjoy, for the simple reason that I do not enjoy anything. Amusements I have *none* . . . The persons who will cut me because I marry Miss Alderson are precisely the persons of whose society I am so anxious to be quit.'

There was an enforced separation lasting six months, but the couple married in London in July 1857, the bridegroom's father and elder brother refusing to attend.

Appearance

As his daughter was forced to admit, Salisbury's dress 'was never his strong point'. He usually wore dull grey trousers and waistcoat under a frock coat grown shiny with age, and at Monte Carlo in 1866 he was refused entry to the casino because he looked so shabby. Occasionally, carelessness lapsed into eccentricity. Once as an old man, he forgot to wear the skull-cap in church that protected him from draughts. Half way through the service he deposited one of his grey woollen gloves on top of his head, keeping it there until he came out of church. As Prime Minister, he went on one occasion to the palace in a mixture of two uniforms, endearingly excusing himself to a shocked Prince of Wales, for whom correct uniform was almost a fetish:

> 'It was a dark morning and I am afraid that my mind must have been occupied by some subject of less importance.'

Château Margaux

During the 1880 election campaign, Disraeli was invited to stay at Hatfield even though Lord and Lady Salisbury were away. Salisbury left instructions to his butler that only Disraeli should be given any of his Grand Château Margaux 1870 to drink. 'I feel awkward,' admitted Disraeli, 'but forget my embarrassment in the exquisite flavour.'

Science

On 15 February 1887, Salisbury admitted to a peer seeking political office who also happened to be a scientist:

> 'I know very little of science, and a good deal of politics: and I would never advise anybody to travel along the intolerably tiresome road on which I have travelled myself – who has the other open to him.'

In fact, he knew enough about science to be able to state after an explosion in his private laboratory, from which he emerged covered in blood, that it had been caused by experimenting with sodium in an insufficiently dried retort. His laboratory had been built in the Hatfield basement, and was connected by a spiral staircase to the corner of his study.

Having experimented successfully with electric lights outside the entrance to Hatfield, he next tried them inside the house, happily disregarding the misgivings of his women guests who felt the harse electric lights at the Hatfield dining room table were far from flattering. Sometimes there were 'miniature storms of lightning ending in complete collapse.' Or alternatively, members of the family would have to interrupt their incessant arguments to throw cushions when the wires sparked.

Hatfield was also one of the first English houses to have telephones installed. The wires ran loosely along the floors so that it was not unknown for guests to trip over them at moments when the electric lights failed. Salisbury used to make his children listen to the ear-pieces in various rooms as he bellowed 'Hey diddle, the cat and the fiddle' into the mouthpiece.

The Recluse

Salisbury was not sociable, avoiding polite society if at all possible. If he had to go out to dinner he would sometimes make no attempt to speak to the ladies sitting next to him. Visitors to Hatfield were particularly resented, and he would occasionally withdraw to a secluded part of the grounds known as the Vineyard where everyone knew his solitude was inviolable. On one occasion when he was asked to say a few words at Hatfield to a group of Conservative voters from his eldest son's constituency he fled to London – only to meet them all at Hatfield station on his return that evening.

Every so often, he recognized his duty to Hatfield guests or to political followers. Then, 'The courtesy with which he greeted his guests was unfailing' his daughter Gwendolen conceded, 'though rendered a trifle impersonal by his constant incapacity to identify them.'

A *National Review* article described one dinner for party supporters given by the Leader of the House of Commons at which Salisbury made an almost superhuman effort, asking for potted biographies of all the guests beforehand and going to tremendous efforts to speak to everyone. When finally he allowed himself to leave he said to his Private Secretary:

> 'I think I have done them all, but there was someone I have not identified, who, you said, made mustard.'

Salisbury and the Queen

Queen Victoria, although she admitted his 'peculiarities', was devoted to Lord Salisbury. Knowing that he was 'bad on his legs' he was the only man she ever asked to sit down. Sometimes, when both were on holiday in France, Queen Victoria would without warning drive over to the Salisbury's house for tea. A fellow guest, Milner, was impressed by their relationship:

'It is easy to see that she is very fond of him. Indeed I never saw two people get on better, their polished manners and deference to and esteem for each other were a delightful sight and one not readily to be forgotten.'

It was a harmony achieved in spite of Salisbury's intense dislike of Balmoral, feelings he had made plain to the Queen's Secretary, Henry Ponsonby:

'He refused to walk out and did not conceal his entire abhorrence of the place and the life there. He positively refused to admire the prospect or the deer which Lady Ely pointed out to him.'

Strict orders were sent to Ponsonby whenever Salisbury was to visit Balmoral that his bedroom must be at least 60 degrees Fahrenheit.

Patronage

Salisbury was notoriously careless about patronage, not at all enjoying his power. 'I declare, they die to spite me,' he said, when it seemed half the bishops in England were disappearing. Once two clergymen with similar names were candidates for a vacant bishopric. He eventually appointed the one not recommended by the Archbishop of Canterbury. 'Oh, I dare say he will do just as well' he explained to those puzzled by his choice.

Hatfield Pineapples

Salisbury took it into his head that too many pineapples were being grown and then consumed by his extravagant household. He ordered that no more were to be grown only to discover, some time later, a large quantity being carefully nurtured in one of his conservatories. He pulled them up and threw them all away.

The Jawbone of an Ass

Lord George Hamilton told the story of a Salisbury dinner party at which a smart young politician and an older country squire quarrelled, the young man accusing the older of being a Philistine. When the country gentleman had the honesty to admit – 'I don't know what you mean by a Philistine', Lord Salisbury interrupted:

'Don't you? A Philistine is a gentleman annoyed by the jawbone of an ass.'

The Tricycle

Lord Salisbury hated most sports but felt the need for active exercise to keep his weight under control. As a young man, he walked a lot, but in later life he took to riding a tricycle around the asphalted paths of Hatfield. For this, he wore a kind of sombrero hat and a short sleeveless cloak with a hole in the middle which made him look like a monk from some obscure order or other. If he planned to ride down some steep slopes he would take his under-coachman with him who would obligingly push him up the hills and then hop on behind as the tricycle returned downwards.

The Paper-knife

Lady Gwendolen and her father were on one of their walks together when he went into a stationer's shop and bought a sharp wooden paper-knife which he had seen in the window. When she asked him why he wanted it, he explained that it would be just the thing for keeping in his pocket and digging into his thigh to keep himself awake when foreign ambassadors came to see him.

Old Age

Always slow to recognize people through vagueness as well as poor eyesight, Salisbury's lack of recognition of even those he knew very well became quite startling in his old age. At the end of the Boer War, he picked up a signed photograph of Edward VII and announced 'Poor Buller [The Commander-in-Chief at the start of the war], what a mess he made of it.'

At a Hatfield garden party in 1903 Salisbury spent most of the afternoon avoiding the guests by remaining in his study but eventually emerged because he wished to speak to Lord Roberts. He found a white-haired man, took him back to his study, and talked with him at length. Only afterwards did he discover that he had been talking, not to Lord Roberts, but to Sir Harry Johnston, the African explorer and administrator.

Near the end of his life, he was out strolling near his London house with his soldier son when a smartly-dressed man raised his hat. 'Who is your guardsman friend?' enquired Lord Salisbury. It was his own butler.

ARCHIBALD PHILIP PRIMROSE

Fifth Earl of Rosebery (1847–1929)

'A dark horse in a loose box.'

Life of Sir William Harcourt, A. G. GARDINER

BORN ON 7 May 1847 in London, Archibald Primrose was the eldest son of Lord Dalmeny and his beautiful overbearing wife, Wilhelmina. Lord Dalmeny, despite a keen interest and belief in physical fitness, died when his eldest son was only three, leaving his widow in charge of the children's upbringing. Archibald was educated at Eton and at Christ Church, Oxford, which he left without taking a degree.

In 1868, he succeeded his grandfather as fifth earl, and ten years later consolidated the family fortunes by marrying Hannah, the only child of Baron Meyer Amschel Rothschild. Meanwhile, he had been a regular attender at the House of Lords, and his organization of Gladstone's Midlothian Campaign brought him to the centre of the political stage. Gladstone appointed Rosebery Under-Secretary at the Home Office (1881–3) and then Foreign Secretary (1886 and again 1892–4). On Gladstone's resignation in March 1894 Rosebery held office for fifteen months as Prime Minister, his job made almost unbearable by a divided Cabinet and a hostile Queen. It was with great relief that he resigned in 1895, and the following year resigned from the leadership of the Liberal party. Although Rosebery lived on until 1929, a lonely widower with two sons, and two daughters, he never held public office again.

Rosebery was an accomplished biographer, publishing works on Chatham, William Pitt, Napoleon and Lord Randolph Churchill.

Eton

At home rather a solitary child, Archie Primrose was in his element at Eton, writing in his diary when he left 'God grant I may never have such a wrench again'. On his last evening there he accompanied some Eton swells to a local theatre where they hurled both abuse and missiles at the actors from the safety of a box until the leading actor could stand it no longer and interrupted his performance to remark: 'I can bear your ridicule, but I would rather not be made a target of.'

As an old man, he asked his servant to buy him a gramophone and said that when it was obvious he was going to die, the Eton Boating Song was to be played. His wishes were carried out.

Christ Church

Despite living the privileged life of the rich aristocrat to the full, Rosebery's Christ Church career was not unsuccessful until he took it into his head that his chief ambition was to win the Derby as an undergraduate. He bought a horse called Ladas, by Lambton out of Zenobia, and ignoring Randolph Churchill's advice that the horse was 'a brute of a beggar', entered it for the 1868 Derby. When challenged by the Christ Church authorities to choose between his race-horse and his degree, there was no hesitation:

> 'Dear Mother,' he wrote, 'I have left Oxford. I have secured a house in Berkeley Square; and I have bought a horse to win the Derby. Your affectionate Archie.'

To make matters worse, the horse came last.

Rosebery had circulated to Christ Church friends the following forecast of the race. After the results, he added the final verse:

> *It is the Derby Wednesday, carrier pigeons come in flights.*
> *There is terror in St James' Street, and agony in White's*
> *From Hayling Isle to Newmarket they have begun to toast*
> *The foremost horse that stayed the course and foremost*
> *   passed the post.*
>
> *From Dan and from Beersheba, from Joppa and Gilgal.*
> *The Israelites are flocking, resolved to stand or fall:*
> *From the Baron* [de Rothschild] *to the broker each one is*
> *   like a lion, he*

Having staked his bottom shekel on the son of a bay
　Hermione.

The Christ Church tutors put a tax on those who came in
　late,
And they were puzzled how to spend the tribute of the Gate.
So they put it on the Derby, and pitched upon a horse
Who took his rise from Lambton's *thighs and cannot stay*
　the course.

There was a wailing in the Common Room, the Censors tore
　their hair,
Some scraped themselves with potsherds, and some began
　to swear,
They d . . . d the race of Lambton *and cursed Zenobia's*
　womb
And wished the race of racehorses a universal tomb.

'They're off!' They stream along the hill at a pace to try the
　bellows,
Which tomorrow will want mending in the 'Drums and
　Masaniellos.'
Bright as a scattered rainbow, swift as the dawn of day,
No living horse can stay the course in that breakneck sort of
　way.

They come along a cracker, now the ruck begins to shirk
Padwick is flogging Ethus, *and the Baron is at work;*
And from the hill arises a wail of souls in pain,
Where Gad and where Jeshurua bewail their vanished gain.

And now from out the beaten crowd a flogging four there
　come,
Pero Gomez *and* Pretender, Ladas *and* Belladrum
They have passed the Judge's tribune – Good heavens, what
　a pot!
And all shout 'What the devil's won?' and Echo answers
　'What?'

Now thank your prophet, Gentlemen, ye who plunged upon
　the Drummer,
Who lumped it upon Rubert *or on* Ladas *went a bummer,*
For he told the first two horses who the Judge's tribune
　passed

> *Then he wrote a warning comma – and the names of the two last.*

Although Rosebery later very much regretted abandoning his Oxford career, his passion for race-horses continued. He loved the excitement and the camaraderie of the Turf, and in 1872 bought The Durdans estate near Epsom where he started a stud. His ambition to win the Derby was eventually achieved three times, including on two successive occasions when he was Prime Minister.

Hannah

Rosebery was introduced to Hannah de Rothschild by Mrs Disraeli at Newmarket in 1868. The two fell in love, and it is fair to say that, although by the time of their marriage Hannah had inherited Mentmore as well as an enormous fortune, her wealth meant little to him. Various members of the family had misgivings, Rosebery's mother confessing:

> 'You can easily suppose how unhappy I must feel in finding that you have chosen as your wife, and the mother of your children, one who has not the faith and hope of Christ.'

Nevertheless, the two were extremely happy, and the religious differences do not appear to have caused trouble. Their children later recalled how their father used to take a tray of food up to his wife's bedroom at the end of the Day of Atonement and how they sat together eating and chatting well into the night. When she died in 1890, it was only to Queen Victoria that he allowed himself to admit:

> 'There is, however, one incident of this tragedy only less painful than the actual loss, which is that at the moment of death the difference of creed makes itself felt, and another religion steps in to claim the body.'

After her death Rosebery always used black-edged writing paper and never allowed her bedroom to be used.

A Splendid Life

Although they disliked large parties and wasteful extravagance, the Roseberys lived extremely well, owning houses in London and Scotland as well as Mentmore and Durdans. Fleets of servants kept each house running efficiently. Gladstone once expressed his regret when one of the horses fetching him from Edinburgh to Dalmeny dropped down dead, only to be informed 'we have two of the same colour at Mentmore.' Paintings, tapestries, and, above all, rare books, were avidly and lovingly collected. Among his treasures were Charles I's copy of the Book of Common Prayer of 1637, Mary Queen of Scots' Bible, Napoleon's travelling library, a 1437 copy of 'De Imitatione Christi' by Thomas à Kempis, and a Shakespeare First Folio.

'Rule Britannia'

When dealing with his Foreign Office boxes, Rosebery was often to be heard humming 'Rule Britannia'. He said it kept his spirits up.

Less Jocular

As Prime Minister, Rosebery was urged by the Queen to be 'less jocular' in his speeches. He had often appeared flippant, a political dilettante, out of place in a sombre world. In August 1881, the day he first took ministerial office, he noted in his Diary:

> Land Bill in the House of Lords, I ordered a grouse punctually at 8 at Brooks; went to eat it, returned in about half an hour, and found I had missed the divisions! A nice beginning for a subordinate of the Government.

In his Diary several years later, he was to describe his appointment as Foreign Secretary as 'an awful scrape'. When Granville passed a note to him at his very first Cabinet meeting asking 'I wonder what you thought of us all?', he sent back the reply 'more numerous than the House of Lords and not so united.'

The Village Pym

Rosebery once made a speech in which he flatteringly likened two leading members of the audience to seventeenth-century parliamentary heroes, calling them 'the village Hampden' and 'the village Pym'. The latter, after bearing this for a while, stalked out furious because he thought he had been called 'the village pimp'.

The Black Side

There was a darker side to Rosebery's nature, described by Churchill in *Great Contemporaries*:

'He could cast a chill over all, and did not hesitate to freeze and snub. On these occasions his face became expressionless, almost a slab, and his eyes lost their light and fire. One saw an altogether different person. But after a bit one knew the real man was there all the time, hiding perversely behind a curtain.'

Sometimes, he did not feel like seeing even those he had invited. He once never appeared at a week-end party at Dalmeny until he suddenly emerged in order to get a paper-knife from his library. He got it, and then disappeared again for the rest of the week-end. At one dinner party when a young lady he did not like the look of confessed to having read a particular book, he was almost cruel:

'It is, indeed, interesting information to us to know that you are capable of so intellectual a pursuit.'

Even royalty was not spared his moods. At a Windsor houseparty Fritz Ponsonby recalled that:

'. . . if anyone tried to draw him into conversation he turned an eye like a fish on them and withered them with biting sarcasm. Although he eventually warmed to his fellow guests he remained extremely frosty towards Edward VII during the whole visit.'

Insomnia

Always prone to sleeplessness, Rosebery's insomnia was at its worst during his fifteen months as Prime Minister. He regularly slept no more than two hours a night, recalling later:

'I cannot forget 1895, to lie night after night, staring wide awake, hopeless of sleep, tormented in nerves, and to realize all that was going on, at which I was present, so to speak, like a disembodied spirit, to watch one's corpse, as it were, day after day, is an experience which no sane man with a conscience would repeat.'

The Wrong Clothes

On at least two occasions, Rosebery appeared before Edward VII, who was meticulous in such matters, in the wrong clothes. The King once 'eyed him angrily' all through dinner on board the royal yacht when he wore a white tie with a Yacht squadron mess-jacket. Another time Rosebery went to a Buckingham Palace reception wearing trousers instead of knee-breeches. 'I presume that you have come in the suite of the American ambassador,' remarked the King.

Last Speech

In August 1918 the vicar at Mentmore talked Rosebery into agreeing to give an address at Mentmore church. The day came, and Rosebery sent off a note to the vicar, 'I have been trying all day to muster up courage to give an address this evening, but I cannot. Rosebery.' Nevertheless, he went to the church, and agreed with the vicar that, when the moment came, if he felt up to speaking he would give a sign. This he did, and made his last speech, on the text 'lift up your hearts'.

An Old Man

Rosebery suffered a stroke in November 1918, and subsequently appalled friends and acquaintances by his appearance. Edmund Gosse saw him in May 1919:

> 'Next moment there emerged a little withered figure in a railway-cap of cloth, who stood blinking in the sun. Snow-white hair, closely-shaven drawn parchment cheeks, dull eyes that gazed out blankly. I should positively, not have known who it was. Lord Reay spoke cheerfully to him, and he shook hands with us both, but said not a word; stood there, without a smile, then turned, still not speaking and was pushed by two servants into the motor, which had the blinds drawn down. Lord Reay, ten years his senior, very much animated by excitement and distress, looked quite young, and turning to me said 'we have seen a dying man! What a rapid and fatal change! We ought not to have stopped, nor have spoken! Who could guess that he had suddenly become like that?' It really was terrible . . .'

Rosebery lived another ten years.

ARTHUR JAMES BALFOUR
First Earl of Balfour (1848–1930)

Playful little Arthur, he
Plays with things so prettily
To him everything's a game
Win or lose it's all the same –
Plays at politics or war
Trivial little games they are –
Plays with souls and plays at golf –
This must never be put off,
Plays with deep philosophies,
Faiths and minor things like these,
Plays with praise and plays with blame
Everything is but a game
Win or lose, it's all the same,
Playful little Arthur, he
Cannot take things seriously.

Poem written by an anonymous friend

ARTHUR JAMES WAS the eldest son and fourth child of James Maitland Balfour by his wife, Lady Blanche, second daughter of the second Marquess of Salisbury. His father was a shadowy figure, a country gentleman who was also, briefly, a member of parliament, but it was his mother who had the more forceful character. After his father's early death, in 1856, her influence was paramount.

Despite almost constant ill health as a boy, Balfour was educated at Eton and at Trinity College, Cambridge, where he obtained a second in the moral sciences tripos. Balfour's first interest upon leaving Cambridge was philosophy. He published a number of philosophical works, chief among which were *A Defence of Philosophic Doubt* (1879) and *The Foundations of Belief* (1895), but even by the date of the earlier work his energies had been directed towards politics. In 1874, he entered parliament, and by 1878 had become Parliamentary Private Secretary to his uncle Lord Salisbury. In 1886 he became Secretary for Scotland, by November of that year had attained Cabinet rank, and in March 1887 accepted the Irish Chief Secretaryship, a position he held with great success until he became Leader of the House of Commons and First Lord of the Treasury. In July 1902, after the conclusion of peace with South Africa, Balfour was the natural successor to Lord Salisbury as Prime Minister. Hampered by being at the helm of a party deeply divided over the question of tariff reform, he still achieved much. The South African war was successfully concluded and the army reconstructed, an entente with France was negotiated, the Committee of Imperial Defence was established, and Balfour himself was largely responsible for the passing of the 1902 Education Act. By the end of 1905 deep divisions within his own party had led him to resign as Prime Minister, and by November 1911 he had resigned his leadership of the Conservative Party.

Paradoxically, it was really only after this date that he began to receive the recognition he deserved as a statesman and a man of exceptional ability and distinction. He again took office in the coalition government of 1915, first as First Lord of the Admiralty and later, on the downfall of Asquith, as Foreign Secretary, a position he held until 1919. Even then, he was ready to serve again. He was Lord President of the Council in Baldwin's administration from 1925 until the year before his death in 1930, so ending a career which had begun decades earlier in the last administration of Benjamin Disraeli.

Upbringing

Balfour was surrounded by remarkable people. His mother, Lady Blanche, had given birth to nine children in a space of eleven years, and far from being exhausted had still managed to combine dazzling charm with staunch religious and moral principles. As a young girl she had so charmed the Duke of Wellington that he presented her with a copy of the map of the field of Waterloo he had had made before the battle.

Devastated by the death of her husband, and burdened by the task of bringing up their eight surviving children alone, she devoted the rest of her life to her children and her religion, announcing that once the children were grown up she would move to the East End and turn her attentions to the poor. In 1862, when the cotton depression was at its worst, she took in two Lancashire girls, at the same time reducing the number of domestic servants at Whittingehame, the family home, and sending the wages saved to the Lancashire Relief Fund. Thereafter no child was spared his share of the chores, and the future Prime Minister found that his job was to black all the boots in the house.

With such a formidable mother, it is not surprising that some of the children were inspired to achieve great things whilst others were almost equal disasters. One sister, Eleanor, became president of Newnham College, Cambridge, whilst another, Alice, was content to keep house for her brother. Frank became professor of Morphology at Cambridge, Gerald was both a scholar and member of Cabinet, but then there was Cecil who forged a cheque in Arthur's name before leaving for Australia, and Eustace, who ended life as a chronic alcoholic.

Women

Balfour is often thought of as a man who enjoyed the company of women (preferably those who managed to combine beauty with cleverness) but who cared for no one deeply. Margot Tennant (later Mrs Asquith) once said to him that he would not care if all his women friends died, to which he replied wickedly: 'I think I should mind if they all died on the same day.'

This is only half the truth. In fact, he had probably become unofficially engaged to May Lyttelton by 1875 and, when she died of typhoid fever, he sent her brother an emerald ring which had belonged to his mother, asking for it to be put into her coffin. Even after that tragedy he did not withdraw completely from close relationships with women, and his friendship with Mary Elcho in particular continued until his death. Whether Lady Elcho (later Countess of Wemyss) whose marriage was not entirely happy, wanted more from Balfour than he was prepared to give is open to question, but their mutual devotion is undoubted. The extent of their relationship was a subject of intense curiosity to their friends and contemporaries, the most accurate description probably being given by Wilfrid Blunt:

> 'She loves, honours and respects him, and he is constant to her, and she has always been constant to him, and she is bound to him by a thousand promises never to give herself to another. On this understanding he has been content that their love should be within certain limits – a little more than friendship a little less than love.'

Women, in general, fell for his charm. 'Oh dear,' sighed Constance Lady Battersea, after a visit to his home in 1895, 'what a gulf between him and most men!' Margot Tennant, according to Lady Jebb, longed to marry him. When questioned about this rumour Balfour replied 'No, that is not so. I rather thought of having a career of my own.'

Newspapers

Unlike other twentieth-century Prime Ministers, Balfour hated reading newspapers. When, in September 1893, he asked one of his sisters what the papers had said about a parliamentary debate the previous night, she replied: 'I can't tell you, for you have none in your house.'

Later, he admitted to Churchill that he did not subscribe to a press-cuttings agency, protesting:

> 'I have never put myself to the trouble of rummaging an immense rubbish-heap on the problematical chance of discovering a cigar end.'

Languor

Perhaps because of childhood ill health, Balfour got into the habit even as a very young man of conserving his energy ready for periodic bouts of feverish activity. He regularly stayed in bed until noon, and always replied to even the simplest letter by telegram. Whenever possible, he lounged rather than sat, 'as if to discover,' wrote the parliamentary correspondent of *Punch*, 'how nearly he could sit on his shoulder blades.'

The Cambridge Philosopher

Throughout his life, Balfour remained donnish. According to Churchill, one day in 1918 as the Supreme Council of the Allies sat at Versailles almost within range of German guns, he spoke on a difficult question for almost ten minutes only to be challenged by a quizzical Clemenceau 'Pour ou contre?'

The MP Ian Malcolm later recalled how he first came across Balfour at the dispatch box. 'Did I say thousands?' asked Balfour in reply to a question. 'Oh, I meant millions, but it makes no difference to my argument.'

He once arrived for an evening party at a great house whose staircase split in two curves. He stood at the bottom for twenty minutes trying to work out a logical reason for choosing one side rather than another.

When his sister, Lady Rayleigh, asked what entertainment she could offer him at her house he suggested, 'Oh something amusing, get some people from Cambridge to talk science.'

Charm

One of the most dined-out men of the time, Balfour had great charm. Churchill wrote:

> 'He was the best-mannered man I ever met – easy, courteous, patient, considerate, in every society and with great and small alike.'

> 'Although he was the best talker I have ever known [said John Buchan] he was not a monopolist of the conversation but one who quickened and elevated the whole discussion and brought out the best of other people.'

Transport

The first Prime Minister to go to Buckingham Palace in a motor car, Balfour had earlier shocked Gladstone when he had, as First Lord of the Treasury, arrived at Hawarden on a bicycle.

On a Colleague

He once said of a colleague, 'If he had a little more brains he would be a half-wit.'

Spiritualism

Although he was never completely convinced of the ability to make contact with the dead, Balfour was very interested in spiritualism. In 1894, he was President of the Society for Psychical Research, and over a number of years he attended several seances. The last of these was in 1929 when a Mrs Willett came to his sitting room and contacted May Lyttelton whilst the gramophone played Beethoven. She returned two days later, apparently fell into a trance, and passed on messages from May 'Tell him he gives me Joy.' It was reported in the Society's Proceedings that Balfour clasped Mrs Willett's hand and told her afterwards that 'he was most profoundly impressed.'

HENRY CAMPBELL-BANNERMAN

(1836–1908)

'A jolly, lazy sort of man with a good dose of sense.'

Diary for 13 May 1886, SIR ALFRED PEASE

HENRY CAMPBELL WAS born near Glasgow on 7 September 1836 the second son of Sir James Campbell, a self-made Glasgow businessman, by Janet, daughter of Henry Bannerman, a rich Manchester manufacturer.

He was educated at Glasgow High School, Glasgow University, and at Trinity College Cambridge, where he took a double honours degree in Classics and Mathematics. At twenty-five, he married Charlotte Bruce, the daughter of a distinguished soldier, and worked in the family tailoring and drapery business until 1868 when he was elected MP for Stirling Burghs, a constituency he represented for the next forty years. In 1871 he was appointed Financial Secretary to the War Office, and the same year inherited the fortune of his maternal uncle, together with the life interest of an estate in Kent, provided he added Bannerman to his name.

For the next twenty years, whenever the Liberals were in office, Campbell-Bannerman held various positions mainly in the War Office or the Admiralty. By 1899, he had become leader of the Liberals in the House of Commons, and on the resignation of Balfour in 1905, he at last became Prime Minister. He at once granted self-government to South Africa and set up the Union, but his short tenure of office was marred by the death of his wife and by his own worsening health. In November 1907 he had another heart attack and died in April 1908 after a bout of influenza.

On His Name

Campbell-Bannerman only very reluctantly agreed to add the Bannerman to his name. Over ten years after he made the change, he wrote to Lord Spencer:

> 'I see you are already tired, as I have long been, of writing my horrid long name. I am always best pleased to be called Campbell *tout court*, and most of my old friends do so . . . An alternative is C.B.'

Charlotte

Shy and retiring as she was, Charlotte exerted tremendous influence over her husband. Many years later, he told Augustine Birrell how she had persuaded him to accept the Chief Secretaryship of Ireland in 1884:

> 'I went home . . . consulted my wife, and having been instructed to telegraph, telegraphed refusal . . . I then proceeded to write a letter giving my reasons why, and I found a difficulty amounting almost to impossibility to get these excellent reasons into a letter. Then arose my domestic adviser and said "See you not why you cannot write the letter? – because it is a false letter. Your conscience is always telling you, as you write, that you ought to accept." After a *grand conseil de nuit*, therefore I telegraphed the next morning recanting my refusal. And this little manoeuvre remained a mystery to Spencer, and to a greater extent than he, Mr G. Thus is a woman ever a man's superior in intuition, and in self-sacrifice.'

The couple remained childless but devoted. Towards the end of her life, Charlotte was almost constantly ill, probably suffering from diabetes which made her so fat that she had to be dressed by two maids. In 1906, her illness suddenly became much worse, and the burden on her husband was almost intolerable. On 24 May, Lord Esher wrote to his son:

> 'C.B. is very much broken. He gets no sleep, and is up three or four times every night. He won't allow anyone but himself to nurse Lady C.B. It cannot possibly go on.'

At the same time, his private secretary, Arthur Ponsonby was telling his wife:

> 'All household business is all over the shop from Lady C.B. never being able to cope with it and it is impossible to expect C.B. to interview scullery maids in the intervals of the Cabinet and H. of Commons.'

When she died in August, it was a blow from which Campbell-Bannerman never really recovered. In 1907 Arthur Ponsonby took in some letters to find him sitting at his desk sobbing.

Who is That?

During a colonial conference in London in April 1907, the Prince of Wales gave a dinner for the Prime Ministers at Marlborough House. Lady Derby turned to her neighbour at the dinner, who happened to be Sir Wilfrid Laurier, the Canadian Prime Minister.

> 'Who [she asked] is the pleasant-looking gentleman next to Lady Laurier, who is enjoying his dinner so much?'
> 'That [said Sir Wilfred] is *your* Prime Minister'

Pets

In 1868, the year he was first elected to the House of Commons, Campbell-Bannerman bought a grey African parrot which outlived him. He also kept French bulldogs at Belmont, once having as many as thirty. He sometimes took one on one of his regular trips to Paris to see, as he put it, the city of its birth.

Marienbad

Every year for thirty years, the Campbell-Bannermans went to Marienbad in Bohemia for the sake of Charlotte's health. By 1905 the King had also become a regular visitor, and in September that year Campbell-Bannerman complained:

> 'I got so mixed up with the King's incessant gaieties, for which his energy and appetite are alike insatiable, that it was no rest or holiday for me. Thus when at last he was gone ... my Doctor ordered me to bed and absolute rest for forty-eight hours.'

The same year, a photograph appeared in an illustrated paper of the King and Campbell-Bannerman talking very earnestly together. The King appeared to be animatedly striking his palm with his clenched fist, and the caption underneath was 'Is it peace or war?' When Campbell-Bannerman asked his secretary if he wanted to know what they had been discussing, he admitted they had been trying to decide whether halibut was better baked or boiled.

HERBERT HENRY ASQUITH

First Earl of Oxford and Asquith (1852–1928)

'Asquith worries too much about small points. If you were buying a large mansion he would come to you and say "Have you thought that there is no accommodation for the cat."'

Letter of 1915 to Lord Riddell from
DAVID LLOYD GEORGE (1863–1945)

HERBERT HENRY ASQUITH was born at Morley, Yorkshire on 12 September 1852, the second son of a noncomformist wool spinner and weaver who died when Asquith was only eight. For a short time he was educated at a school near Leeds, but in 1863 he and his elder brother were sent to live with relatives in London and to attend the City of London School. At the age of seventeen, he won a classical scholarship to Balliol College, Oxford and by 1874 had been awarded a first in Greats, the highly-prized Craven scholarship, and a Balliol fellowship. The following year he entered as a student at Lincoln's Inn and began his career at the Bar.

By 1877 Asquith had married Helen Melland, the daughter of a Manchester physician and had settled in Hampstead. Over the next few years she gave birth to five children (four sons and a daughter) whilst her husband supplemented his fairly erratic earnings from the Bar with money for articles contributed to the *Economist* and the *Spectator*.

Asquith regarded his career at the Bar as a stepping stone towards his real career in politics. By 1886 he had been elected Member of Parliament for East Fife and soon impressed the House of Commons with his abilities as a speaker. His wife died of typhoid in 1891 but, though shattered, Asquith did not allow domestic unhappiness to delay his political success. Gladstone appointed him Home

Secretary in 1892 at the age of thirty-nine, and by 1894 his domestic happiness had been restored with his marriage to Margot Tennant. With the downfall of the Liberal government in 1895, Asquith again found himself out of political office and returned for the next ten and a half years to what had now become an extremely successful legal practice.

When the Liberals again took office Asquith was appointed Chancellor of the Exchequer, and it was not until Campbell-Bannerman became so ill that his resignation became imperative that Asquith took over as Prime Minister.

Asquith held on to his office continuously for a period of eight years and eight months, a record unequalled since Lord Liverpool's administration almost a century earlier. Among the administration's achievements were the introduction of old age pensions and of national insurance, the payment of MPs, the Parliament Act of 1911 by which the powers of the House of Lords were reduced, and the Welsh Disestablishment Act. Divisions within the party appeared first with the attempt to introduce Irish Home Rule, and later over policy during the First World War. In May 1915 Asquith formed a Coalition in which Unionist leaders and one member of the Labour Party were included, but his popularity continued to decline. By December 1916 he had been forced out of office and in the election of 1919 he lost the seat he had held continuously for the previous thirty-two years. He returned to the House of Commons from 1920 to 1924 as member for Paisley but after a second electoral defeat accepted the King's offer of a peerage. In the last few years before his death in 1928 he turned to writing and published the *Genesis of the War* (1923) and *Fifty Years of Parliament* (1926).

His Wives

Few men can have had wives as dissimilar as Helen and Margot Asquith. Asquith himself paid tribute to his first wife in a letter to Mrs Horner written on the first anniversary of her death.

'She cared little for society, shrank from every kind of publicity and self-advertisement, hardly knew what ambition meant. She was more wrapped up in her children than any woman I have ever known. To me she was always perfect, loyal, sympathetic, devoted; not without pride in such successes as I had; but not the least anxious for me to "get on", never sanguine or confident, and as a rule inclined to take a less hopeful view of things. I used sometimes to reproach her with her "pessimism". What has happened to me lately would have given her little real pleasure; indeed I doubt whether, if she had been here, I would have taken such a step. She was the gentlest and best of companions, a restricting rather than a stimulating influence, and knowing myself as I do I have often wondered that we walked so evenly together. I was only eighteen when I fell in love with her, and we married when we were little more than boy and girl. In the cant phrase our marriage was a "great success"; from first to last it was never clouded by any kind of sorrow or dissension; and when the sun went down it was in an unclouded sky.'

By the time Helen died, Asquith had already met Margot Tennant. The latter described in her autobiography how she behaved when she met the first Mrs Asquith:

'I found out from something he [Asquith] said to me that he was married and lived at Hampstead and that his days were divided between 1 Paper Buildings and the House of Commons . . . When I discovered he was married, I asked him to bring his wife to dinner, which he did, and directly I saw her I said: "I do hope, Mrs Asquith, you have not minded your husband dining here without you, but I rather gathered Hampstead was too far away for him to get back to you from the House of Commons. You must always let me know and come with him whenever it suits you."'

The two women can have had nothing in common. Margot later dismissed Helen with the words: 'She lived in Hampstead and had no clothes.' She herself shone both in Leicestershire hunting society and amongst the exclusive set in London known as 'The Souls'. Wherever she was, she had to be at the centre of the stage, and she attracted around her men as different as Gladstone, Balfour, and Benjamin Jowett, the distinguished Master of Balliol, who conducted a correspondence with her. It is difficult to imagine how a man who claimed to have been completely happy with a woman as unassuming and retiring as Helen Asquith can have selected as his next wife a woman who combined charm, directness and spontaneity with vanity, selfishness and tactlessness.

Other Women

Asquith himself admitted to 'a slight weakness for the companionship of clever and attractive women'. In 1908 Pamela Jekyll drew a diagram for him showing his heart divided between 'Viola' [Tree], Dorothy [Beresford], Lillian [Tennant], Venetia [Stanley] and herself. By 1912 most of these had faded from view, but Venetia Stanley, his daughter Violet's closest friend, had come to dominate his attentions to an almost dangerous extent. He saw her frequently but also wrote endless letters; during the first three months of 1915 he wrote to her 151 times. Although it is unlikely that they were lovers in the physical sense, there is no doubt that he loved her and needed her. On 26 April 1915 he wrote:

> 'To see you again, and be with you and hear your voice, and above all to find everything is unchanged, has made a new creature of me. You are the best and richest of life-givers.'

He was devastated when, only a month later, she decided to marry Edwin Montagu, a suitor she had earlier rejected and who had himself been one of Asquith's private secretaries.

Drink

Asquith sometimes drank too much. During the Committee stage of the Parliament Bill he appeared on the front bench too drunk to speak and at two o'clock in the morning an Opposition speaker pointedly drew attention to 'the very happy manner in which the Prime Minister in the earlier hours of the evening chose to withdraw from the barricades'.

His Reading

Asquith read voraciously throughout his life. During the First World War, he developed the habit, when parliament was not sitting, of hiding in the Athenaeum Library. On 21 January 1915 he wrote to Venetia Stanley:

> 'After writing to you, and writing my Cabinet letter, and disposing of a lot of smaller things, I walked across after six to the Athenaeum, and took up a novel. *Sir Perryworm's Wife* (a

good title) wh. with judicious skipping I read from cover to cover . . . I found it readable and *rather* soothing.'

Never a demonstrative man, his books were a solace to him, and a means by which he could retreat from harsher realities. His daughter Violet found, through his love of books, a way to comfort him after his final election defeat in 1924:

'We had a difficult send-off, at Glasgow, saying good-bye to faithful old supporters there, who came with tears and flowers. As we steamed out of the station, I lay back feeling bruised from head to foot – and recoiling instinctively from the pile of newspapers that lay by my side – their head-lines stinging me like adders. I looked across at Father in an agony of solicitude (for I knew how the good-byes had moved him) – then meeting his calm gaze I realised suddenly that he had already made his peace with events. Groping wildly for a life-line that might draw me into smooth waters by his side, I asked him in as steady a voice as possible: "I suppose you haven't by any chance got an old P.G. Wodehouse in your bag that you could lend me?" A smile of instant response, mingled, I thought with relief, lit up his face as he replied triumphantly "Being a provident man I have got in my bag, not one, but *four brand new* ones!" My wounds were healed – for I knew that he was invulnerable.'

A Visit to Windsor

In June 1908 the Asquiths spend a weekend at Windsor. All went well until Asquith failed to join Their Majesties in the Castle Courtyard at 4 p.m. to motor to the gardens and then to Virginia Water, where they were to have tea. The King, who hated being kept waiting, looked first at his watch and then at the Castle clock, becoming more and more irritated. Margot Asquith described the event:

'Seeing affairs at a standstill I went up to the Queen and said I feared there had been a scandal at Court, and that Henry must have eloped with one of the maids of honour. I begged her to save my blushes by commanding the King to proceed, at which she walked up to him with her amazing grace, and, in her charming way, tapping him firmly on the arm pointed with a sweeping gesture to his motor and invited Graicie Raincliffe and Alice Keppel to accompany him: at which they all drove off . . .

'When we returned to the Castle we found that Henry had gone for a long walk with the Hon. Violet Vivian, one of the Queen's maids of honour, over which the King was jovial and even eloquent.'

Cruising with the Churchills

For three consecutive summers before the First World War, he and his wife were guests of the Churchills on the Admiralty yacht. According to Churchill, despite facing growing problems both at home and abroad:

> '. . . you would not have supposed he had a care in the world. He was the most painstaking tourist. He mastered Baedeker, examined the ladies upon it, explained and illuminated much, and evidently enjoyed every hour. He frequently set the whole party competing who could write down in five minutes the most Generals beginning with L, or Poets beginning with T, or Historians with some other initial. He had innumerable varieties of these games and always excelled in them. He talked a great deal to the Captain and the navigators about the ship and the course and the weather . . .
>
> 'For the rest he basked in the sunshine and read Greek. He fashioned with deep thought impeccable verses in complicated metre, and recast in terser form classical inscriptions which displeased him.'

Raymond's Death

Asquith's eldest son Raymond had, as a young man, surpassed his father's outstanding academic record by obtaining an All Souls Fellowship. Effortlessly clever, a brilliant future was predicted for him at the Bar, to which he was called in 1904, and in politics. His death in the trenches in 1916 shocked even those who had become immune to the carnage of the First World War. Cynthia Asquith, his sister-in-law, wrote in her diary:

> 'Darling, brilliant, magically charming Raymond – how much delight and laughter goes with him! It seems to take away

one's last remains of courage. One might have known that
nothing so brilliant and precious would escape, but after each
blow one's hopes revive, and one reinvests one's love and
interest.'

Only three days after Raymond's death, his father wrote typically:

'Whatever pride I had in the past and whatever hope I had for
the far future – by much the largest part of both was invested
in him. Now all that is gone. It will take me a few days more to
get back to my bearings.'

His Earldom

When Asquith selected his title, he encountered some raised
eyebrows, particularly amongst Oxford conservatives. 'It is like a
suburban villa calling itself Versailles', complained Lady Salisbury.

DAVID LLOYD GEORGE

First Earl Lloyd George of Dwyfor (1863–1945)

Lloyd George no doubt when his life ebbs out,
Will ride on a flaming chariot
Seated in state on a red hot plate
'Twixt Satan and Judas Iscariot,
Ananias that day to the Devil will say
'My claim for precedence fails
So move me up higher, away from the fire,
And make way for that liar – from Wales.

Anonymous contemporary rhyme

THE FIRST SON of William and Elizabeth George, David Lloyd George was born on 7 January 1863 at Chorlton-up-Medlock near Manchester. William George was a schoolteacher who returned to farm in Wales only two months after the birth of his son. Little more than a year later he died of pneumonia and his widow and children were taken under the protection of Richard Lloyd, Elizabeth's brother. The children went to the village school at Llanystumdwy, and David subsequently qualified as a solicitor and set up an office in Criccieth.

Lloyd George entered the House of Commons in 1890 as Liberal member for Carnarvon. His opposition to the Boer War brought him to the national attention, and when the Liberals came into office in 1905 he was first President of the Board of Trade (1905–8) and then Chancellor of the Exchequer (1908–1915). In Asquith's Coalition Government, he was Minister of Munitions followed by Secretary of State for War. In December 1916, at the age of fifty-four, he replaced Asquith as Prime Minister, immediately providing the dynamic leadership vital to the prosecution of the war. He secured a massive majority for the Coalition in the 1918 general election and for his remaining years in office devoted his enormous energy to the pacification and economic recovery of Europe, to the problems of Ireland, and to domestic depression and unemployment. By 1922, it was feared that Lloyd George was ready to plunge the country into a war against Turkey, and the Conservatives withdrew their support from the Coalition.

For the remaining twenty-three years of his life, Lloyd George was to remain out of office. He was leader of the Liberals from 1926 to 1931, and leader of the Independent Liberals from 1931 to 1945 but was disliked and mistrusted by many. He resigned as an MP in 1945 and died on 26 March of the same year, not long after he had been made an earl.

Lloyd George was first married to Margaret Owen, the daughter of a Criccieth farmer. They had two sons and three daughters. Two years after her death in 1941 he married Frances Stevenson, who had been his mistress and secretary for many years.

The Oak Tree

As a child, Lloyd George used to relax in the woods near his uncle's home. One oak tree was a particular favourite and he used to climb to the top taking his books with him –

> 'On one occasion when I did this, the singular thought struck me, "What a remarkable fellow am I, to read Euclid on top of an oak tree. Why am I doing this?" I asked myself. And quick as a flash, I answered myself, "I am special. I am astonishing, 'Duw, I believe I am a genius!"'

Margaret Owen

Maggie Owen first attracted Lloyd George's attention in 1885 when she was twenty-one. Despite her parents' disapproval of the penniless young suitor, they continued to meet, and soon she was in love, not at all put off by the ruthless ambition he was too impatient to hide:

> 'My supreme idea is to get on. To this idea I shall sacrifice everything – except, I trust, honesty. I am prepared to thrust even love itself under the wheels of my Juggernaut, if it obstructs the way . . . Believe me – and may Heaven attest the truth of my statement – my love for you is sincere and strong. In this I never waver. But I must not forget that I have a purpose in life, And however painful the sacrifice I may have to make to attain this ambition I must not flinch – otherwise success will be remote indeed . . .'

They married in 1888, but within the first few years Maggie was already refusing to spend much time in London which she hated. The signs of danger were obvious to anyone, but she chose to ignore them. Sometimes, he was almost pathetic:

> '. . . When am I to get little Dickie's photo? I want it badly. I can't stand this solitude much longer. It is unbearable. Here the House adjourns in a few minutes [from] now, that is at 6, and I go to my lodgings like a hermit or a prisoner to his cell. Dark gloomy dungeon my room is. I don't know what I would give now for an hour of your company. It would scatter all the gloom and make all the room so cheerful.'

So when the affairs began then, Maggie was herself partly responsible as Lloyd George was the first to point out:

> '. . . Be candid with yourself. Drop that infernal Methodism which is the curse of your bitter nature and reflect whether you have not rather neglected your husband. I have more than once gone without breakfast, I have scores of times come home in the dead of night to a cold dark and comfortless flat without a soul to greet me. When you were surrounded by your pets. I am not the nature either physically or morally that ought to have been left thus . . . You have been a good mother. You have not – and I say this not in anger – not always been a good wife. I can point you even amongst those whom you affect to look down upon – much better wives. You may be a blessing to your children. Oh, Maggie . . . beware lest you be a curse to your husband.'

It is a tribute to their genuine affection for each other that the marriage lasted at all, even after their children had grown up and left home. Over the years, Maggie learned largely to ignore her husband's affairs, even the one with Frances Stevenson, and when they were together they lived tranquilly enough. On 24 January 1938 the Churchills gave a Golden Wedding party for them at Cannes. Lloyd George's speech was typically outrageous:

> 'We have lived together in perfect harmony for fifty years. One of us is contentious, combative, and stormy. That is my wife. Then there is the other partner, placid, calm, peaceful and patient. That is me.'

The Other Women

Lloyd George was clearly indefatigable in his pursuit of other women, telling Sir Oswald Mosley 'Love is all right if you lose no time.' He once gave a large dinner in a private room of a hotel. Sir Oswald was invited and looked at the guest list which included a strangely assorted collection of warring politicians. He remarked:

'This will lift the roof if it gets out'.

Lloyd George sought to pacify him:

'My dear boy, if everything I have done in this hotel during the last forty years had got out, you have no idea how many times I would have had to retire from politics.'

Wherever he was, and whoever he was with, he was eyeing the ladies. His son Richard had watched what was going on since the time when, as a small boy, he had seen his father 'eating' Mrs Timothy Davie's hand and had reported the strange incident to his furious mother.

Later, his father had shown slightly more discretion:

'I remember sitting in a restaurant with him, through which passed cohorts of fashionable, handsome creatures. A most statuesque enchantress passed our table, conscious of being the centre of masculine attention, dipping and swaying like a yacht with all its sails engaged. I made some youthfully appreciative remark, but father hardly raised his eyes from his soup plate. "Handsome, like one of Rosebery's fillies. And about as exciting," was his indifferent comment. Another queen of the follies passed by a little later, all pink and white perfection. "I've lost my taste for sugar mice," father said a little testily after another effusion of praise from me. Then, a little later, a pale, dark-eyed woman, in her late thirties, her hair in a severe unfashionable bun, appeared; and father sat up and watched her lingeringly as she passed, otherwise unnoticed, to some obscure table. "Now, she's *interesting*" he said. "She has something. She's a deep one, I'll wager." He leaned forward confidentially and I waited, my ears at the alert – but then, becoming aware of our relationship, he sat back and addressed himself to his pressed duck.'

Lucy Masterman once went to an evening service with him at a church in Nice. Lloyd George was singularly inattentive, taking the opportunity of a loud hymn to remark: 'That is a very nice looking girl! I wonder who she is?'

Frances Stevenson

Frances Stevenson was twenty-three when she met Lloyd George in 1911. She was a teacher at Allenswood, a girls' boarding school in Wimbledon, and that summer coached Megan in Wales. By the end of 1912 Lloyd George had invited her to become both his secretary and his mistress, making it quite plain that he had absolutely no intention of leaving his wife. Frances Stevenson accepted his terms and stayed with him until his death. Lloyd George virtually led a double life, switching from one household to another with apparent ease. Given the circumstances, it is astonishing that his private life did not cause a scandal. Stories about his escapades were circulated privately but there was no hint in the Press of his long-standing affair with Miss Stevenson even after she had given birth to a daughter in 1928.

Frances Stevenson's diary clearly reveals the depth of their passion:

> '*April 23rd 1917*
> ... We went down to Walton H on Saturday afternoon [21 April], and had a perfect weekend. I do not think we have ever loved each other so much. D says that ours is a love that comes to very few people and I wonder more and more at the beauty and happiness of it. It is a thing that nothing but death can harm, and even death has no terrors for me now, for D asked me yesterday if I would come with him when he went. He begged me not to stay behind, but for both of us to go together, and I promised him to do so, unless I have any children of his to claim me. So, I am not afraid now of the misery if D is taken away, for then I shall go too and his end will be my end, and until then everything is happiness, if our love stays. I hope by any chance, I shall not go first, for I know his misery would be great, and he could not leave his work, which is a great one. I am so happy now that we have decided this, for sometimes my heart would stop beating with terror at the thought of life without D.'

Equally clear was the fact that Lloyd George managed to get what he wanted from both his wife and his mistress and still pursue whoever else took his eye.

Spilling the Beans

When Lloyd George became Chancellor of the Exchequer in April 1908 he was so excited that he could not resist telling the editor of the *Daily Chronicle* about his own promotion and that of several other people. Although he naturally told the editor to keep the information to himself, on 10 April the *Daily Chronicle* published a list of nearly all the proposed Cabinet changes. Asquith was furious. Lloyd George's denial of his indiscretion was quite shameless:

> 'Winston told me last night [he wrote] that some of my colleagues had rushed to you immediately on your arrival with the amiable suggestion that I had been responsible for the publication of the *Chronicle* list. I need hardly tell you that I feel very hurt at the accusation and I think I ought to know who it is among my colleagues who deems me capable of what is not merely a gross indiscretion but a downright and discreditable breach of trust. Men whose promotion is not sustained by birth or other favouring conditions are always liable to be assailed with unkind suspicions of this sort. I would ask it therefore as a favour that you should not entertain them without satisfying that they have some basis of truth.'

The Breakdown

From about 1914, Lloyd George spent as much time as possible at his house at Walton Heath. This sometimes caused problems, especially when he had to attend evening functions in London. Late one night he was being driven back from a City function where he had been required to wear his elaborate Privy Councillor's uniform, including knee breeches, long stockings, and silver buckled pumps. Suddenly his car broke down in the middle of nowhere. The chauffeur got out to investigate, failing to notice that Lloyd George had also got out of the car to stretch his legs. All too soon, Lloyd George heard the car engine splutter into life before it disappeared down the country lane without him. It was some time before the chauffeur noticed that the back seat was empty. Appalled at what he had done, he sped back along the same road and finally saw in the headlights of the car the weary figure of his employer trudging down the middle of the road. The incident became one of Lloyd George's favourite stories. In its final version he used to add that he eventually came to the doors of a lunatic asylum and in desperation rang the bell:

> '"I'm the Chancellor of the Exchequer" he announced as the warden answered the door. "Come in," invited the warden calmly. "The rest of the Cabinet is expecting you."'

The Welsh Embassy

During Lloyd George's occupancy both 11 and 10 Downing Street took on the appearance of a Welsh embassy. The family spoke to each other in Welsh, there were two or three Welsh-speaking maids, and one of Lloyd George's favourite methods of relaxation was to sing Welsh hymns at the piano. The food, sadly, was not of embassy standards: Lloyd George liked best to eat bacon and beans, and insisted on apple pasties every Saturday. All in all, the atmosphere was very homely:

> 'So far as the food, service and appointments were concerned, it looked as if a small suburban household were picnicking in Downing Street – the same simple food, the same little domestic servant, the same mixture of tea and dinner.'

The Pets

Lloyd George was never without a dog – Welsh terriers inevitably, but Alsatians, Chows, Airedales, and even a St Bernard turned up at various stages. For ten years, he also had a white pigeon called Doodie who had been presented to him in America. After dinner, she was allowed out of her cage and would perch on Lloyd George's shoulder. She hated the steel-rimmed pince-nez he used to wear and would get the edge of the frames in her beak and toss them off his nose, then stroke his eyebrows with her beak or even smooth his eyelashes and eyelids. Eventually, the pigeon had to be put to sleep after contracting a leg infection.

China Tea

On Wednesday 29 July 1931 Lloyd George had an operation for the

removal of a prostate gland. The nurse gave him a cup of tea when he
came round: 'This isn't China tea,' he complained quickly.

. . . *and Margot again*

Lloyd George was not one of Margot Asquith's conquests. 'He can
never,' she pronounced, 'see a belt without hitting below it.'

ANDREW BONAR LAW
(1858–1923)

'It is fitting that we should have buried the Unknown
Prime Minister by the side of the Unknown Soldier.'

ASQUITH, on leaving Law's funeral
service at Westminster Abbey, 1923

BORN ON 16 September 1858 in New Brunswick, Canada, Bonar Law
was the fourth son of the Rev. James Law, a Presbyterian minister.
His mother died when he was two, and at the age of twelve Law
travelled to Scotland with his mother's sister to be educated at her
family's expense. He went to Gilbertsfield School, Hamilton, and to
Glasgow High School, before starting out to make his living in
business.

Having achieved some success, Law turned his attention to politics and in 1900 entered the House of Commons as a Unionist Tariff
Reformer for one of the Glasgow constituencies, and as early as 1902
became Parliamentary Secretary to the Board of Trade. After the
resignation of Balfour as Conservative party leader in 1911, Law
took his place, and in 1915 took office as Colonial Secretary in the
first Coalition. Under Lloyd George, Law was Leader of the House of
Commons and Chancellor of the Exchequer, exchanging the
Exchequer for the Privy Seal in 1919. Ill health led to his resignation
from office in 1921, but he returned to become Prime Minister on 23
October 1922. He was in office for only 209 days being forced to
resign through illness on 20 May 1923. He died from cancer of the
throat five months later.

In 1891 Law married Annie Pitcairn Robley, the daughter of a
Glasgow shipbuilder. They had four sons and two daughters. His
wife died in 1909, and two sons were killed in the First World
War.

The Name

Bonar Law's mother, Elizabeth, wanted to call her son after the Reverend Robert Murray McCheyne, a preacher she much admired. There was a problem, however, since she already had a son called Robert. For some reason she decided that the next best thing was to call him after the preacher's biographer, Andrew A. Bonar.

The Teetotaller

Although Law smoked the whole time, he never touched alcohol. After the results of the 1906 election were in and it was clear that Law had lost his seat, another Scottish Unionist candidate went up to him to commiserate, saw what he was drinking, and declared in disbelief: 'Ma God! Milk!'

Beaverbrook later recalled his first lunch with Law:

> 'The food was not very good, and I noticed with a little annoyance that I was given one glass of whisky and water, whereas my host helped himself twice to what appeared to be a special whisky out of his own bottle. This keeping of a special tap in one's own house is a thing I have a prejudice against.
>
> 'It was a week after that when I found out that he was a teetotaller and his 'special whisky' was a bottle of lime juice.'

The Loyal Daughter

When Law lost his seat in the 1906 election, his eldest daughter was ten. That night, she cried herself to sleep and the next day to the consternation of visitors, wrapped herself in a sack and poured ashes over her head.

The Party Leader

When Law was chosen party leader in preference to either Austen Chamberlain or Walter Long, it was said by a wit that 'he rose between two stools.'

At the time, Liberals suggested that the Litany should be extended for Conservatives to read 'Lord have mercy upon us and incline our hearts, to Bonar Law'. Resolutely unglamorous, Law was given a lecture by his much more flamboyant friend, Lord Beaverbrook: 'You are a great man now. You must talk like a great man, behave like a great man.'

Law's reply was characteristic: 'If I am a great man then a good many great men must have been frauds.'

Totally lacking magnetism, Law succeeded only in winning grudging respect rather than enthusiasm for his leadership.

The Visit to Windsor

Lord Sysonby recorded a weekend spent at Windsor Castle by Bonar Law and his daughter:

'In April 1921 Bonar Law and his daughter came to stay at Windsor Castle from Saturday to Monday . . . On Sunday, the King said to me that he and the Queen were motoring to see somebody, and I was therefore to find out what Bonar Law would like to do and make the necessary arrangements. I asked Bonar Law to say frankly what he would like most to do. Would he like to go round the pictures and furniture? But he said this would bore him.

'I then suggested the library, but he said that he would want a week at least to see this even superficially. He would rather go out. I suggested the farms, but he said this would be worse than the pictures. After I had exhausted all the usual sights with no success, I said he had better propose something himself. He said he would like to go for a drive in the park with his daughter, and I replied that nothing would be easier.

'I asked whether he would care to play bridge when he returned, but he said he had quite given up cards, and added that what he would really like was a game of chess. He warned me, however, that it was no use asking him to play "bumble-puppy" chess, as that was tiresome. He had of late years studied chess very thoroughly and now invariably played with professionals, but of course he could not expect anything of this sort at Windsor; all he asked was someone who could play a first-class game. I said I quite understood and would arrange all this.

'I went away and ordered the carriage, but scratched my head over the chess. My own chess was infantile and therefore out of the question, and although I knew that some of the Household played chess, I was quite sure that their games came under the head of "bumble-puppy" and that it was a waste of time to ask them to take on Bonar Law. It suddenly occurred to me that Sir Walter Parratt had in his day been a first-rate player, and that I remembered his telling me that he found all the chess problems in the newspapers never took him more than ten minutes to solve.

'So I wrote a note to him asking him to come and play Bonar Law at chess soon after six; that is, after the evening service at St George's Chapel. Then a short scribble to Bonar Law explaining who Parratt was. When I thought I had arranged everything I found there was some difficulty about the board and chessmen. There were innumerable and valuable sets under glass cases, but a common or garden board seemed impossible to find. I consulted Derek Keppel, the Master of the Household, and he at once started his myrmidons on the scent of one. Eventually, an ordinary set was found in the cupboard of the room that was formerly where Princess Mary worked with her governess.

'Keppel arranged a charming setting for the game with a small table, two comfortable arm-chairs and shaded electric light lamps.

'I went to the room soon after six and talked to Bonar Law. When Parratt came in I introduced them, and while a footman handed cigars and offered tea or coffee, Bonar Law whispered in my ear: "Isn't my opponent a bit old?" I merely replied that he knew the game; as a matter of fact, Parratt was 80 or more. So I left them.

'I heard afterwards that they played in dead silence for an hour and that Parratt then said: "*That* is checkmate." Bonar Law replied: "Not at all, I have seven different moves." "Precisely," said Parratt, "but if you move one, I do so and so. Checkmate. If you move two, I do so and so; again checkmate." He went through the whole seven moves and described what would happen in each case.

'Bonar Law studied this for twenty minutes and then said: "That is right." I told the King and, not very tactfully, when His Majesty came to dinner he said to Bonar Law: "I hear old Parratt beat your head off at chess." Bonar Law merely said he had had a very interesting game.'

The Death of his Sons

After the death of his wife as the result of an operation, Law was often melancholy. With the death of his two eldest sons in 1917 he grew much worse. Charlie, a second lieutenant, was reported missing after the battle of Gaza. For a time, it was thought he was a Turkish prisoner and his father, full of hope, sent a postcard:

> '*My dearest Charlie*,
> I am sending this on the chance of its reaching you. For three days until a German paper announced that you were a prisoner I was in utter despair, as we all were, and I knew then how dear you are to me.'

Months later, the postcard was returned by the Ottoman Red Crescent.

James, in the Royal Flying Corps, himself insisted on being put in the fighter squadron in September 1917. He lasted a week. His devastated father, accompanied by Lord Beaverbrook, visited the headquarters of his son's squadron in France. He asked to see a plane which his son had flown and sat alone in the cockpit for two or three hours.

Dick's Bike

In 1919 Law bought his son Dick a motor bike, and one day decided to try it out himself with Sir Archibald Geddes (the President of the Board of Trade) as his passenger and with Dick in the side-car. He set off down the steep drive of his new house at Kingston Hill to discover that not only did he not know how to stop the machine, but also that he was going to collide with an enormous steam roller that just happened to be slowly passing the end of his drive. He managed to swerve into the gate at the entrance to the drive, and no one was hurt.

On the Strikers

After the First World War, there was a spate of strikes in England. Dining out after addressing a political meeting, Law was asked by his hostess: 'Now do tell me, Mr Bonar Law, what do these people really want?'

Law looked round the grand dining room. 'Perhaps they want just a little of all this,' he replied.

STANLEY BALDWIN
First Earl Baldwin of Bewdley (1867–1947)

'A man of no experience, and of the utmost insignificance'

LORD CURZON in 1923

THE ONLY SON of Alfred Baldwin, a wealthy ironmaster, and his wife Louisa, Stanley Baldwin was born at Bewdley on 3 August 1867. It was not until he was almost eleven that he was finally dispatched to a preparatory school, Hawtrey's, from where he went on to Harrow and to Trinity College, Cambridge.

In 1888, Baldwin entered the family business, and after his father's death in 1908 took his place as Conservative MP for West Worcestershire. He played little part in the House of Commons until 1916 when he became Andrew Bonar Law's Parliamentary Private Secretary, and the following year became joint financial secretary to the Treasury. He was Chancellor of the Exchequer under Bonar Law and on the latter's resignation in 1923 became, unexpectedly, Prime Minister. He was later to tell Asquith:

> 'The position of leader came to me when I was inexperienced, before I was really fitted for it, by a succession of curious chances that could not have been foreseen. I had never expected it.'

He was to hold the office three times – in 1923, from 1924 to 1929, and from 1935 to 1937. He finally retired to his country house, Astley, exhausted by the cares of office and especially by the abdication crisis; and died there in December 1947.

Baldwin was married for over fifty years to Lucy Ridsdale, the daughter of a former Master of the Mint, by whom he had four sons and three daughters.

Held Aloft

The day he was born, the infant Stanley Baldwin was carried by the family cook up to the top of the house and held up high on a chair. It was a local belief that babies shown in this way would rise in the world.

Cousins

Baldwin's mother Louisa came from a remarkable family. Her father was a Wesleyan minister from Wolverhampton. Of his five daughters, four, including Louisa, married distinguished men, Alice married John Kipling and produced Rudyard, Georgina married Sir Edward Burne-Jones, and Agnes married Sir Edward Poynter, the President of the Royal Academy.

Stanley and his cousin Rudyard Kipling were good friends throughout their lives. On Sunday 19 January 1936 Edward, Prince of Wales, went to see Baldwin at 10 Downing Street to inform him of the King's illness. He found Baldwin preoccupied:

> 'I wonder if you know, Sir, that another great Englishmen, a contemporary of your father's, died yesterday?'

When the Prince failed to respond, Baldwin went on:

> 'But of course, Sir, you have a great deal on your mind. I should not have expected you to know. It was Rudyard Kipling, my first cousin'.

Trouble at School

All seemed to be going well at Harrow until, in the middle of Baldwin's third year, Alfred Baldwin received a telegram from the headmaster and an angry letter complaining about his son's behaviour. Apparently Stanley had produced a pornographic composition and, what was worse in the eyes of the headmaster, had sent it to his cousin at Eton where it had been detected. Baldwin was duly flogged, and his relations with the school soured although his father tried to make light of the incident, writing to his wife:

'the whole affair was much exaggerated and far more folly than anything else . . . the upshot is a flogging, which is now over and done with.'

When he proceeded to Trinity after a year's break from full-time education, Baldwin was not pleased to learn that his former head-master was now installed as Master of Trinity.

The Simple Man

Part of Baldwin's success as a politician came from his reputation as the best sort of honest, straightforward Englishman who never concerned himself too much with the machinations of politics. As his career progressed, more observant contemporaries began to wonder how much of this was true. Harold Nicolson remarked:

> 'There is something very strange about Stanley Baldwin. At first sight he is a solid English gentleman, but then one observes odd nervous tricks. He has an extraordinarily unpleasant habit of smelling at his notes and licking the edges slightly as if they were the flap of an envelope. He scratches himself continuously. There are russet patches across his head and face. And a strange movement of the head, with half-closed eyes, like some tortoise half-awake smelling the air – blinking, snuffy, neurotic.'

Austen Chamberlain was more positive in his denunciation:

> 'Yes, I should like to write about Stanley Baldwin but it is wiser not to do so, for the Stanley Baldwin whom we know does not fit in at any point with the picture which the public have made of him for themselves. They think him a simple, hardworking, unambitious man, not a "politician" in the abusive sense in which they so often use the word, whom nothing but a stern sense of duty keeps at his ungrateful talk, a man too of wide and liberal mind who has educated his party.
>
> 'And we know him as self-centred, selfish and idle, yet one of the shrewdest politicians, but without a constructive idea in his head and with an amazing ignorance of Indian and foreign affairs and of the real value of political life. "Sly, devilishly sly!" would be my chapter heading and egotism and

idleness the principal characteristics that I should assign to him.'

The Great Walker

Never a keen sportsman, Baldwin's favourite activity, until arthritis struck, was taking long walks. In 1917, for example, he spent a long weekend walking sixty miles in the Cotswolds. Every summer, the Baldwins took a holiday at Aix-les-Bains from where Baldwin regularly reported on his walks:
In 1921:

> 'My walks are a daily joy and I am rapidly getting into some sort of condition. I find I can now do six hours climbing to a couple of thousand feet, with ease, and though I am very happy by myself I often feel I want someone for a minute to enjoy the beauty of it all and shout "Thank God".'

and again in 1922:

> 'I have got into training again and yesterday I did a 5000-foot little mountain, to the top and back on my own legs in about seven hours and fit as a fiddle after it. I couldn't have done it three weeks ago to save my life. My agility in the descent surprised me and I can only conclude that living with *goats* made me sure footed among rocks.'

The War Debt

In 1919 there appeared an anonymous letter in *The Times* appealing to the wealthy to tax themselves voluntarily and announcing 'that the writer, having estimated his estate at £580,000, would buy £150,000 of the War Loan for cancellation. Although the letter was signed 'F.S.T.' it was unknown even to the Chancellor of the Exchequer that the author was Stanley Baldwin, Financial Secretary to the Treasury, who had anonymously given £150,000 to the nation.

Leaving Downing Street

After the 1923 election, all the staff and servants of 10 Downing Street were lined up in the hall as Mr and Mrs Baldwin came down the stairs.

'"I'm glad we are leaving these lodgings, Cissy" remarked the ex-Prime Minister in an attempt to be cheerful, "the beds are damp."

"But, Stan dear," protested his wife, "they're our *own* beds."'

The other Stanley Baldwin

On his return to office in 1924, Stanley Baldwin received a letter of congratulation from a ten-year-old Canadian who also happened to be called Stanley Baldwin. He wrote back personally:

'Dear namesake, I am glad you wrote to me and don't ever forget that you have got a name worth taking care of when you grow up. I will try and not let it down so long as I bear it and you do the same after my work is finished. Good luck to you.'

The Chancellor of Cambridge University

Baldwin himself described his installation as Chancellor in 1930:

'It was a heavy day: the installation at noon, the lunch in Caius Hall, the degree ceremony, a garden party at Magdalene, a dinner at Trinity and a reception at the Lodge. I had the perfect page in attendance all day. He was in court dress and acted as to the manner born. Two funny things happened. Of course a Trinity dinner is always a family party, no reporters, absolutely private. Dawes [the new American ambassador] sent his speech to the Press Association and so it was published. But funnier still, an American movie man turned up. Would we stop the procession on its way to the Senate House from Trinity for the American Ambassador to make a speech? On explaining to him that this wasn't done, he replied: "But the American Ambassador has given his consent."'

The old School Tie

During a week-end at Cliveden in 1935, Baldwin admitted it was true that during his previous premiership he had been wearing his old school tie in a railway compartment and had been asked by a fellow-traveller:

'Were you not at Harrow in my time? What have you been doing since?'

R.A.B.'s Dog

In July 1935, Baldwin visited a Conservative Party fête held in the grounds of Stanstead Hall, R.A. Butler's country house in Essex. He was not at all put out when bitten by the family dog:

> 'I quite understand how you feel; I want to do that to every supplementary question in the House at this time of year.'

He had in his pocket an iodine pencil, calmly produced it, and painted it on the scratch.

The House of Lords

After having been created Earl Baldwin of Bewdley, he admitted to Inskip that he did not much want to go to the House of Lords, adding:

> 'There is perhaps a certain retributive justice in it, as I have sent so many others there hoping I should never see their faces again.'

Last Public Appearance

In 1947, Baldwin attended the unveiling by George VI of the statue of his father, George V, in Old Palace Yard opposite the House of Commons. Few recognized him but there was a faint cheer as his car sped away from the crowds. The deaf, enfeebled ex-Prime Minister, turned to his companion sadly and asked, 'Are they booing me?'

JAMES RAMSAY MACDONALD

(1866–1937)

'If God were to come and ask "Ramsay, would
you rather be a country gentleman than a P.M.?"
I should reply "Please God, a country gentleman"'

Diary for 5 October 1930, HAROLD NICOLSON

THE ILLEGITIMATE SON of Anne Ramsay, James Ramsay Macdonald was brought up at Lossiemouth, Morayshire, and attended a local school. After a spell as pupil-teacher there, Macdonald left Scotland in 1886 and soon took a job as secretary to a radical politician, supplementing his income by freelance socialist journalism. He stood as Independent Labour Party candidate at the general elections of 1895 and 1900, and from 1900 to 1912 acted as secretary to the Labour Representation Committee, the embryo from which the Labour Party grew.

In 1906, Macdonald finally entered the House of Commons as Labour MP for Leicester, one of twenty-nine successful Labour candidates. Politicians of all persuasions quickly recognized his abilities as a parliamentarian, and by 1911 he had become chairman of the parliamentary Labour group. A passionate opponent of the First World War, Macdonald was wrongly but universally condemned as a pacifist. By 1918, his popularity in Leicester had been eroded to such an extent that he was defeated by over 14,000 votes. In 1922, the growing reaction against Lloyd George's coalition, brought him back to the House of Commons and in 1924 he became the first Labour Prime Minister as well as Foreign Secretary. Preoccupied with foreign affairs, he made little effort to conciliate the Liberals on whom the Labour government depended. As a result, it fell in October 1924.

Macdonald returned for a second period in office in 1929 at the age of sixty-three, and again his chief concern was with foreign affairs. At home, a deepening economic depression precipitated the financial crisis of 1931. Labour ministers were unable to agree on a method of tackling the crisis and Macdonald, after attempting to resign, was persuaded by the King to head an all-party National Government which he intended to last only as long as the immediate crisis. Instead, it continued until 1937, with Macdonald as its head, vilified by most of his former colleagues, until ill health forced him to be replaced by Baldwin in 1935. Even then, he lingered on until 1937 as Lord President of the Council, and died only a few months later, on 9 November, on board a ship bound for South America.

In 1896 Macdonald married a London social worker, Margaret Gladstone, the daughter of a distinguished scientist. They had six children, one of whom died of diphtheria in 1910. His wife died in 1911.

The Illegitimate Child

Ramsay Macdonald's mother never married. His father was probably a ploughman called John Macdonald. The minute-book of the Kirk Session of the local Kirk reveals the birth and the stigma attached to it:

> '14th December 1866 compeared of their own accord John Macdonald foreman at Sweethillock, and with him Anne Ramsay residing at Lossiemouth, who being acknowledged that she had borne a male child on the 12th of October last, and she now named as the father of her child John Macdonald, sometime fellow servant with her at Claydale. The said John Macdonald being present was asked by the Moderator to say whether he acknowledged the truth of the charge, to which he answered that he did. The parties were then solemnly addressed by the Moderator as to the evil of the sin they had committed and were exhorted to seek repentance and forgiveness and divine grace to guide them in time to come. They received the same in a becoming manner and professed their sorrow and their desire to be forgiven and led in the way of divine commandment. The Kirk Session were satisfied with the same, and considering that one of the parties resides at a distance agreed that they be now absolved from Church censure and be restored to Church privileges, which was done accordingly.'

What is not known is the story behind the bare facts of the birth. Malcolm Macdonald puts forward two suggestions. One was that the engaged couple quarrelled violently and Annie refused to marry John Macdonald. The other was that Annie's mother did not think John Macdonald good enough for her daughter and forbade the union. Whatever the truth, the result was that Ramsay Macdonald was brought up by his mother and his grandmother, two poor but determined women in a tiny 'but-and-ben' cottage in Lossiemouth. Both women earned some sort of living by sewing, but it is said too that Annie used to gut fish for the herring fleet in the summer.

Marriage

When Macdonald got engaged on the steps of the British Museum to Margaret Gladstone, a London girl of independent mind and means, the latter was at pains to win the affections of her fiancé's mother, apologizing for not immediately coming to Lossiemouth:

'*My dear Mrs Macdonald*,
Your son tells me that he has told you that we love one another, and that you send me kind thoughts and words. I thank you for them from the bottom of my heart. I never knew my mother, and I always hoped that if I ever married, my husband's mother would be living and would like me. That I shall like her I never feel any doubt; and if you need any promise that I will not try to take him away from you (I could not do it if I did try) here it is.

'I cannot tell you how sorry I am that I am tied in London just at this time when I want to come to Lossiemouth and get to know you and his home. But if you could see my grand-mother you would see how any excitement is utterly out of the question . . . There is one thing that I should be very glad if you would tell me, and that is by what name I am to call your son. I only know him as Mr MacDonald and really don't know what Christian name he uses. Mine is Margaret.

'He tells me that you asked him if I could cook and keep a house clean, and that he did not know. I have done a little both of cooking and of housework, but I have not had much practice, and I am afraid you would not think much of my performances, though I liked what I did of both. I often make butter when I am staying at a farmhouse which my grandmother goes to every summer and I always long to milk the cows there, but have never screwed up the courage to ask if I may.

'I am nothing like so good as my mother must have been according to the accounts of her in the book [enclosed life of her grandfather]; but nothing could help to make me better like your son's love, and if you will love me too it will help me. I am, if you will let me be, yours affectionately,

Margaret Gladstone

She kept the reply her future mother-in-law sent her:

My dear Margaret
Many thanks for the Book and letter; shall read it and return it my Dear Gural i am sorry to here of your grandmothers illness i do hope she is better i now wat nursing is i nursed my Grandmother my Aunt and then My Dear Mother was confined to bed for 4 years and 6 months and a dear person in trouble she was but i trust your Granmother will soon get over this bad turn My Dear Gural you ask me for my Young Mans christian name it is Jamie Ramsay Macdonald we call him Ramsay My own name is Anniee Ramsay My son is as good son to me and i trust if it please God that you and Ramsay be happy i trust got will go with you in all your ups and downs in life and I shall be verry glad to sea you in Lossiemouth My Dear Gural you spoke of milking cows i have Milked cows and made Butter and all that work but for the last 29 years i have been doing little but sowing in my dear little home Now my dear i will not forget to pray god for you as i have done for him in the past that god may be with you both and that you may be happy Ramsay will soon be Back to London and i will be all alone again with Much Love and i hopes you will writ me soon

from your frind
Mrs A Ramsay

After their marriage the couple lived in a small flat with no bathroom at Lincoln's Inn Fields. Margaret, herself a convinced socialist, was a founding member of the Womens Labour League, an active campaigner for the rights of women, as well as a supporter of innumerable welfare and charitable organizations in the East End. She was less than zealous about either her appearance or the state of her flat. Fellow members of one committee of which she was chairman once presented her with a new blouse to wear at an important delegation only to find that she wore it back to front. A secretary later recalled the chaos of their flat:

> '. . . They were very untidy – he wasn't, I think he wanted to be tidy, but she never. There was a great big armchair, an enormous one full of papers; and I think she kept all the clothes she ever had, because clearing up was rather difficult. You never knew where you might have to go . . . I might have to take the baby up to the bath . . . or attend to the little girl who was sitting on her pot, or if they were out to take garlands from an Indian visitor.'

The couple were devoted to each other and to their six children, although pressure of work meant that the latter were often left in the care of the maid, Ada, or of the cross-eyed charlady, Mrs Gurling. Malcolm Macdonald remembered often being invited back to her garret home 'where we guzzled fish-and-chips picked from newspaper wrappings and winkles gouged from their boiled shells.'

This happy chaotic world was shattered, first by the death of David in 1910, and then for ever in the following year by the early death from blood-poisoning of Margaret Macdonald. She was only forty-one and her desolate husband never really got over the loss. On the first anniversary of her death Malcolm Macdonald remembered that he gathered all his surviving children around him and, looking at his watch to see the actual moment of her death spoke to what must have been a terrified family about their mother 'with this terrible tear-stained agony of grief'. Three years later, he wrote in his diary on 12 September:

> 'This is the fourth anniversary of the funeral. This year I had had to spend the 8th in a Bristol hotel. The afternoon was strangely like that when she died, bright, sunny, peaceful. I was very weary both in mind and spirit and as I sat through the hours of the death agony alone in my room, it was not sorrow that came to me but a sad weariness and a wonder if she was or was not, if she cared, or knew, or what.'

The year before he died a foreign visitor asked him why he had never remarried. 'My heart', he replied, 'has been in the grave for a quarter of a century.'

Life at Number 10

Ramsay Macdonald never seemed at all comfortable in 10 Downing Street. Harold Nicolson described how he once bumped into the Prime Minister in the street and was taken home for a drink:

> 'Walking across St Stephen's Yard I observe a small figure in front of me with collar turned up. He turns to see who is behind him and I see it is Ramsay Macdonald. I say "Hullo, sir, How are you?" He greets me warmly. We walked across to Downing Street and people take off their hats as he passes. The traffic is stopped. He talks about Vita's broacast on Persia: the best he has ever heard. He asks me to come in and have a drink. We reach the door of No. 10. He knocks. The porter opens and stands to attention. Ramsay asks him. "Is Berry in?" "No, sir, he has gone." "Is Ishbel in?" (not Miss Ishbel) "Yes, sir." "Would you ask her to bring two glasses to my room?" We then go upstairs. The room has an unlived-in appearance. Turners over the fireplace. Ishbel is there. He asks her to get us a drink. She goes out and returns with two tooth-glasses and a syphon. Says she can't find any whisky. Ramsay says it is in the drawer of his table. He finds it. "What about some champagne," he says, "to celebrate the victory?" [passing of Trades Disputes Bill] I say I will not have champagne. Malcolm comes in. "A cigarette?" I say I will. "Malcolm, we have got cigarettes, haven't we – in that Egyptian box?" Malcolm goes to search for the Egyptian box. Then there are no matches.'

Whilst he was in office, the family groceries were delivered to Number 10 in a co-op van, and to save money the family ate their meals in the official banqueting rooms which were heated at Government expense. There can have been little family life there since Macdonald proved himself to be incapable of delegation. It is said that he was even to be found looking up train times for one of his secretaries and he started out as Prime Minister by opening all his letters himself.

The Ladies

Ramsay Macdonald, as his enemies were quick to notice, enjoyed the company of women. Although the void created by Margaret's death was never filled, he was much comforted at various times by the friendship of women like Lady Margaret Sackville, Molly Hamilton, Cecily Gordon-Cumming and Lady Londonderry. He met Lady Londonderry at a dinner at Buckingham Palace in 1924 and by 1930 both she and her husband were good friends, visiting him at Chequers and inviting him to glittering receptions at Londonderry House. He wrote her poems; she sent him medieval Latin love lyrics, and for a while at least his sense of desolation was forgotten.

> 'I have been away for a day or two [he wrote after one visit] . . . I have to tell my hostess how she mothered me, and try and tell her how I loved it. One evening she rubbed a startled nerve and soothed it by the magic of her hand and I could hardly bear her going away. I felt so miserable and deserted . . .
>
> 'Then, when I said "good bye", she asked me not to write at all but just telephone. Ah! those moderns who live in a mechanical world and come to regard the engines of motor cars as the wings of angels bringing us to heaven, and the quiverings of telephones as the means of conveying affection. How can I convey by telephone the happy delusion that for three days I seemed to be living an old existence, that my hostess and I had known each other from the beginning when there was only the Word, and would know each other until the Word resumed its empire, that with her I wandered in rich autumn pastures where gentle winds blew and the air was benign?'

With Cecily Gordon-Cumming, who was in her early twenties when they met on a cross-channel steamer, he was more paternal. Until she married in 1931 they wrote, and saw each other, regularly. Miss Gordon-Cumming admitted later that he might have been 'in a small, far-away way . . . slightly in love with me' and that when they drove together in the back of his car he sometimes held her hand under a rug.

The Country-House Life

Whatever the actual nature of his relationships with other women, there were many who disapproved and who accused him of betraying his class. He appeared to derive far too much enjoyment from the company of the upper classes. Beatrice Webb was particularly distressed about it all, complaining in her diary:

> 'Alas! Alas! Balmoral is inevitable; but why the castles of the wealthiest, most aristocratic, most reactionary and by no means the most intellectual of the Conservative Party? "Because," J.R.M. would answer if he laid bare his heart, "I am more at home with them than I should be with you or any other member of the Labour Party." . . . It argues a perverted taste and a vanishing faith.'

The Walker

Macdonald did not want to spend all his time relaxing in the country houses of the rich. His chief relaxation was always hill-walking. After the 1924 election he went on a walking tour in the West Country, writing afterwards:

> 'If friends fail, the hill road never does. When you are up it never blames; it has no grievances if not put in a Cabinet and its ruts are not made in reverence; when you are down it does not attribute its misfortunes to you.'

Nor was he only a fair-weather walker. He once described a typical night's sleep on a walking holiday in the Cairngorms:

> 'I lay down that night under shelter of a great granite boulder, which in times when the poor earth was convulsed with pain, came down like an angel from the heights to minister to the comforts of man. The wind moaned like a wild beast prowling around; I could hear the drip, drip of the rain in the little pools round the stone; the rush of the streams was like a gale in a wood . . . At eight o'clock we stretched ourselves out to sleep without a dry square inch of clothing on us and with the brittle stalks of heather, which had mercifully been left by whoever had last taken a night's lodging in this free "hotel for travellers", pricking us.
>
> 'And we did sleep – a happy, dreamless sleep. Now and again the bed became too hard, or the heather too sharp, or the wind puffs too cold, but the dark moments of wakefulness only added to the pleasure. No king in his feather bed was

happier. We were alone amidst the clouds, the companions of
the storm and the rushing waters. We were to have started
again at four: we slept till six.'

King George VI's Coronation
Harold Nicolson found Ramsay Macdonald looking very distinguished in his Trinity House uniform. He told him how well he
looked:

'Yes [replied Macdonald] when I was a visitor to a lunatic
asylum, I always noticed how well the worst lunatics looked.'

ARTHUR NEVILLE CHAMBERLAIN

(1869–1940)

'I was very fond of him. I like all unlovable men'

His physician LORD HORDER (1871–1955)

'He might have been the Secretary of a firm of undertakers reading the Minutes of the last meeting'

HAROLD NICOLSON

THE SECOND SON of Joseph Chamberlain, the radical MP from Birmingham, Neville was born at Edgbaston, Birmingham on 18 March 1869 and was educated at Rugby and at Mason College, Birmingham, where he studied metallurgy and engineering design. From 1890–97 he lived in the Bahamas, attempting unsuccessfully to establish a sisal plantation for his father. He returned to Birmingham to make his own way as a businessman, and gravitated towards city politics, becoming a councillor in 1911 and Lord Mayor in 1915.

In 1918, at the age of fifty, Chamberlain entered the House of Commons, and in the 1920s and 1930s held a number of offices, notably Minister of Health and Chancellor of the Exchequer. On Baldwin's resignation, he was the obvious choice to become Prime Minister at the age of sixty-eight when, as he admitted in the House of Commons, 'most people are thinking of retiring from active work'. Foreign affairs dominated, his twin aims of appeasement and rearmament apparently successful until Hitler's invasion of Czechoslovakia shattered the dream. Resigning the premiership in May 1940, Chamberlain stayed on as Lord President of the Council until ill-health forced his withdrawal from public affairs in October 1940. He died two months later having declined all honours, preferring to remain plain Mr Chamberlain like his father before him.

In 1911 Chamberlain married Annie Vere Cole, by whom he had

one son and one daughter. He himself admitted his debt to his wife in a letter to his sister Hilda:

> 'I should never have been Prime Minister if I hadn't had Annie to help me. It isn't only that she charms everyone into good humour and makes them think that a man can't be so bad who has a wife like that. She has undoubtedly made countless friends and supporters . . . and she has kept many who might have left me if I had been alone, but are devoted to her . . .'

Dull

Neville Chamberlain was not made of the stuff of which anecdotes were written. He was a devoted husband and father, and a loyal, affectionate elder brother to his three younger sisters, named Ida, Hilda and Beatrice. He won the admiration of George VI and of countless others, but he had little style, warmth or even eccentricity, a quality much admired in a British Prime Minister. Churchill could only recall one intimate social occasion with Chamberlain 'amid all the business we did together over nearly twenty years'. Even his butler had to admit to Samuel Hoare that 'you can't know Mr Chamberlain till you have been with him five years.' One of the few endearing traits about him was his capacity for self-criticism, admitting after he had seen himself on film:

> '. . . if I had not previously seen the person who addressed us from the screen, I should call him pompous, unsufferably slow in diction and unspeakably repellent in person.'

The Motherless Boy

Neville was six when both his mother and his grandmother died. His father's youngest sister, Clara, took over as a sort of foster-mother but lacked any maternal affection. When Neville rushed into her arms having arrived home after his first term at Rugby he always remembered that she said only 'Neville, your cap's crooked', and he made a vow there and then never to kiss her again.

The Late Victorian Man

Neville Chamberlain never managed to move with the times. He hated motor cars and telephones, and never used a modern fountain pen. Intellectually, too, his outlook was Victorian. He disliked modern art, describing paintings by Stanley Spencer as 'hideous, distorted, grotesque productions' and was convinced that Epstein's *Christ* was a joke. Equally, the emergence of the Labour Party was anathema to him, Baldwin having to beg him to remember that when addressing Labour MPs he was still addressing gentlemen, 'I always gave him the impression, he said, when I spoke in the House of Commons, that I looked on the Labour Party as dirt.'

The Country Lover

Despite his Birmingham upbringing, Chamberlain was very much the country gentleman in his love of fishing, shooting and gardening. He sent occasional articles to the *Countryman* on botany, took an active interest in the garden at Chequers, and submitted letters to *The Times* and *Daily Telegraph*, not on matters of state, but on the habits of a blackbird in the garden of 11 Downing Street or the appearance of a grey wagtail in St James's Park.

My Tenants the Ribbentrops

In 1936 Chamberlain let his house in Eaton Square for a while to Ribbentrop, the German ambassador and his family. 'I think it is very amusing considering my affections for Germans in general and Ribbentrop in particular.'

Munich

Chamberlain was fêted as a hero on his return from his peace-mission to Germany in 1938. Besides a chorus of praise in the British press, tributes arrived at 10 Downing Street from all over the world. Innumerable fishing rods and salmon flies arrived, four thousand tulips were sent from Holland, and cases of Alsatian wine were delivered. The strangest request came from a man in Greece who asked for a piece of Chamberlain's umbrella to make a relic in an icon.

Dinner with the Churchills

The 'social occasion' with the Churchills, to which a reference has already been made, was a dinner party for four at Admiralty House on 13 October 1939. At first, Chamberlain fascinated Churchill with an account of his sisal-growing struggles in the Bahamas, but events soon became more exciting. Churchill himself described the dinner:

'During dinner the war went on and things happened. With the soup an officer came up from the War Room below to report that a U-boat had been sunk. With the sweet he came again and reported that a second U-boat had been sunk; and just before the ladies left the dining room he came a third time reporting that a third U-boat had been sunk. Nothing like this had ever happened before in a single day, and it was more than a year before such a record was repeated.

'As the ladies left us, Mrs Chamberlain, with a naïve and a charming glance, said to me, "Did you arrange all this on purpose?" I assured her that if she would come again we would produce a similar result.'

A Quiet Abbey Funeral

Chips Channon noted in his diary that the date of Chamberlain's funeral was not published 'lest the Germans would stage a raid and get Winston and the entire Government with one bomb.' He added his own impression of the event:

'There in the Abbey, and it angered me to see them, were all the little men who had torpedoed poor Neville's heroic efforts to preserve peace, and made his life a misery: some seemed to be gloating. Winston, followed by the War Cabinet, however, had the decency to cry as he stood by the coffin . . .'

WINSTON LEONARD SPENCER CHURCHILL

(1874–1965)

> 'We are all worms. But I do believe that I am
> a "glow worm".'
>
> WINSTON CHURCHILL to Violet Bonham Carter

BORN AT BLENHEIM PALACE on 30 September 1874, the elder son of Lord Randolph Churchill by his American wife, the former Jenny Jerome, Winston Churchill was educated first at two preparatory schools, then Harrow and Sandhurst. Commissioned in the 4th Hussars, Churchill served between 1895 and 1898 in Cuba, India and Egypt. In South Africa in 1899 he acted as war correspondent for the *Morning Post* and the following year entered the House of Commons as Conservative MP for Oldham.

Crossing over to the Liberals in 1904, Churchill served under Campbell-Bannerman and Asquith as Under-Secretary of State for the Colonies (1906–8), President of the Board of Trade (1908–10), Home Secretary (1910–11) and First Lord of the Admiralty (1911–15). In Asquith's Coalition Churchill was, briefly, Chancellor of the Duchy of Lancaster but resigned in 1915 to command a battalion in France. Lloyd George made him Minister of Munitions (1917), Secretary of State for War (1919–21) and Secretary of State for the Colonies (1921–2).

Out of office and of Parliament from October 1922 for two years, Churchill bounced back in October 1924 to become Chancellor of the Exchequer in Baldwin's Conservative Government (1924–9). Viewed by many in the Thirties as unduly alarmist with his insistence on rearmament, Churchill's return to office was inevitable once war had been declared.

In September 1939 he became First Lord of the Admiralty. In May 1940 he replaced Chamberlain as Prime Minister and formed an all-party coalition committed to 'victory at all costs'. As a war leader, he was outstanding, inspiring his countrymen by his stirring oratory and by his own pugnacious courage.

On 26 July 1945, defeated in the general election, Churchill resigned. He refused to bow out of politics and returned, aged and infirm, for a last tenure of office from 1951 to 1955.

In retirement, Churchill's health gradually deteriorated and he died on 25 January 1965. He was given a state funeral and buried at Bladon near Blenheim.

In 1908 Churchill married Clementine Hozier, the daughter of Colonel Sir H.M. Hozier and Lady Blanche Ogilvie. They had one son and three daughters. A fourth daughter died before she was three.

Churchill was also a very successful writer and painter. In 1953 he received the Nobel Prize for Literature. Among his books are *My Early Life*, *The World Crisis*, *Marlborough*, *The Second World War*, and *A History of the English Speaking Peoples*.

Ambition

Churchill never deigned to hide his ambition. As a young politician, he modelled his speeches on Gibbon and Macaulay, and scoured the pages of the *Annual Register* in order to work out what he would have said on particular issues.

He first met Violet Asquith, who became a lifelong friend, at a dinner party in 1906. He asked how old she was, and she replied that she was nineteen.

> 'And I [he complained] am 32 already. Younger than anyone else who *counts* though.'

Clementine

Churchill himself wrote that he married Clementine Hozier and they 'lived happily ever after'. They were indeed devoted to each other although Churchill was not always an easy husband. As a bride, Clementine learned very quickly that she was never going to be able to monopolize her husband's attention. It is said that in the vestry after their wedding Churchill talked politics with Lloyd George. On their honeymoon he worked on his book *My African Journey* and sent letters on current affairs to his colleagues.

Clementine was never overawed by her husband. She argued

against buying Chartwell, on which he had set his heart (he went ahead just the same). In the 1930s she sometimes escaped from the pressures of home life to travel with friends. For the first four months of 1935 she travelled to the Dutch East Indies on board 'Rosaura', Lord Moyne's yacht, and during the voyage, according to her daughter fell 'romantically in love' with one of her fellow passengers, a debonair art dealer. This passing attachment did nothing to undermine the strength of their marriage, and Clementine had more influence over her husband than anyone else. In the dark days of June 1940 when it seemed to his colleagues that Churchill was becoming more and more tyrannical under the strain, only Clementine could broach the subject:

> 'One of the men in your entourage (a devoted friend) has been to me and told me that there is a danger of your being generally disliked by your colleagues and subordinates because of your rough sarcastic and overbearing manner . . .
>
> My Darling Winston. I must confess that I have noticed a deterioration in your manner; and you are not as kind as you used to be.'

It is not known how Churchill replied, but the fact that he kept Clementine's letter is significant.

Accidents

Quite apart from Churchill's exploits as a soldier, it is surprising that he ever survived to become Prime Minister. As a boy, his closest escape came when he was eighteen and staying near Bournemouth with his aunt, Lady Wimborne. He was being chased by his brother and a cousin and was trapped half-way across a bridge over a deep gulley. Undaunted, Churchill leapt off the bridge, hoping to slide down a tree. Instead, he fell nearly thirty feet to the ground, ruptured a kidney, and was unconscious for three days. It took him more than three months to recover properly.

As early as 1914, Clementine had tried to persuade Winston not to pursue a hobby she viewed with alarm: flying. He had already gone up almost 140 times and had been judged by a future Marshal of the RAF, Lord Trenchard, as 'altogether too impatient for a good pupil'. After the war, as Secretary of State for Air, he flew many times. His pilot was Colonel Jack Scott, but his plane had dual controls and Churchill often flew himself part of the way to Paris or back. In July

1919 he took off himself from Croydon and soon found, to his alarm, that the controls were not working properly. Scott was unable to prevent the plane from crashing, and whereas Churchill himself escaped virtually unhurt, Scott was knocked unconscious and had both legs broken. After that, Churchill's enthusiasm for flying waned.

On a trip to the States in 1929 Churchill got out of a taxi in New York and forgot for a moment that cars used the right hand side of the road. He was knocked down immediately and lay in hospital for eight days.

> 'It was the equivalent of falling thirty feet on to a pavement . . . of stopping 10 pounds of buckshot dropped 600 feet, or two charges of buckshot at point-blank range. I do not understand why I was not broken like an egg-shell or squashed like a gooseberry . . .'

On the Birth of His First Child

Churchill told Lloyd George that Diana, his daughter, was the prettiest child ever seen. 'Like her mother, I suppose?' remarked Lloyd George gallantly.

'No, she is exactly like me.'

Clothes

The *Tailor and Cutter* did not approve of the clothes Churchill wore on his wedding day. It was, they pronounced:

> 'neither fish, flesh, nor fowl, and was one of the greatest failures as a wedding garment we have ever seen, giving the wearer a sort of glorified coachman appearance.'

Churchill never cared much about the opinion of others and went on wearing exactly what he wished. In later years, he was often seen in his much-loved siren suit, a comfortable garment resembling an outsize rompersuit.

Churchill's taste in underwear is less well-known, but soon after his marriage an appalled Clementine confided to Violet Asquith that her husband bought fine pale pink silk underwear from the Army and Navy Stores and that it cost about £80 a year. When Violet Asquith challenged him about his extravagance, he replied gravely:

> 'It is essential to my well-being. I have a very delicate and

sensitive cuticle – feel it . . . I have a cuticle without a blemish – except on one small portion of my anatomy where I sacrificed a piece of skin to accommodate a wounded brother officer on my way back from the Sudan campaign.'

The Orator

During the war Harold Nicolson wrote an article in the *Spectator* on Churchill's oratory. When Churchill thanked him for what he had said, Nicolson expressed the hope that he had been right in stating that Winston was not a born orator. 'You are perfectly right,' Churchill agreed. 'Not born in the very least – just hard, hard, work.'

After giving his 'blood, sweat and tears' speech to the House of Commons it is said that he spotted an old friend as he was leaving the chamber and muttered to him 'That got the sods, didn't it?'

According to Harold Nicolson, when Churchill had finished giving his 'We shall fight on the beaches' speech he put his hand over the microphone and added:

'We will hit 'em over the head with beer bottles, which is all we have to fight them with.'

The Soldier Manqué

Churchill loved fighting and rather regretted not being able to get on to a battlefield during the Second World War. He admitted as much to Alexander:

'I envy you the command of armies in the field. That's what I should have liked.'

The King himself had to order Churchill not to sail with the D-Day invasion fleet, a plan on which the Prime Minister had set his heart. He was not pleased:

'A man who has to play an effectual part in taking with the highest responsibility, grave and terrible decisions of war may need the refreshment of adventure.'

Even so, when Churchill finally inspected the Normandy bridgehead on 12 June he arranged a trip home on a destroyer and managed to persuade its admiral to shell the enemy-held coastline. To his great disappointment, the Germans did not return fire.

The Sentimental Patriot

Churchill could always be moved to tears by the courage of his countrymen. Lord Ismay observed him on a visit to London dockland during the Blitz:

> '"Good old Winnie," they cried, "We thought you'd come and see us. We can take it. Give it 'em back."
>
> 'Churchill broke down, and as I was struggling to get him through the crowd, I heard an old woman say, "You see, he really cares. He's crying."'

The man who, as Lord Riddell recorded, had once moved a worm off a golf-course to the safety of some bracken saying 'Poor fellow. If I leave you here, you will be trampled by some ruthless boot', was easily moved to tears by simple things. John Peck tells how:

> 'Driving down to Chequers one Friday evening, when the bombing was at its worst, he saw a very long queue of people lined up outside a shop in a poor quarter of London, and he stopped and sent his detective to see what the shortage was that had caused it. It was a queue for birdseed. Winston wept.'

By the end of the war, Churchill's capacity for weeping had become rather a joke. Anthony Eden told Harold Nicolson that when Churchill received the Freedom of Paris he did not stop crying for one moment and could have filled buckets by the time he received the honour.

Working for Churchill

Sir George Mallarby, Under-Secretary in the Cabinet Office, best described what it was like working for Churchill:

> 'Anybody who served anywhere near him was devoted to him. It is hard to say why. He was not kind or considerate. He bothered nothing about us. He knew the names only of those very close to him and would hardly let anyone else come into his presence. He was free with abuse and complaint. He was exacting beyond reason and ruthlessly critical. He continuously exhibited all the characteristics

which one morally deplores and abominates in the boss. Not only did he get away with it but nobody really wanted him otherwise. He was unusual, unpredictable, exciting, original, stimulating, provocative, outrageous, uniquely experienced, abundantly talented, humorous, entertaining – almost everything a man could be, a great man.'

Ellen Wilkinson, one of his Cabinet, compared Churchill's performance at meetings with that of Attlee:

'When Mr Attlee is presiding in the absence of the Prime Minister the Cabinet meets on time, goes systematically through its agenda, makes the necessary decisions, and goes home after three or four hours' work. When Mr Churchill presides we never reach the agenda and we decide nothing. But we go home to bed at midnight conscious of having been present at an historic occasion.'

Attlee at one stage wrote to Churchill complaining bitterly of 'the method or rather lack of method of dealing with matters requiring Cabinet decisions'. Churchill sulked in bed for a while and then collared one of his private secretaries: 'Let us think no more of Hitlee or Attler; let us go and see a film.'

He was a hard task master, once rebuking an exhausted secretary: 'We must go on like gun-horses till we drop.' Finding it easy himself to keep going with the help of his famous cat-naps, he expected others to keep up. When Lord Halifax asked him once to postpone a Cabinet meeting arranged for 10 p.m., he rescheduled it for 10.30 p.m. It was not what Lord Halifax had had in mind.

What endeared him to many was his unflagging ebullience, his unquenchable zest for life. Sir Alan Brooke, Chief of Imperial General Staff, once found him at 3 o'clock one morning. He was wearing a multi-coloured dressing-gown over one of his siren suits, one hand was held aloft with a sandwich and the other with watercress and he was dancing round the room giving occasional skips in time to the music blaring forth on the gramophone.

On another occasion, Sir Alan flew with Churchill from Stranraer to the States. Churchill strode purposefully up to the plane dressed in zip-up shoes and carrying a gold-topped cane, singing to himself 'We are here because we're here – we are here because we're here.' He was in high spirits, ate and drank enormously, and warned his pilot that it would not look too good if they crashed into the Washington Monument.

The Bricklayer

One of Churchill's many forms of relaxation was bricklaying. He spent the whole of August 1928 at Chartwell 'building a cottage and dictating a book: 200 bricks and 2,000 words a day.' The Southern Counties divisional secretary of the Amalgamated Union of Building Trade Workers tried to recruit Churchill as a member of his union. Churchill was willing to join, but the Executive Council decided he was not eligible.

On Old Etonians

Churchill used the phrase *'primus inter pares'* in the course of a speech in the House of Commons in 1941. Immediately, there were demands from Labour members for a translation. Churchill's response was swift:

> 'Certainly I shall translate – (pause) – for the benefit of any Old Etonians who may be present.'

Visit to the White House

According to Harry Hopkins, during Churchill's visit to the White House at the end of 1941, Roosevelt walked into Churchill's room, and found his guest in the bath. Churchill was not at all put out:

> 'The Prime Minister of Great Britain has nothing to hide from the President of the United States.'

Food and Drink

Churchill loved both. He habitually ate an enormous breakfast, once spurning the idea of breakfasting off salmon: 'No! No! I will have meat. Carnivores will win this war.'

Both lunch and dinner were usually lavish and accompanied by champagne or white wine. Brandy usually followed, and periods between meals were filled with periodic weak whiskies and soda. Churchill disliked both tea and coffee.

In 1944 Anthony Eden told Harold Nicolson that after a late night in Cairo, Churchill boarded an aeroplane the next morning complaining that he had lost his voice and was extremely ill. He was plunged into deepest gloom, and in despair his servant suggested a cough lozenge:

'No, you bloody fool,' Churchill croaked, 'a whisky and soda of course.'

Churchill was honest about his drinking: 'I have taken more out of alcohol than alcohol has taken out of me.'

He tried to persuade King Ibn Saud of Arabia, a strict Moslem, that cigars and alcohol were part of his religion.

Even during his final retirement, he still enjoyed food and drink. Macmillan took him to Buck's Club when he was 79. He enthusiastically ploughed through a huge meal of a dozen oysters, cream soup, chicken pie, and ice cream, all washed down with Moselle and brandy. When he left amidst cheering onlookers he remarked to Macmillan, 'I think I may still be not all on the debit side.'

On His 1945 Defeat

When Clementine tried to comfort him during lunch arguing gamely, 'It may well be a blessing in disguise,' Winston refused to be cheerful: 'At the moment it seems quite effectively disguised.'

He was soon pouring scorn on the Socialist government both in public and in private. He particularly disliked its use of jargon and used to attempt to sing 'Home Sweet Home' substituting the popular socialist term 'accommodation unit.' Sir Hartley Shawcross, one of the leading members of the government, was dubbed 'Sir Shortly Floorcross.'

On Modern Art

Churchill painted a lot during his retirement. He disliked modern art. Sir Alfred Munnings, the President of the Royal Academy, once asked him: 'What would you do if you saw Picasso walking ahead of you down Piccadilly?'

Churchill did not hestitate: 'I would kick him up the arse, Alfred.'

On his eightieth birthday, at a special meeting of both Houses of Parliament, Churchill received a portrait of himself by Graham Sutherland. He hated it on sight and after his wife's death it was revealed that the portrait had been destroyed. It was not the first portrait of her husband that Clementine had destroyed. Mary

Soames stated that her mother had also put her foot through a sketch of Winston done around 1927 by Sickert.

The Retirement

Lord Moran's controversial book about Churchill's state of health ended five years before Churchill's death because he 'thought it proper to omit the painful details of the state of apathy and indifference into which he sank after his resignation.'

At seventy-five, the old spirit was still there: 'I'm ready to meet my Maker. Whether my Maker is prepared for the great ordeal of meeting me is another matter.' On his eighty-fifth birthday, he was much gloomier:

'I feel very well. I hope I don't go on feeling very well. I don't want to waste time reading novels and playing cards.'

The Funeral

'It wasn't a funeral: it was a triumph.'

Clementine Churchill to Mary Soames

Churchill was the first statesman since Gladstone to lie in state in Westminster Hall. Three hundred and twenty thousand people queued for hours to pass his coffin, shrouded in the Union Jack and with the insignia of the Garter lying on it. For a short time, the four service-men keeping guard at the corners of the catafalque were replaced by the Speaker of the House of Commons and the leaders of the three main political parties.

Between Churchill's death and his funeral the American flag wherever it flew was at half-mast – the first time a foreign commoner had been honoured in this way. On the day of the funeral, Big Ben was silent from early morning till midnight. In St Paul's Cathedral, the Queen waived her prerogative and waited inside for the coffin and the family mourners to arrive. It was a moving ceremony, lightened by the singing of Churchill's favourite hymn, 'Battle Hymn of the Republic'. As the coffin appeared at the water's edge to be taken by launch from Tower Hill to Waterloo all the crane drivers in the Pool of London dipped their cranes in salute. The ceremony was watched on television all over the world by an estimated 350 million people, but to those who were there it seemed an intimate affair.

CLEMENT RICHARD ATTLEE

First Earl Attlee (1883–1967)

'A sheep in sheep's clothing'

WINSTON CHURCHILL (1874–1965)

BORN AT PUTNEY on 3 January 1883, Clement Attlee was the seventh child of a City solicitor, Henry Attlee. He was educated at Haileybury College and at University College, Oxford and then began a career at the Bar. Attlee was soon converted to socialism when he began doing some voluntary social work in the East End. By 1909 his career at the Bar had ended and for the next few years he spent his time in social work, lecturing, and local politics. Unlike some socialist politicians, he did not hesitate to fight during the First World War, returning from active service in Gallipoli, Mesopotamia and France to become Mayor of Stepney in 1919.

In 1922 Attlee entered the House of Commons as MP for Limehouse and the same year married Violet Millar, the daughter of a family friend. He served under Ramsay Macdonald as Under Secretary of State for War (1924), Chancellor of the Duchy of Lancaster (1930–1) and Postmaster-General (1931) but went into opposition during the years of the National Government. Elected Leader of the Labour Opposition in 1935, he guided his party into coalition with Churchill in 1940 becoming Lord Privy Seal and, from 1942, deputy Prime Minister. After the 1945 election, Labour was swept into power by a landslide victory and Attlee at last became Prime Minister, at the age of sixty-two. At home, his ministry saw the introduction of the National Health Service and the nationalization of the Bank of England, coal mines, gas, electricity, railways, road transport, and the steel industry. Independence was granted to India and Pakistan, the Marshall Plan was supported, NATO established, and the decision taken for British atomic bombs to be built.

From 1951–5 Attlee again led the Labour Party in opposition. At the age of 72, he finally retired to the Lords and died almost twelve years later on 8 October 1967.

Life at Haileybury

At the age of thirteen, Attlee was sent to Haileybury College, which at the time was going through a fairly bad patch. In order to encourage more pupils, fees were reduced, and once there, boys were discouraged from progressing through the lower forms too quickly. Attlee described conditions in his autobiographical notes:

> 'There were only two baths for eighty boys, the rest using zinc "toe pans". Our sanitary needs were supplied by three rows of earth closets . . . Many of the form rooms opened straight on to the quadrangle. In winter one was either frozen or roasted according to one's geographical position between the fire and the door. Forks and spoons were washed by being thrown in a large tub of hot water and stirred with a brush . . . The general arrangements were very rough. Lower boys had to pig it in the form rooms or class rooms where there was no privacy and a good deal of opportunity for bullying. The food was extremely bad at first but improved later. It was disgustingly served. I can clearly remember thinking often that one of the blessings of leaving would be decent food properly served . . .'

The Poet

Attlee's secret dream was to be a poet. He wrote a considerable amount of poetry, including the following sonnet, written before the First World War:

> *My life is passing like a lonely stream*
> *Winding through meadows flecked with white and gold*
> *That farseen distant castled hills enfold*
> *Yearnings and visions, memories of a dream*
> *Like tributary brooks my friendship seem*
> *Into the volume of the river rolled*
> *So in my heart their added wealth I hold*
> *But still my life is lonely like the stream.*
> *Sudden a change in this calm life I see*
> *The cataracts and shoals of Love are near*

Life is a torrent and within my heart
The calling of another stream I hear
This is the waters meet, never to part
Love let us flow together to the sea.

The Soldier

Attlee saw active service throughout the First World War. One of the incidents he recorded revealed his toughness as well as his compassion. A recalcitrant soldier had been brought before him in handcuffs:

'He had accumulated sentences of twelve years' imprisonment which would await him at the end of the war. I told him that he must now set to work to get remission and that we would help him. Our lads, too, were all determined to help. As one lad of nineteen said, "I reckon that poor lad has never had a chance. He's been dragged up." I think myself that he was not entirely sane.

'However, we all set out to help him. He volunteered for every patrol. He lay out between the lines sniping and in a few weeks I got about six years of his sentence remitted. A little later I recommended the remission of the rest. Next evening I found him and his sergeant outside my dug out. The sergeant said that he refused to go back to the line. On my questioning him, he talked wildly about being fed up and so on. I was much annoyed that all our trouble should go for nothing, so I adopted a method that I found useful with disobedient boys. I took out my watch and said "You've got one minute to return to duty", and then counted slowly. At forty-five seconds he sloped arms and returned to the trench. I suppose it was irregular, but I did not put him on a charge, and when I left the unit he was still doing well.'

The Perfect Husband and Father

Attlee's wife, Violet, was never a socialist, once declaring:

'Most of our friends are Conservatives. Clem was never really a socialist, were you, darling? Well, not a rabid one.'

Despite this, and problems caused by her ill health and possessiveness, Attlee was a model husband and father. Every house they lived in had an odd-job room where Attlee could produce book-shelves or cupboards on demand, upholster chairs or mend broken toys. A Wren brought in to help at Chequers was once surprised to find that the Prime Minister could re-cover her ironing table.

Atlee was an equally dutiful godfather. After the end of the war a godson wrote him a sharp letter on the subject of Hornby trains:

> '*My dear Godfather*
> 'It's long past time you started the Hornby factories going again. Shooly they should be started by now.'

Attlee was able to assure the small boy that the trains were back in production, and sent a postal order so that he could buy one. Another time, when a private secretary told him that he would not have time to take his children to the Trooping of the Colour, the Prime Minister insisted on taking them himself.

The Family Quiz

After lunch on Sundays, the Attlee family used to be quizzed by its head on matters of general knowledge, including questions on the names of foreign statesmen and on topics in the news. The questions were graded, the youngest getting the easiest questions. The children discovered many years later that these games were at least in part intended as a tactful way of briefing Violet on subjects she would be expected to know about.

'*Philip*'

In 1929, Attlee made an official visit to India. His bearer was a man called A.N.A. Aseervatham, whom Attlee for some reason called 'Philip', and the two became friends. They kept in touch and in the 1950s Attlee provided references enabling 'Philip' to obtain a licence to open a bar in Bangalore. The Indian still pays for an annual Requiem Mass to be said in a cathedral in Bangalore on Attlee's birthday.

Reserve

Widely recognized as a man of integrity, Attlee's shyness and reserve prevented him from gaining universal popularity. Sir John Colville once suggested to Winston Churchill that Attlee might be elected to 'The Other Club', an exclusive dining club, only to be told:

'I think not. He is an admirable character, but not a man with whom it is agreeable to dine.'

Even one of his own supporters, George Strauss, confessed that it was:

'very difficult to have a relaxed discussion with him on any subject except bishops or cricket. I once went by car with him to Harwell and I had about the most painful one and a half hours I have ever spent in my life.'

Sometimes, he disarmed colleagues by admitting his shyness, as when he told his junior ministers in 1945:

'One more thing: if I pass you in the corridor and don't acknowledge you, remember it's only because I'm shy.'

On other occasions, he appeared curt to the point of rudeness; as in his interview with one junior minister who rushed to Downing Street expecting praise only to be told:

'I want your job.'
'But . . . why, Prime Minister?'
'Afraid you're not up to it.'

That was the end of the interview. When asking older colleagues to resign he used to say more politely:

'Well, you had a good innings. Time to put your bat up in the pavilion.'

Interview with Crossman

In 1946 Richard Crossman asked to see Attlee, anxious to prove to him the determination of Jews in displacement camps to go to Palestine. Attlee listened to Crossman for about twenty minutes, and then, during a pause in the monologue, asked:

'"How's your mother, Dick?"
"She's very well. I'm seeing her next week" replied Crossman.
"Good, give her my regards" said Attlee, and Crossman had to leave.'

Chequers

The regime at Chequers under the Attlees was fairly spartan. When Dean Acheson, the U.S. Ambassador, was taken there for lunch by Ernest Bevin he later complained that he had never been so cold in his life. During lunch, he claimed, all the windows were open and the blowing curtains parallel to the floor. After asking for a martini he was given just vermouth. When offered another drink he requested neat gin in the hope that it would warm him up.

1951 Election Campaign

The *Daily Mirror* set the scene:

> 'While his wife drives, Mr Attlee puts on his glasses, rests on a brown and green folk-weave cushion, and does newspaper crossword puzzles. Occasionally when they are driving he unwraps a mint from a blue tin marked "biscuits" and pops one into his wife's mouth. If their car is held up at a level crossing, Mrs Attlee gets out her knitting – a pair of grey socks.
>
> Like a good wife, before they set out every morning, Mrs Attlee puts a crease in her husband's trousers with a portable electric iron.'

The Garter

When he became a Knight of the Garter, he thought of a verse:

> *Few thought he was even a starter*
> *There were many who thought themselves smarter*
> *But he ended* PM
> CH *and* OM
> *An earl and a knight of the garter.*

At Eighty

On being asked what it was like to be eighty:

> 'Better than the alternative.'

ROBERT ANTHONY EDEN
First Earl of Avon (1897–1977)

'Straight from charm school.'

LORD VANSITTART (1881–1957)

BORN ON 12 June 1897 at Windlestone Hall in County Durham, Anthony Eden was the third son of Sir William and Lady Eden. He went to Eton, volunteered in 1915 and fought until the end of the war, finishing up as Brigade Major and in possession of a Military Cross. At Christ Church, after the war, he read oriental languages, particularly Persian and Turkish and entered the House of Commons in 1923 as MP for Warwick and Leamington.

Eden's appointment as Parliamentary Private Secretary to Austen Chamberlain in 1926 began his long association with foreign affairs. He was Foreign Secretary (1939–40); Secretary of State for War (1940) and Churchill's Foreign Secretary from 1940 to 1945. When Churchill returned to power in 1951 Eden was again Foreign Secretary and a Deputy Prime Minister eagerly awaiting the moment when he would replace his leader. Even after suffering a stroke in 1953 Churchill still delayed his resignation and so it was not until 1955 that Eden at last became Prime Minister. He was to remain in office only twenty-one months, during which time he ordered British and French forces to occupy the Suez Canal Zone. Forced into resignation in 1957, because of his handling of the Suez crisis, Eden lived in retirement for another twenty years, despite frequent attacks of ill health. He accepted an earldom in 1961 and died at home on 14 January 1977.

In 1923 Eden married Beatrice Beckett, the daughter of a banker, but they separated in 1946. In 1952 he married Clarissa Churchill, the niece of Sir Winston Churchill.

Parents

Sir William was splendidly eccentric. His son remembered him with affection in his book *Another World*, recalling, alongside his discerning taste in contemporary paintings, some of his wilder outbursts. One day, for example, Sir William looked out on the rain beating down on hounds, huntsmen and followers assembling outside Windlestone Hall:

> 'As my father came through the front hall to join them, his eye fell on a barometer hanging on the panelled wall. He walked up to it and tapped: it read "Set Fair". He tapped again: it still replied "Set Fair". He took it off the wall, walked through the front door to the top of the flight of steps and sent it clattering down before the assembled company saying "Go and see for yourself, you damned fool." '

Sybil, Anthony's mother, was beautiful but remote. It was not that she neglected her five children: she visited them assiduously at their boarding schools, packed their trunks, and arranged doctors, dentists, and – until stopped by her husband – manicurists. Yet, her son confessed:

> 'I think my mother preferred the simpler relationship which existed between donor and recipient to the more complicated one between mother and child. No doubt she often found her children mystifying, wilful or even ungrateful, though she was always conscientious about us.'

The Onion Flower

One night, amidst the horror of the trenches, 'the Boy' (as he was called in the division) stumbled on a flower in full bloom. Thrilled, he picked it carefully and took it back to the dug-out, planning to press it and send it home to Windlestone. When one of his fellow-soldiers returned to the dug-out, he was blunt:

> 'What is the filthy stink in here?'

The plant was an onion in flower.

Military Cross

In August 1916 Eden's battalion was ordered to carry out a surprise raid on the German trenches. Discovered by the enemy, they were forced to retreat under a hail of bullets. Eden, realizing that his platoon sergeant was missing, went back to the forward position. He found the wounded man and brought him back safely through the wire. He was later awarded the Military Cross.

Clichés

Eden's speeches, especially those on domestic matters in which he had little interest, were often ridden with clichés. In a speech at Wellington on 22 October 1951, he proclaimed:

> 'the present situation is far too serious to make any promises, but we must have opportunity and incentive at home and peace and stability abroad.'

One of his aides once looked at Eden's draft of a speech and suggested, tongue in cheek, that the only possible improvement would be to add that there would be 'no stone unturned in the search for agreement'. Eden, to the aide's consternation, took the suggestion seriously and amended his speech.

The Divorced Foreign Minister

When Eden married for a second time, the *Church Times* protested that not so many years previously a Foreign Secretary would have had to resign rather than take a second wife whilst the first was still alive:

> 'Mr Eden's action this week shows how far the climate of public opinion has changed for the worse ... the world is openly rejecting the law of Christ in this as in so much else.'

Clarissa was a devoted wife, nursing a frequently-ill husband for the remaining twenty-five years of his life.

The Difficult Master

Both as Foreign Secretary and as Prime Minister, Eden was an unpredictable, irritable taskmaster. Evelyn Shuckburgh, one of his private secretaries, found him more than difficult:

'Mid February 1952
. . . easily the worst scene I have so far had with A.E. The
chauffeur and detective [in Lisbon], thinking they knew better than our instructions, had taken us off to the American
[instead of the French] Embassy . . . Being already late . . . this
extra delay seemed intolerable, and the annoyance was for
some minutes uncontrolled. It developed into a physical
struggle between me trying to shut the window between us
and the driver, so that the lower classes might be insulated
from these troubles, and A.E. leaning forward to wind it down
so that he might call them bloody fools! All ended amicably as
usual.'

As Prime Minister, Eden was ill and overworked. He was a poor
delegator, interfering with both senior and junior ministers, holding
meetings at all hours of the day, sometimes when he was getting
dressed, or even, it is said, in the bathtub. Butler was one of those
persecuted:

'. . . the Prime Minister paid me the compliment of expecting
me, more than the Chairman of the party, to be responsible
for Conservative success in the country. I was therefore at the
receiving end of those innumerable telephone calls, on every
day of the week and at every hour of the day, which char-
acterized his conscientious but highly-strung supervision of
our affairs.'

MAURICE HAROLD MACMILLAN
First Earl of Stockton (1894–   )

'Interesting work. Fine town house. Nice place in the country. Servants. Plenty of foreign travel. I wouldn't give it up if I were you.'

HAROLD MACMILLAN to James Callaghan,
who was then Prime Minister.

HAROLD MACMILLAN WAS born in London on 10 February 1894, the third son of Maurice and Helen Macmillan. He was educated at Summerfields, Eton and Balliol College, Oxford. By August 1915 he was with the Grenadier Guards in France, but after being wounded on the Somme in 1916 he spent the rest of the war in hospital.

In 1919 Macmillan went to Canada as ADC to the Governor General, the ninth Duke of Devonshire. The following year, he married the Duke's daughter, Lady Dorothy Cavendish. They had one son and two daughters.

After spending several years in the family publishing firm, Macmillan entered the House of Commons as Conservative MP for Stockton-on-Tees. For many years considered an unorthodox Tory rebel, it was not until 1940 that Macmillan took political office when he became Parliamentary Secretary to the Ministry of Supply. It was in December 1942 that Churchill gave him the recognition he deserved when he was appointed Minister of State in North Africa. Liaising between Churchill and Eisenhower, he had an important political and diplomatic role to play, and he made the most of it. After the war, he joined other Conservatives in Opposition, and under Churchill and Eden was successively Minister of Housing, Minister of Defence, and Foreign Secretary. At last, in January 1957 he replaced Anthony Eden as Prime Minister. He was sixty-two. In the first half of his administration there were many successes: he restored the confidence of a Conservative government battered by the Suez fiasco, restored good relations with the United States and presided over a period of economic boom. After 1960, economic difficulties, the French veto on British entry into the EEC and the Profumo scandal combined to undermine Macmillan's prestige. In October 1963 he underwent an operation on his prostate gland and resigned.

In retirement, Macmillan has devoted himself to six volumes of memoirs, to his publishing interests, and to the University of Oxford, of which he is Chancellor. He was created Earl of Stockton in 1984.

Summerfields

In 1964 Macmillan was asked to write a foreword to a book about his old preparatory school. 'I could not refuse', he admitted, 'for I still stand in great awe of a headmaster.'

The Wounded Soldier

In 1916 Macmillan was shot and seriously wounded in the thigh. He lay dazed in no-man's land for a whole day, passing the time by reading a copy of Aeschylus which he happened to have in his pocket. Whenever German soldiers passed, he pretended to be dead, and eventually at the end of the day he was spotted by a rescue party. Refusing to allow stretcher-bearers to risk their lives on his behalf Macmillan crawled his own way out of danger.

Back in England, Macmillan was in hospital for two years, undergoing a number of operations to remove pieces of metal and bone in his thigh. He described hospital life in a letter to Hermione Lyttelton in August 1918:

> 'The man in the bed next to me is stone deaf as a result of shell shock. He is a very voluble talker, but, as he can hear absolutely nothing that one says it's one of the easiest conversations to maintain. He is talking all the time to me now. I just say "Rhubarb, Mr Benson" from time to time and he is quite delighted . . .'

A Society Wedding

Macmillan's wedding to Lady Dorothy Cavendish at St Margaret's, Westminster was a grand affair. Among the Cavendish guests were Queen Alexandra, Princess Victoria and the future George VI. Not to be outdone the Macmillans managed to produce no less than three

OMS, including Thomas Hardy, paying what proved to be his last London visit. It is said that the Duke, another of whose daughters had married a brewer, consoled himself with the thought 'Well, books is better than beer.'

Lady Dorothy sometimes behaved like a character from one of Nancy Mitford's novels. At Number 10, she loved to gather her grandchildren around her, sometimes managing to create the atmosphere of a country-house week-end. It was even found necessary to write a notice stating firmly 'roller skating not allowed on Cabinet days.' It was at Birch Grove, their Sussex home, that she was happiest where she was occasionally to be seen gardening in the dark by torchlight with hot water bottles strapped to her legs to keep them warm. When the nights were warm she regularly ordered her bed to be moved into the garden and slept outside.

The crash Landing

On 21 February 1943 Macmillan, accompanied by his private secretary John Wyndham, set off on a flight from Algiers to Alexandria. The small aircraft set off down the runway successfully enough but completely failed to get airborne. Instead it crashed into flames in a vineyard close to the airfield. Wyndham crawled out of the plane, found his spectacles, and looked around in vain for his Minister:

> 'Suddenly, a familiar figure was seen to be struggling to get out of the pilot's side window, his moustache burning with a bright blue flame. He was quite out of reach. We shouted: "Push Minister, push." He landed on the ground with a thump, very badly burnt.'

Three days later Macmillan wryly described the incident in his diary:

> 'Middle-aged and rather portly publishers, encumbered by the weight of their own dignity and a large green Ulster overcoat, trying to spring through a smallish hole ... to be reached by scrambling over a confused mass of driving-wheels, levers and other mechanical devices of a jagged and impeding kind, if they are to achieve success in such an operation, must be inspired by a powerful and overwhelming motive. For lesser exertions, such as to enter Parliament, to struggle through years of political failure and frustration, lesser motives may serve. Ambition, patriotism, pride – all

these can impel a man and finally bring him within the hallowed precincts of the Privy Council and the Cabinet. But to do what I did in the early hours of last Monday morning, only one motive in the world is sufficient – FEAR (not fame) is the spur.'

Greeks in a Roman Empire

Richard Crossman, in Algiers during the war as Director of Psychological Warfare, described his first meeting with Macmillan:

'Macmillan sent for me straight away. No doubt the speech he made to me was made to every other arrival, but it impressed itself indelibly on my memory. "Remember," he said, "when you go to the Hotel St George, you will regularly enter a room and see an American colonel, his cigar in his mouth and his feet on the table. When your eyes get used to the darkness, you will see in a corner an English captain, his feet down, his shoulders hunched, writing like mad, with a full in-tray and a full out-tray, and no cigar.

"Mr Crossman, you will never call attention to this discrepancy. When you install a similar arrangement in your own office, you will always permit your American colleague not only to have a superior rank to yourself and much higher pay, but also the feeling that he is running the show. This will enable you to run it yourself.

"We, my dear Crossman, are Greeks in this American empire. You will find the Americans much as the Greeks found the Romans – great big, vulgar, bustling people, more vigorous than we are and also more idle, with more unspoiled virtues but more corrupt. We must run A.F.H.Q. as the Greek slaves ran the operations of the Emperor Claudius."'

The Unflappable Prime Minister

Macmillan always cultivated an air of calmness, and usually managed to give the impression that he never worked very hard. He wrote out a text from *The Gondoliers* for his aides: 'Quiet, calm deliberation disentangles every knot.' John Wyndham never knew him to fuss or flap, even on one occasion when a speech prepared for him was not ready at the crucial moment:

'It was during the Foreign Ministers' Conference in Geneva. One day, in the middle of luncheon at the Foreign Secretary's villa, I rose to excuse myself saying that I wanted to make sure that Mr Macmillan's speech was in order before he went down to the Palais des Nations for the afternoon meeting. Kirkpatrick, the Permanent Head of the Foreign Office said that there was no hurry because Mr Macmillan was due to speak last. Mr Macmillan told me to stop fussing and to sit down and finish my lunch: I could stay behind in the villa and bring the speech down when it was ready. I remained in the villa, checking the speech at leisure. But when all the Ministers were gathered together at the Palais des Nations, Molotov, who was due to speak first, said: "I pass". Dulles said the same. So did the French Foreign Minister. All eyes turned to Macmillan, who without looking round put his right hand behind him for his speech. But behind him was a vacant chair and no speech, no Wyndham. He withdrew his empty hand, feeling more amazement – as I learned later – than he showed on his face, and straightaway suggested that the Foreign Ministers should adjourn for refreshment.'

The man who had a copy of 'Aeschylus' at hand in the trenches resorted to *Pride and Prejudice* when he was waiting to hear whether he or R.A. Butler was to become Prime Minister. If a problem seemed insoluble, he would withdraw to his study and read from one of his favourite authors – Trollope, Thackeray, Dickens or Jane Austen. After Mrs Thatcher had been elected leader of the Conservative Party in 1975, Macmillan thought that she seemed to be doing far too much. When told of her busy schedule of August engagements, Macmillan was heard to remark:

'She would do much better to stay at home in her garden – has she got a garden? – and read Moneypenny and Buckle's *Life of Disraeli*.'

Chancellor of Oxford University
From the time of his installation as Chancellor of Oxford University in 1959 when, it is said, he wore his mortar board the wrong way round, Macmillan has never refused an invitation there. He visits Oxford about three times a term and makes innumerable speeches. Recently, he paid a visit to Oxford during August, noticed that there were very few undergraduates around, and on being reminded that it was the long vacation, remarked:

'Ah, yes, I suppose they have all gone north for the grouse
shooting.'

Walter Bagehot Centenary Speech

At a centenary dinner, Macmillan referred to a report of his death
which had appeared in a national newspaper:

'When I died last summer, I was tempted to bring it all to an
end. I thought I'd go to Coutts Bank, draw out my money and
disappear. I'd live in Provence. After lunch I could play a
game of boule or dominoes and read the *Echo de Lyons*. I
would not exist. But it all went wrong when people started
ringing up. One man said, "the *Daily Telegraph*, which is a
very respectable paper, says you are dead, so you must be." I
replied "Like Mark Twain's, the reports of my death have
been greatly exaggerated," at which the young man asked,
"Who is Mark Twain?" I think that would have amused
Bagehot.'

The Grand Old Man

As Prime Minister, Macmillan had his critics, but as the G.O.M. of
British politics, he is universally admired. Now that he is in his nineties,
his shuffling gait and air of decrepitude is at last appropriate. His maiden
speech in the House of Lords on 13 November 1984 was a sensation,
bringing his peers to their feet for the first time in living memory. Walking
uncertainly with the aid of a silver-topped cane, the newly created Earl of
Stockton referred to himself as 'a sort of political Rip Van Winkle'. He
had used exactly the same phrase to describe himself in a speech in the
House of Commons some thirty-nine years earlier in December 1945. At
one moment in his speech, he used the idiom of another age to describe
the opposing arguments of neo-Keynesians and monetarists:

'There are two points of view, and it goes right through. Many
of your Lordships will remember that it operated in the
nursery. How do you treat a cold? One nanny said, "Feed a
cold" – she was a neo-Keynesian. Another nanny said,
"Starve a cold" – she was a monetarist. It is natural.'

ALEXANDER FREDERICK DOUGLAS-HOME
Lord Home of the Hirsel (1903–)

'An elegant anachronism.'

HAROLD WILSON (1916–)

BORN IN LONDON on 2 July 1903, Alec Douglas-Home was the eldest son of Lord Dunglass, heir to the 12th Earl of Home. He was educated at Ludgrove, Eton, and Christ Church, Oxford, and entered the House of Commons as MP for South Lanark in 1931. He was Parliamentary Private Secretary to Neville Chamberlain (1937–40), Minister of State at the Scottish Office (1951–5), Secretary of State for Commonwealth Relations (1955–60), Leader of the House of Lords and Lord President of the Council (1957–60), and Foreign Secretary (1960–63). When Macmillan was forced to resign as Prime Minister in October 1963, Lord Home was an unexpected choice as his successor. Four days later, he disclaimed his peerage for life, and during the next twelve months largely succeeded in reuniting the Conservative Party and reviving their fortunes after the disasters of the Profumo affair and the collapse of negotiations over British entry into the Common Market. After the defeat of the Conservatives in the 1964 election, Sir Alec remained their leader until 1965 when he was replaced by Edward Heath. From 1970–74 he returned to office as Foreign Secretary.

In 1936 Alec Douglas-Home married Elizabeth Alington, the second daughter of the headmaster of Eton. They have one son and three daughters.

The Eton Hero
At Eton, Alec Douglas-Home shone effortlessly. His success was best described by Cyril Connolly:

'He was a votary of the esoteric Eton religion, the kind of graceful, tolerant, sleepy boy who is showered with all the laurels, who is liked by the masters and admired by the boys without any apparent exertion on his part, without experiencing the ill-effects of success himself or arousing the pangs of envy in others. In the eighteenth century he would have become Prime Minister before he was thirty; as it was he appeared honourably ineligible for the struggle of life.'

The Reluctant Horseman

Alec's father thought his eldest son ought to be a good rider. One morning they set off together to tour the estate. After ten minutes Lord Home slowed down to see how his eldest son was progressing and was confronted with the sight of a riderless horse. Alarmed, he turned back and found Alec in a ditch, unhurt and totally absorbed in studying a butterfly on a shrub.

More Butterflies

On 27 August 1947 Alec wrote triumphantly to the *Scotsman* that he had seen a yellow clouded butterfly near West Linton and asking whether any more had been seen in Scotland. Two days later the following crushing reply appeared in print:

> 'In answer to Lord Dunglass's letter I saw one specimen of the clouded yellow butterfly yesterday three miles north of Abington, Lanarkshire, and another today five miles west of Lanark.'

The letter was written by Edward Douglas-Home.

On His Back

Between 1940 and 1942 Lord Dunglass spent two years lying flat on his back and encased in plaster. He had earlier injured his back by falling on a tree stump whilst trying to pull up a lilac bush and by 1940 an X-ray revealed both a hole in the spine and tuberculosis in the surrounding area. During the summer his bed used to be taken outside on a pulley system. Even in the depths of winter, Alec was so anxious to be able to look at the countryside that his summerhouse was moved on to the drive and given a revolving base so that he could have a change of view at different times of the day.

Help With 3,000 Women

In the middle of drafting a review of foreign affairs one evening at The Hirsel, Sir Alec was interrupted twice by telephone calls from a practical joker within the family. When the telephone rang for the third time and a Scottish voice asked, 'Lord Home, can you help me with three thousand women?' Alec bellowed rudely down the telephone and slammed down the receiver. Five minutes later the telephone rang yet again but this time Lady Home had to pacify an irate Scottish clergyman who was complaining about Lord Home's rudeness when invited to address three thousand members of the Women's Guild.

The Vague Foreign Secretary

When he flew around the world as Foreign Secretary his wife used to remind him where he was by repeatedly hissing the name of the place in his ear as he walked down the steps of the aeroplane. 'Peking, Alec, Peking, Peking.' Otherwise, there was every likelihood that the Foreign Secretary would offend his hosts by declaring he was very happy to be back in some other place at the other side of the globe.

Fourteenth Earl

On Lord Home's appointment as Prime Minister, Harold Wilson much enjoyed attacking the choice of a fourteenth earl to lead the country's government. In a television interview Lord Home took the opportunity of pointing out:

> 'I suppose Mr Wilson, when you come to think of it, is the fourteenth Mr Wilson.'

The Honest Mother

A *Daily Express* reporter telephoned Lady Home after her son had become Conservative Prime Minister: 'You must be a proud mother, Lady Home.'

Lady Home did not hesitate. 'I think it should have been Mr Butler.'

The Flower Arranger

R.A. Butler, looking back on Sir Alec Douglas-Home's career as Prime Minister, declared:

> 'I will give away his secret. Whenever things became most tense he would go away on his own for half an hour and arrange a vast bowl of flowers.'

JAMES HAROLD WILSON
Lord Wilson of Rievaulx (1916–   )

'The man who is running the Government one day was sped on his way the next, with just about as much ceremony as a shop assistant found with his hands in the till.'

MARCIA WILLIAMS (Lady Falkender) (1932–   ), following Harold Wilson's loss of the June 1970 General Election

BORN NEAR HUDDERSFIELD on 11 March 1916, the son of a nonconformist industrial chemist, Harold Wilson was educated at Royds Hall Secondary School, Huddersfield and then, when his family moved to Cheshire, at the Wirral Grammar School. He won a scholarship to Jesus College, Oxford where he gained a First in PPE and won the Gladstone Memorial Prize. He became a don at New College and in 1938 was elected a Fellow of University College where he worked as a research assistant to the new Master, Sir William Beveridge.

During the war, Wilson was drafted into the Civil Service, but immediately the war was over entered the House of Commons as Labour MP for Ormskirk. Recognition came almost immediately: he was a junior minister before he was thirty and at the age of thirty-one in 1947 became President of the Board of Trade, the youngest Cabinet minister for a hundred and fifty years. In 1951 he suddenly resigned, with Nye Bevan, over the question of cuts in social services.

After the death of Hugh Gaitskell in 1963, Wilson was elected Labour Party Leader. He succeeded in uniting the party sufficiently to win the 1964 election by a small majority, and remained in office until 1970. In 1974 he returned to power as Prime Minister of a minority Labour government. Two years later he unexpectedly accepted the Garter and returned to the backbenches. He was made a Life Peer in 1983.

In 1940, Wilson married Gladys Mary Baldwin, the daughter of a Congregational Minister. They have two sons.

The Background

Harold Wilson has absorbed much less of the upper-middle class way of life than any of the other men who, like him, rose from a modest background to become Prime Minister. He still sounds and behaves like the down-to-earth Yorkshireman he was born. His way of life, even at the height of his power, was immensely ordinary, his natural habitat suburbia, and his preferences deliberately unexotic. He once declared:

> 'If I had the choice between smoked salmon and tinned salmon, I'd have it tinned. With vinegar.'

Not that his background was quite as unprivileged as he has sometimes liked to make out. His father was not a manual worker but an industrial chemist with an exceptionally gifted mathematical brain. Wilson has still not succeeded in living down a remark made in a speech in Birmingham in July 1948 and quoted in the *Daily Telegraph*:

> '... the school I went to in the North was one where more than half the children in my class never had boots or shoes to their feet.'

In fact, poor as many of their neighbours probably were, the Wilson family could afford to send the ten-year-old Harold and his mother to Western Australia to visit an uncle who was an Australian MP.

The Youthful Socialist

There are those who have doubted Harold Wilson's youthful socialist convictions but there is a well-known story that on General Election Day, December 1923, when Harold Wilson was seven and in hospital following appendicitis, he ordered his parents not to stay with him too long in case they missed their vote for the Socialist candidate.

Eighteen months later, Herbert Wilson took his son to London and showed him the Houses of Parliament and Downing Street. Harold posed for a photograph on the steps of Number 10.

At the Board of Trade

As President of the Board of Trade after the war, Wilson had to cope with the problems of rationing. A lady once wrote enclosing two vests and complaining bitterly that they had been bought with a number of precious coupons, but had shrunk terribly. He replied politely:

> *'Dear Madam*
> The Board of Trade does not make vests.'

The Platform Speaker

Wilson's skill as a speaker improved tremendously over the years. Where he excelled was in dealing with the unexpected interruption or the irreverent heckler. At one of his meetings in 1964 a mother, embarrassed by her baby's yells, rose to leave the hall:

> 'Don't take him out, madam [bellowed Wilson] this election is about his future.'

At a speech in Glasgow during the same campaign, Wilson was talking about the vast sums of money spent on the 'Blue Streak' missile system. A heckler shouted 'Groundnuts', and was immediately rounded on by Wilson:

> 'There's an ageing young Conservative ... His only contribution to the Blue Streak argument is to shout groundnuts. ... Where have you been, Rip van Winkle?'

The Nervous Wife

Mrs William Waldegrave, the wife of the then Education Minister, was sitting in the House of Commons Gallery listening to a speech her husband was making. Suddenly the middle-aged woman sitting quietly next to her spoke up:

> '"You look very nervous, my dear."
> "Oh yes I am," agreed Mrs Waldegrave, "you see that's my husband down there."'

The stranger was not silenced by this:

> 'Ah yes, I do know what it's like. You see my husband was Prime Minister for quite a few years and I'm afraid you'll find that it gets worse.'

It was Mrs Wilson.

Working Methods
One of those who probably knew him best, having worked with him since 1956, is Marcia Falkender. His habits did not make her task of running his Private Office in Opposition, or of being his Personal and Political Secretary at 10 Downing Street, particularly easy – especially as he often worked late.

> 'Although his work methods are extremely organized and neat – in the sense of annotating papers and so forth – there is only one word to describe the room in which he worked: untidy. His study, both at Number 10 and in Opposition, was littered with books and papers – all of which he expected to find in proper order, neatly arranged and easily available, first thing the next day.'

No Profound Thoughts
Harold Wilson was leader of the Labour Party from 1963, but even those close to him were not always clear where he intended leading it. One of those who worked with him both in and out of government, Richard Crossman, recorded in his diary of December 1966 that:

> '. . . he certainly doesn't confide in me any profound thoughts about the future of the Labour Party, and I'm prepared to say as of today that I don't think he has any.'

The Middle-Class Monarchist
Despite – or perhaps because of – leading the Labour Party, Harold Wilson was devoted to the monarchy as an institution and to the Queen personally. He enjoyed going to Court, and was very proud that the Queen liked his visits to her. When Prince Philip stated on American television in 1969 (perhaps with deliberate exaggeration) that the Royal Family would 'go into the red next year', Harold Wilson gave one of his best parliamentary performances ever, defusing a potentially embarrassing situation for his government by managing to convey the message that the Opposition was playing party politics with the monarchy and the constitution, while he was putting Queen and country first.

'That Man' Resigns
Harold Wilson's announcement in early March 1976 that he intended to retire from the premiership took almost everyone by

surprise, causing considerable speculation as to whether some scandal was about to be revealed. His timing was such that, after the announcement, his first appearance in the Commons, was for Prime Minister's questions, which had often provided him with his greatest triumphs. The chamber was full nearly fifteen minutes before he was expected there, with even the Peers' Gallery crowded – something that generally happens only when war (or sexual scandal) is in the air. However, he managed to get through Question Time without indicating who was to be his successor, fending off Opposition queries by saying that the Labour Party had 'long had a practice of democratic election, not the scatty system you introduced'. (This system had recently brought Mrs Thatcher to the leadership of the Conservative Party.)

The occasion was perhaps most notable for the claim of one Labour MP that Mr Wilson had resigned 'without any knives in the back whatsoever'. 'Of course, that is true,' he replied; but Frank Johnson, a parliamentary sketchwriter in the Press Box, claimed that other shoulderblades along the front bench did all the twitching necessary for the time being.

No major scandal broke, and Woodrow Wyatt put down the resignation – probably correctly – to Wilson's being bored with politics, 'world-weary', and observed that it was nice for his wife, Mary, who 'loathed the tawdry atmosphere of political intrigue'. Her husband, however, does not seem always to have been aware of this, telling Crossman that she had enjoyed a 1966 campaign meeting in Birmingham when her neck was scratched by something thrown at her. 'Who told you that?' she asked him. *That man?*

EDWARD RICHARD GEORGE HEATH
(1916–   )

'Ted's a fellow I'd go tiger-shooting with.'

HAROLD MACMILLAN

'. . . what a wonderful country, what a marvellous country, where the Prime Minister – the Prime Minister – turns to me and says "That chord – was it D sharp or D sharp minor?"'

SIR GEORGE SOLTI

BORN ON 9 July 1916 the elder son of William and Edith Heath of Broadstairs, Kent, Edward Heath was educated at Chatham House School and Balliol College, Oxford. During the war he served as an artillery officer, in 1945 becoming second in command of the second regiment of the Honourable Artillery Company.

After spells in the Civil Service, in a merchant bank, and as a journalist on the *Church Times*, Heath was elected Conservative MP for Bexley in 1950. He joined the Whip's Office in 1951 and from 1955 to 1959 was both Chief Whip and Parliamentary Secretary to the Treasury. In 1959, Macmillan made him Minister of Labour and in 1960, Lord Privy Seal with special responsibility for negotiating Britain's entry into the EEC. In 1965, he replaced Sir Alec Douglas-Home as leader of the Conservatives, and from 1970–74 was Prime Minister. Never widely popular either in his own party or in the country, Heath was replaced as Conservative leader by Margaret Thatcher in 1975.

Edward Heath has never married. He is an accomplished musician and is the author of several books, on politics and on sailing.

The Background

Edward Heath was brought up in a modest semi-detached house in Broadstairs. His father was a carpenter who married a twenty-five-year-old lady's maid. They worked and saved hard, put a deposit on a house, and eked out the family living by taking in summer visitors.

Although William Heath later became a master builder, the Heaths were never well-off. For twelve years after their marriage they never had an evening out together. At last, they planned a trip to the local cinema, leaving the nine-year-old Edward in charge of his younger brother. During the evening, the young Edward Heath telephoned a rather startled cinema manager asking him to pass a message to his parents that he and his brother were fine.

Edward Heath was not the first Conservative Prime Minister to gain the office despite not coming from the traditional upper-class, public school mould. Having got himself to Balliol and having become President of the Oxford Union it was not so strange that Edward Heath should later have become Conservative Party leader. To the fathers of men like Heath and Wilson, though, their sons' achievements were really remarkable. A few days after Heath had become Party Leader, Harold Wilson's father, himself glowing with fatherly pride, wrote a letter to William Heath:

> '*Dear Mr Heath*
>   Please accept my congratulations to you on the election of your son Edward to the leadership of his party. I can imagine your feelings of pride on his success as I underwent the same elation on my son's election as leader of his party a little over two years ago. I am afraid that in my case there is a difference of age of some years as I am rapidly approaching eighty-three, but even so it is a great thrill to me to see and hear my son in the House of Commons. When I do so I look back on his years as a boy, a Boy Scout, etc., etc., and undoubtedly you have the same feelings at times. Trusting that you will have many years of good health to enjoy your son's success, I am, Yours very sincerely,
>
> *J. Herbert Wilson.*'

The Enigma

To a lucky few who penetrate the mask of reserve, Edward Heath is kind, amusing, and altogether agreeable. To the rest of the world he appears difficult, ill at ease, and cold. Even when he was Chief Whip, his manner was sometimes unfortunate. When Airey Neave revealed to him that he would have to retire from junior office because of a mild heart condition, Heath's sympathy was none too obvious:

'Well, that's the end of your political career, then.'

Many years later, in 1973, he was positively prickly, even to loyal supporters. John Nott, then a junior Treasury minister, met him in a Westminster corridor and hoped to discuss financial policy. He was soon thwarted: 'If you want to resign, put it in writing.'

Friends of Mr Heath claimed this was intended as a joke.

Even at social functions his manner was often awkward. At one grand dinner he sat next to Vittoria Leoni, the beautiful and amusing wife of the then President of the Italian Republic. All he managed to say to her all evening was 'How is the President?'

Marriage

When he became Party leader, the question of Edward Heath's bachelor status assumed national importance. Heath himself dealt with the matter sensibly enough. Asked by Kenneth Harris of the *Observer* if he thought a Prime Minister ought to be married, he replied:

> 'I don't know. It would depend to some extent on the woman, wouldn't it? What I do know is that a man who got married in order to be a better Prime Minister wouldn't be either a good Prime Minister or a good husband.'

The Musician

Music has always been important to Edward Heath. Not least, it provided him with a much-needed organ scholarship within a month of his arrival at Balliol. Soon he had started the Balliol Choir, joined the Bach Choir, and begun organizing the annual Broadstairs carol concert. During the arduous Common Market negotiations in the early 1960s it was said that he carried around with him the score of Britten's War Requiem together with all his other official papers. At one stage during the negotiations he was to be found reviving his spirits by playing a Bach toccata and fugue in St Stephen's Cathedral in Vienna.

Sometimes, music was used more practically as a means of escape:

> 'The devoted team of secretaries in No. 10 are constantly lying in wait to fill every moment of the Prime Minister's time with red boxes, Parliamentary questions, Foreign Office telegrams

and all the other demands of the office, but I have noticed that the best way I can fend them off is go and play something on the piano. They creep up to the door with their red boxes and creep away again with the boxes unopened. "Heath is at his exercises," they murmur to themselves . . .'

The Sailor

Despite having been brought up in the seaside town of Broadstairs, Heath was not always a sailor. It was only after he became Party leader that he took up sailing as a hobby. Typically, by 1969 he was a leading yachtsman, winning, in *Morning Cloud*, the prestigious Australian race from Sydney to Hobart. 'We have shown,' he declared prosaically, 'that planning and preparation pay.'

Mr Heath's first book was called *Sailing – A Course of My Life*. He joked that the second one might be about cookery, entitled *Cooking – Three Courses of My Life*.

LEONARD JAMES CALLAGHAN

(1912–   )

'When I am shaving in the morning, I say to myself that if I were a young man I would emigrate. By the time I am sitting down to breakfast I ask myself, "Where would I go?"'

JAMES CALLAGHAN

'He's got a certain charm, you know: Uncle Jim. He used that very often.'

LORD SHINWELL (1884–1986)

BORN ON 27 March 1912 at 38 Funtington Road, Portsmouth, James Callaghan was the son of a seaman who had wisely turned down an offer to go on Scott's South Pole expedition in 1911. His father, injured at the battle of Jutland, died when James was nine. Educated at Portsmouth North Secondary School, Callaghan left when he was seventeen to become a clerk in the Inland Revenue.

After seven years, Callaghan became assistant secretary of the Inland Revenue Staff Federation. In 1942 he served on the staff of the Director of Naval Intelligence, and in 1945 entered the House of Commons as Labour member of Cardiff South. Two years later he became parliamentary secretary at the Ministry of Transport. After Attlee's defeat in 1951, he was out of office until 1964 when he became Harold Wilson's Chancellor of the Exchequer. The devaluation of the pound in 1967 led to him being moved from the Exchequer. In the 1974 Labour Ministry he was appointed Foreign Secretary, and after Harold Wilson's resignation in 1976 became Prime Minister for three years until defeated by Margaret Thatcher in 1979. In 1980 he returned to the back benches, leaving the leadership of the Labour Party to Michael Foot.

In 1938 Callaghan married Audrey Moulton. They have one son and two daughters.

Over Ambitious

Jim Callaghan regretted not having had a university education, and some of those who knew him well believed that the lack of it made him feel inferior and inclined to bluster, though at the same time providing him with an impetus to prove he could get to the top. Certainly, the nervous Woodrow Wyatt (who entered Parliament at the same time, in 1945), waiting to make his maiden speech and listening to Callaghan, judged his performance as already an accomplished one. By November 1964, however, Dick Crossman described him as Chancellor of the Exchequer, sitting in a Cabinet Committee and 'sort of bleating amiably what he feels'.

Perhaps over nearly twenty years early enthusiasm and idealism had left him. Woodrow Wyatt used to cnjoy Sunday lunches in Blackheath with the Callaghan family, shortly after they had both been elected:

> 'When our seniors intrigued together against each other, he said "we of our generation are never going to behave like that." He forgot that precept as he got older.'

In fact, Attlee thought him over ambitious and refused – to his annoyance – to give him a post higher than that of junior minister, telling him that no one had a prescriptive right to promotion.

Uncle Jim

Even before he was Prime Minister, Jim Callaghan was conscious of his avuncular public image, and promoted it. His colleagues, too, were aware of it – though they didn't in fact think of him like that (indeed the discrepancy between his public and more private images might explain why he was against the televising of Parliamentary proceedings).

Dick Crossman noted in January 1969 that he was in no doubt Callaghan was building up his position in the public eye:

> '. . . on everything you see, there is Jim Callaghan, sensible, constructive, sturdy, thoroughly English, doing his job, a big man who could keep the movement going even when it is defeated and gets rid of Harold Wilson.'

Sober Decision

On the evening of 28 March 1979, Callaghan's government, after being defeated on the bill to devolve governmental power to Scotland and Wales, faced a motion of no confidence.This coincided with a strike by the Commons' catering staff, and the *Guardian*'s political columnist is reported to have pointed out that, should the government lose, it would not only be the first time for over fifty years that a government had lost a vote of this nature, it would probably also be the first time it had lost one with everyone on both sides sober.

The government lost the vote, and Mr Callaghan called an election which he also lost.

Personality

An amiable, avuncular figure, Jim Callaghan often seemed to be just outside the limelight. His fellow Labour MPs were clearly intrigued by his political success. On 5 September 1969 Roy Jenkins remarked to Richard Crossman:

> 'You know there is nobody in politics I can remember and no case I can think of in history where a man combined such a powerful political personality with so little intelligence.'

Crossman himself was only marginally less damning:

> 'Right inside he's a coward with a wonderful outside image and a likeable personality.'

Barbara Castle, herself no friend of Callaghan, revealed him in his best light at a 1974 diplomatic banquet at the Royal Naval College, Greenwich:

> 'Jim makes a brief, relaxed and highly competent after-dinner speech to that glittering audience. His poise in these matters is remarkable.'

Finally, Marcia Falkender, who later became Harold Wilson's Personal and Political Secretary, has admitted that when Callaghan gave her a wedding present of table linen she was so thrilled that she felt it had to be put away and not used:

> 'At the time [1955] I felt a present from such a distinguished Labour leader was something that really could not be used for every-day living.'

MARGARET HILDA THATCHER

(1925–   )

'It wasn't an election. It was an assumption.'

NORMAN ST JOHN STEVAS on her election as party leader.

MARGARET ROBERTS WAS born in Grantham on 13 October 1925, the second daughter of Beatrice and Alfred Roberts, a self-made shopkeeper. She was educated at Huntingdon Tower Road elementary school, Kesteven and Grantham Girls School, and Somerville College, Oxford, where she read chemistry.

By the time she had begun her first job at a plastics factory in Essex, Margaret Roberts knew that what she really wanted to do was to read for the Bar and to enter politics. In the 1950s she did both, finally entering the House of Commons in 1959 as Conservative MP for Finchley. Under Macmillan she was a Junior Minister for Pensions and National Insurance (1961–4) and Heath made her his Secretary of State for Education (1970–74). In 1975 Margaret Thatcher replaced Edward Heath as leader of the Conservative Party, and in 1979 became Britain's first woman Prime Minister.

In 1951 Margaret Roberts married Denis Thatcher, a divorced businessman, and in 1953 her twins, Mark and Carol, were born.

Family Background

The flat above the shop in Grantham was modest, possessing neither bath, running hot water, nor indoor lavatory. Beatrice and Alfred Roberts both worked all their lives with a ferocious energy matched only by that of their younger daughter. Alfred, besides working long hours to make the shop a success, was a Methodist lay preacher, a Rotarian, a school-governor, a JP, a local councillor, and for a time, Mayor of Grantham. Beatrice Roberts's energies were directed towards exclusively domestic objects, but were almost equally alarming. Besides serving in the shop and doing all the housework, she baked, decorated, sewed and upholstered to perfection. Even when they holidayed they went at separate times so that the shop would not have to be shut: Beatrice used to take the girls to a boarding house in Skegness for a fortnight whilst Alfred would go there for a week later in the year. Neither did the two girls escape from their share of the chores. Mrs Thatcher recalls helping with deliveries, weighing out sugar and butter, as well as helping to serve in the shop.

One would have sympathized with the Roberts family if they had passed their Sundays in a stupor brought on by exhaustion. In fact they spent much of the day at the Finkin Street Methodist Church, both daughters attending Sunday School followed by morning service, then afternoon school and usually evening service as well. When they returned home for supper games were forbidden.

At Somerville

Dame Janet Vaughan, later a distinguished Principal of Somerville College, remembered Margaret Roberts at Oxford:

> 'She fascinated me. I used to talk to her a great deal, she was an oddity. Why? She was a Conservative – she stood out. Somerville had always been a radical establishment and there weren't many Conservatives about then. We used to argue about politics; she was so set in steel as a Conservative. She just had this one line . . . We used to entertain a good deal at weekends, but she didn't get invited. She had nothing to contribute, you see.'

Mrs Thatcher's Energy

As Prime Minister, her stamina has become legendary. Regularly surviving on four or five hours sleep, Mrs Thatcher's day time schedule daunts many a follower. At Oxford, where most undergraduates lead a far from arduous existence, she used to get up at six and end her working day at eight in the evening. A few years later she passed her Bar finals only four months after the birth of the twins. During her first election campaign, the vice-chairman of the Conservatives, Janet Young, asked her one morning if she had managed to sleep after a particularly gruelling nineteen-hour day. 'Oh I couldn't get to sleep for ages,' Mrs Thatcher confessed, 'so I lay in bed and read Aristotle.'

The more punishing her schedule, the more she seems to thrive. Even after the Brighton bomb, when she'd had a completely sleepless night, she delivered her final speech to the party conference next day without any visible sign of fatigue.

Asked by Brian Connel of *The Times* how she coped with the strain of office, she replied:

> 'I've no idea, it's just that I'm a round peg in a round hole. I don't feel any sign of physical strain at all. I've always led an onerous timetable but I like it. I have a tremendous amount of energy and for the first time in my life it is fully used. I have always a little bit in reserve. In public life you must, because no matter how busy you are, there will be some time when you need a little bit extra. But when you are going flat out, you never feel tired, it's when you've stopped.'

Toughness

It was as Minister of Education that Mrs Thatcher's unpopularity was probably at its height. She had just stopped free milk in secondary schools and, during a demonstration, was hit on the chest by a stone egg. The obvious question was put to her: 'Does it hurt?'

'It hurt like mad,' she admitted.

The interviewer persisted: 'And what did you do?'

'I went on speaking, what else could I do?'

Sir Geoffrey and the Roast Lamb

Sir John Junor, editor of the *Sunday Express*, once reported on television that, at a Chequers dinner, a Wren waiting at table had accidentally poured a helping of roast lamb and gravy down Sir Geoffrey Howe's front. Mrs Thatcher's concern was not for her shocked colleague but for the embarrassed Wren: 'Don't worry, my dear, it could happen to anyone.'

A Middle-aged Lady

It has to be admitted that Mrs Thatcher is not often amusing but then, to be fair, neither were her three predecessors in office. Stories of her kindness and consideration to employees abound, but few can remember any jokes she has made. Occasionally, there are attempts at levity: at her first party conference after being made leader she descended on the rostrum and with a blue feather duster playfully dusted the nose of Peter Thomas, who was trying to introduce her. One has to be the loyallest of Conservatives before one can really laugh uproariously at that sort of joke. It is not clear yet whether Mrs Thatcher can laugh at herself. During a discussion lunch at the Institute of Economic Affairs in February 1974, Christopher Tugendhat unwisely suggested that abstruse economic points could not be explained to constituency parties dominated by middle-aged women in flowery hats. Mrs Thatcher leapt upon him:

'Speaking as a middle-aged lady who likes hats . . .'

Prime Ministers' Portraits

Portraits of every Prime Minister hang up the stairs at Number 10. When questioned about the fact that there is no room for one of herself, Mrs Thatcher is said to have replied – 'Don't worry, I'll push all the others down.'

The Face That Never Slips

Clive Limpkin, a press photographer, has spent a lot of time trying to catch Mrs Thatcher off-guard. To this end, he lay in wait at a party conference:

'I was watching her at that conference and waiting for an interesting facial expression and I suddenly realized that she was yawning with her mouth shut; at that point I knew I'd been beaten.'

The Children's Party

At a Palace of Westminster children's party organized by Westminster journalists one year, Mrs Thatcher tried to put all the young guests at their ease. A four-year-old made a plaintive appeal to her: 'Miss, miss! They've given me blancmange and I don't like blancmange.'

'That,' she instructed him, 'is what parties are all about: eating food you don't like!'

SOURCES

SIR ROBERT WALPOLE, *First Earl of Orford* (1676–1745)

C. Hanbury Williams, *Works*, 3 vols, 1822.

Lord Hervey, *Memoirs*, ed. R. Sedgwick (London: William Kimber, 1952).

R. W. Ketton-Cremer, *Horace Walpole* (London: Duckworths, 1940).

Milton Percival. ed., *Ballads Illustrating the Administration of Sir Robert Walpole* (Oxford Historical and Literary Studies, 1916).

Sir J. H. Plumb, *Sir Robert Walpole*, 2 vols, vol. 1, *The Making of a Statesman*, vol. 2, *The King's Minister* (London: Cresset Press, 1956, 1960).

SPENCER COMPTON, *First Earl of Wilmington* (1673–1743)

C. Hanbury Williams, *Works*, 3 vols, 1822.

Lord Hervey, *Memoirs*, ed. R. Sedgwick (London: William Kimber, 1952).

Horace Walpole, *Letters*, ed. P. Cunningham (London: Richard Bentley & Son, 1891).

HENRY PELHAM (1696–1754)

J. B. Owen, *The Rise of the Pelhams* (London: Methuen, 1957).

Alexander Pope, *Epilogue to the Satires* (1738).

Horace Walpole, *Memoirs of the Reign of King George II*, ed. Lord Holland, 3 vols (London: Henry Colborn, 1846).

THOMAS PELHAM-HOLLES, *Duke of Newcastle* (1693–1768)

Reginald Lucas, *George II and His Ministers* (London: Arthur L. Humphreys, 1910).

Lewis Namier, *England in the Age of the American Revolution* (London: Macmillan, 1930).

Lord Hervey, *Memoirs*, ed. R. Sedgwick (London: William Kimber, 1952).

Brian Tunstall, *William Pitt, Earl of Chatham* (London: Hodder & Stoughton, 1938).

Horace Walpole, *Letters*, ed. P. Cunningham (London: Richard Bentley & Son, 1891).

Horace Walpole, *Memoirs of the Reign of King George II*, ed. Lord Holland, 3 vols (London: Henry Colborn, 1846).

T. White, *The Age of Scandal* (London: Jonathan Cape, 1950).

WILLIAM CAVENDISH,
Fourth Duke of Devonshire (1720–1764)

Lady Mary Wortley Montagu, *The Letters and Works of Lady Mary Wortley Montagu*, ed. Lord Wharncliffe, 2 vols (London: George Bell & Sons, 1898).

Lord Waldegrave, *Memoirs 1754–1758* (London: John Murray, 1821).

Horace Walpole, *Correspondence*, ed. W. S. Lewis, 48 vols (London: Oxford University Press, 1973).

JOHN STUART, *Third Earl of Bute* (1713–1792)

Stanley Ayling, *George the Third* (London: Collins, 1972).

Lord Edmund Fitzmaurice, *The Life of William, Earl of Shelburne*, 3 vols (London: Macmillan, 1876).

John Stuart, *Letters* (Historical MSS Comm.).

Herbert van Thal, ed., *The Prime Ministers* (London: George Allen & Unwin, 1975).

Horace Walpole, *Memoirs of the Reign of King George III*, 4 vols (London: R. Bentley, 1845).

GEORGE GRENVILLE (1712–1770)

Edmund Burke, *Works of the Rt Hon. E. Burke*, 2 vols (London: Holdsworth & Ball, 1834).

Philip Lawson, *George Grenville* (Oxford, Clarendon Press, 1984).

Herbert van Thal, ed., *The Prime Ministers* (London: George Allen & Unwin, 1975).

Horace Walpole, *Letters*, ed. P. Cunningham (London: Richard Bentley & Son, 1891).

Horace Walpole, *Memoirs of the Reign of King George III*, 4 vols (London: R. Bentley, 1845).

CHARLES WATSON-WENTWORTH, *Second Marquess of Rockingham* (1730–1782)

Stanley Ayling, *George the Third* (London: Collins, 1972).

George Thomas, Earl of Albemarle, *Memoirs of the Marquis of Rockingham and his Contemporaries*, 2 vols (London, 1852).

Horace Walpole, *Correspondence*, ed. W. S. Lewis, 48 vols (London: Oxford University Press, 1973).

Horace Walpole, *Letters*, ed. P. Cunningham (London: Richard Bentley & Son, 1981).

Horace Walpole, *Memoirs of the Reign of King George III*, 4 vols (London: R. Bentley, 1845).

Arthur Young, *A Six Months Tour through the North of England*, 4 vols, 1770.

WILLIAM PITT, *First Earl of Chatham* (1709–1778)

John Timbs, *Anecdote Biography. William Pitt, Earl of Chatham and Edmund Burke* (London, 1862).

Brian Tunstall, *William Pitt, Earl of Chatham* (London: Hodder & Stoughton, 1938).

Horace Walpole, *Memoirs of the Reign of King George II*, ed. Lord Holland, 3 vols (London: Henry Colborn, 1846).

AUGUSTUS HENRY FITZROY, *Third Duke of Grafton* (1735–1811)

Clive Bigham, *The Prime Ministers of Britain 1721–1921* (London: John Murray, 1923).

W. J. Smith, ed., *The Grenville Papers*, 4 vols (London: John Murray, 1852).

Horace Walpole, *Letters*, ed. P. Cunningham (London: Richard Bentley & Son, 1891).

FREDERICK NORTH,
Second Earl of Guilford (1732–1792)

W. Adams, ed., *Modern Anecdotes* (London: Hamilton Adams & Co., 1886).

Lord Broughton, *Recollections of a Long Life* (London: John Murray, 1911).

Lord Glenbervie, *Diaries of Sylvester Douglas*, ed. F. Bickley, 2 vols (London: Constable, 1928).

G. H. Jennings, *Anecdotal History of the British Parliament from the earliest period to the present time* (London: H. Cox, 1890).

R. Lucas, *Lord North*, 2 vols (London: Arthur L. Humphreys, 1913).

Alan Valentine, *Lord North* (University of Oklahoma Press, 1967).

Horace Walpole, *Letters*, ed. P. Cunningham (London: Richard Bentley & Son, 1891).

WILLIAM PETTY, *Second Earl of Shelburne, First Marquess of Lansdowne* (1737–1805)

Jeremy Bentham, *The Works of Jeremy Bentham* (Edinburgh: William Tait, 1843).

Francis Hardy, *Memoirs of the Political and Private Life of James Caulfield, Earl of Charlemont* (London, 1810).

Horace Walpole, *Journals of the Reign of King George III*, 4 vols (London: R. Bentley, 1845).

Sir N. W. Wraxall, *Historical and Posthumous Memoirs of My Own Time* 5 vols (London: Bickers & Son, 1884).

WILLIAM HENRY CAVENDISH-BENTINCK,
Third Duke of Portland (1738–1809)

Clive Bigham, *The Prime Ministers of Britain 1721–1921* (London: John Murray, 1923).

Denis Gray, *Spencer Perceval, The Evangelical Prime Minister* (Manchester University Press, 1963).

Dictionary of National Biography (London: Oxford University Press, 1975).

WILLIAM PITT (1759–1806)

John Ehrman, *The Younger Pitt: The Years of Acclaim* (London: Constable, 1969).

Joseph Farington, *Diary*, ed. James Greig, 8 vols (London: Hutchinson, 1928).

Robin Furneaux, *William Wilberforce* (London: Hamish Hamilton, 1974).

Derek Jarrett, *Pitt the Younger* (London: Weidenfeld & Nicolson, 1974).

Sir N. W. Wraxall, *Historical Memoirs of My Own Time*, 2 vols (London: T. Cadell & W. Davies, 1815).

Philip Ziegler, *Addington* (London: Collins, 1965).

HENRY ADDINGTON,
First Viscount Sidmouth (1757–1844)

John Ehrman, *The Younger Pitt: The Years of Acclaim* (London: Constable, 1969).

Joseph Farington, *Diary*, ed. James Greig, 8 vols (London: Hutchinson, 1928).

Lord Granville Leveson-Gower, *Private Correspondence 1781–1821*, ed. Castalia, Countess Granville (London: John Murray, 1917).

Lord Holland, *Memoirs of the Whig Party in my Time* (nd).

George Pellew, *Life and Correspondence of the Right Honourable Henry Addington first Viscount Sidmouth* (London, 1847).

Philip Ziegler, *Addington* (London: Collins, 1965).

WILLIAM WYNDHAM, *Baron Grenville* (1759–1834)

Lord Auckland, *The Journal and Correspondence of William, Lord Auckland*, 4 vols (London: Richard Bentley, 1860–2).

E. V. Boyle, *Seven Gardens and a Palace*, 1900.

Duke of Buckingham and Chandos, *Memoirs of the Court and Cabinets of George III from original family documents*, 1853.

THE HON. SPENCER PERCEVAL (1762–1812)

Robin Furneaux, *William Wilberforce* (London: Hamish Hamilton, 1974).

Denis Gray, *Spencer Perceval, The Evangelical Prime Minister* (Manchester University Press, 1963).

National Adviser, 20–3 May 1812.

ROBERT BANKS JENKINSON,
Second Earl of Liverpool (1770–1828)

Harriet Arbuthnot, *The Journal of Mrs Arbuthnot 1820–32*, eds. Francis Bamford and the Duke of Wellington, 2 vols (London: Macmillan, 1950).

Norman Gash, *Lord Liverpool* (London: Weidenfeld & Nicolson, 1984).

Princess Lieven, *The Private Letters of Princess Lieven to Prince Metternich 1820–26* (London: John Murray, 1937).

Dorothy Marshall, *The Rise of George Canning* (London: Longman & Co., 1938).

M. Villiers, *The Grand Whiggery*, (London: John Murray, 1939).

GEORGE CANNING (1770–1827)

W. Adams, ed., *Modern Anecdotes* (London: Hamilton Adams & Co., 1886).

Charles Greville, *Diary*, ed. P. W. Wilson, 2 vols (London: Heinemann, 1927).

Wendy Hinde, *Canning* (London: Collins, 1973).

FREDERICK JOHN ROBINSON,
First Viscount Goderich, First Earl of Ripon (1782–1859)

Wilbur Devereux Jones, *Prosperity Robinson* (London: Macmillan, 1967).

Emily Eden, *Miss Eden's Letters*, ed. Violet Dickinson (London, 1919).

Charles Greville, *Diary*, ed. P. W. Wilson, 2 vols (London: Heinemann, 1927).

L. Jennings, ed., *The Croker Papers*, 3 vols (London: John Murray, 1884–5).

J. Morley, *Life of W. E. Gladstone*, 3 vols (London: Macmillan, 1903).

ARTHUR WELLESLEY,
First Duke of Wellington (1769–1852)

Richard Aldington, *Wellington* (London: Heinemann, 1946).

Annual Register, 1830.

Harriet Arbuthnot, *The Journal of Mrs Arbuthnot 1820–32*, eds. Francis Bamford and the Duke of Wellington, 2 vols (London: Macmillan, 1950).

G. R. Gleig, ed., *The Life of Arthur, Duke of Wellington*. From the French of M. Brialmont, 4 vols (London: Longmans, 1858).

Charles Elvin, *A History of Walmer Castle* (privately printed, 1894).

Sir William Fraser, *Words on Wellington* (London: John Nimmo, 1889).

Frances Mary Gascoyne-Cecil, *The Gascoyne Heiress, The Life and Diaries of Frances Mary Gascoyne-Cecil 1802–1839*, ed. Carola Oman (London: Hodder & Stoughton, 1968).

Daniel George, ed., *A Book of Anecdotes* (London: Hulton Press, 1957).

C. T. Herrick, ed., with extracts from Miss J's Diary, *Letters of the Duke of Wellington to Miss J* (London: Fisher Unwin, 1924).

L. Jennings, ed., *The Croker Papers*, 3 vols (London: John Murray, 1884–5).

Elizabeth Longford, *The Years of the Sword* (London: Weidenfeld & Nicolson, 1969).

Elizabeth Longford, *Pillar of State* (London: Weidenfeld & Nicolson, 1972).

Sir Herbert Maxwell, *The Life of Wellington*, 2 vols (London: Sampson Low & Co., 1899).

Frances, Lady Shelley, *Diary, 1787–1817*, ed. Richard Edgcumbe, 2 vols (London, 1912).

Philip, 5th Earl of Stanhope, ed., *Notes of Conversations with the Duke of Wellington 1850* (London: John Murray, 1888).

John Timbs, *Wellingtonania, anecdotes, maxims and characteristics of the Duke of Wellington* (London, 1852).

John Timbs, *A Century of Anecdote from 1760 to 1860*, 2 vols (London: Richard Bentley & Son, 1864).

CHARLES GREY, *Second Earl Grey* (1764–1845)

Georgiana, Duchess of Devonshire, *Letters*, ed. Lord Bessborough (London: John Murray, 1955).

G. H. Jennings, *Anecdotal History of the British Parliament from the earliest period to the present time* (London: H. Cox, 1890).

Earl of Malmesbury, *Memoirs of an ex-Minister*, 2 vols (London: Longmans, Green & Co., 1884).

Brian Masters, *Georgiana* (London: Hamish Hamilton, 1981).

G. M. Trevelyan, *Lord Grey of the Reform Bill* (London: Longmans, 1920).

WILLIAM LAMB, *Second Viscount Melbourne* (1779–1848)

Lord Beaconsfield, *Letters*, ed. Ralph Disraeli (London: John Murray, 1887).

Lady Harriet Cavendish, *Hary-o, The letters of Lady Harriet Cavendish, 1796–1809*, eds. Sir G. Leveson-Gower and Iris Palmer (London: John Murray, 1940).

David Cecil, *Lord M* (London: Constable, 1954).

Viscount Esher, ed., *The Girlhood of Queen Victoria*. A selection from Her Majesty's diaries between the years 1832 and 1840 (London, 1912).

Abraham Howard, *Sketches of Eminent Statesmen and Writers* (London, 1880).

Elizabeth Longford, *Victoria R. I.* (London: Weidenfeld & Nicolson, 1964).

Hariette Wilton, *Memoirs* (London: Eveleigh Nash, 1909).

Philip Ziegler, *Melbourne* (London: Collins, 1976).

SIR ROBERT PEEL (1788–1850)

Norman Gash, *Mr Secretary Peel* (London: Longmans, 1962).

Norman Gash, *Sir Robert Peel* (London: Longmans, 1972).

Daniel George, ed., *A Book of Anecdotes* (London: Hulton Press, 1957).

Lady Gregory, ed., *Sir William Gregory*, 1894.

Macmillan's Magazine, November 1874

JOHN, *First Earl Russell* (1792–1878)

Lord Broughton, *Recollections of a Long Life* (London: John Murray, 1911).

Ethel Peel, *Recollections of Lady Georgiana Peel*, 1920.

John Prest, *Lord John Russell* (London: Macmillan, 1972).

G. W. E. Russell, *Collections and Recollections* (London: Smith, Elder & Co., 1898).

J. R. Russell, 13th Duke of Bedford, *A Silver-plated Spoon* (London: Cassell, 1959).

Lady John Russell, *A Memoir with selections from her diaries and correspondence*, eds. D. MacCarthy and A. Russell (London: Methuen, 1910).

Sir Spencer Walpole, *The Life of Lord John Russell*, 2 vols (London: Longman & Co., 1889).

G. M. Young, ed., *Early Victorian England*, 1830–1865, 2 vols (London: Oxford University Press, 1934).

EDWARD GEORGE GEOFFREY STANLEY,
14th Earl of Derby (1799–1869)

W. Adams, ed., *Modern Anecdotes* (London: Hamilton Adams & Co., 1886).

Lady Burghclere, ed., *A Great Lady's Friendships* (London: Macmillan, 1933).

Wilbur Devereux Jones, *Lord Derby and Victorian Conservatism* (Oxford: Blackwells, 1956).

Charles Greville, *Diary*, ed. P. W. Wilson, 2 vols (London: Heinemann, 1927).

Lord Redesdale, *Memories*, 2 vols (London: Hutchinson, 1915).

Edward Stanley, *Journal of a Tour in America 1824–5*.

GEORGE HAMILTON GORDON,
Fourth Earl of Aberdeen (1784–1860)

Muriel Chamberlain, *Lord Aberdeen* (London: Longman, 1983).

Princess Lieven, *Correspondence of Princess Lieven and Earl Grey*, 3 vols (London: Richard Bentley, 1890).

V. Surtees, *Charlotte Canning* (London: John Murray, 1975).

H. W. V. Temperley, *England and the Near East* (London: Longman & Co., 1936).

John Timbs, *A Century of Anecdote* from 1760 to 1860, 2 vols (London: Richard Bentley & Son, 1864).

Mrs Hugh Wyndham, ed., *Correspondence of Sarah Spencer, Lady Lyttelton 1787–1870*, 1912.

HENRY JOHN TEMPLE,
Third Viscount Palmerston (1784–1865)

William Day, *Reminiscences of the Turf* (London: Richard Bentley & Son, 1886).

Speaker Denison, Journal, 1865.

Charles Greville, *Diary*, ed. P. W. Wilson, 2 vols (London: Heinemann, 1927).

T. Lever, ed., *The Letters of Lady Palmerston* (London: John Murray, 1957).

Jasper Ridley, *Lord Palmerston* (London: Constable, 1970).

BENJAMIN DISRAELI,
First Earl of Beaconsfield (1804–1881)

Robert Blake, *Disraeli* (London: Eyre & Spottiswoode, 1966).

Cornhill Magazine, January 1912.

Louisa Devey, *Life of Rosina, Lady Lytton* (London: Swan Sonnenschein, Lowrey & Co., 1887).

Sir W. Fraser, *Disraeli and His Day* (London: Kegan Paul, Trench, Trubner, 1891).

Daniel George, ed., *A Book of Anecdotes* (London: Hulton Press, 1957).

W. Meynell, *The Man Disraeli* (London: Hutchinson, 1927).

W. F. Monypenny and G. E. Buckle, *The Life of Benjamin Disraeli*, 6 vols (London: John Murray, 1910–20).

Philip Snow and Stefanie Waine, *The People from the Horizon* (London: Phaidon, 1979).

W. M. Torrens, *Memoirs of the Right Honourable William, second Viscount Melbourne* (London, 1878).

WILLIAM EWART GLADSTONE (1809–1898)

Margot Asquith, *An Autobiography* (Butterworth, 1920).

Joseph Dean, *Hatred, Ridicule or Contempt* (London: Constable, 1953).

Philip Guedalla, *The Queen and Mr Gladstone* (London: Hodder & Stoughton, 1958).

R. R. James, *Rosebery* (London: Weidenfeld & Nicolson, 1963).

Philip Magnus, *Gladstone* (London: John Murray, 1954).

Joyce Marlow, *Mr and Mrs Gladstone* (London: Weidenfeld & Nicolson, 1977).

John Wilson, *A Life of Campbell-Bannerman* (London: Constable, 1973).

ROBERT ARTHUR TALBOT GASCOYNE CECIL,
Third Marquess of Salisbury (1830–1903)

E. F. Benson, *As We Were* (London: Longmans, 1930).

Robert Blake, *Disraeli* (London: Eyre & Spottiswoode, 1966).

Lady Gwendolen Cecil, *Life of Robert, Marquess of Salisbury*, 2 vols (London: Hodder & Stoughton, 1921).

A. L. Kennedy, *Salisbury* (London: John Murray, 1953).

Sir George Granville Leveson-Gower, *Mixed Grill* (London: Frederick Muller, 1947).

Viscountess Milner, *My Picture Gallery 1886–1901* (London: John Murray, 1951).

National Review, November 1931.

Arthur Ponsonby, *Henry Ponsonby* (London: Macmillan, 1942).

Kenneth Rose, *The Later Cecils* (Weidenfeld and Nicolson, 1975).

Sir Ernest Scott, ed., *Lord Robert Cecil's Gold Field Diary*, 1935.

ARCHIBALD PHILIP PRIMROSE,
Fifth Earl of Rosebery (1847–1929)

Evan Charteris, *Life and Letters of Sir Edmund Gosse* (London: Heinemann, 1931).

Winston Churchill, *Great Contemporaries* (London: Butterworth, 1937).

Christopher Hibbert, *Edward VII* (London: Allen Lane, 1976).

Robert Rhodes James, *Rosebery* (London: Weidenfeld & Nicolson, 1963).

Lord Sysonby, *Recollections of Three Reigns* (London: Eyre & Spottiswoode, 1955).

ARTHUR JAMES BALFOUR,
First Earl of Balfour (1848–1930)

Margot Asquith, *Autobiography* (London: Butterworth, 1920).

Winston Churchill, *Great Contemporaries* (London: Butterworth, 1937).

Max Egremont, *Balfour* (London: Collins, 1980).

Ian Malcolm, *Lord Balfour* (London: Macmillan, 1930).

Barbara Tuchman, *The Proud Tower* (London: Hamish Hamilton, 1966).

HENRY CAMPBELL-BANNERMAN (1836–1908)

Austen Chamberlain, *Politics from the Inside* (London: Cassell, 1936).

Viscount Esher, *Journal and Letters*, 4 vols (London: Ivor Nicholson & Watson, 1934).

Christopher Hibbert, *Edward VII* (London: Allen Lane, 1976).

J. A. Spender, *Life of the Rt. Hon. Sir Henry Campbell-Bannerman*, 2 vols (London: Hodder & Stoughton, 1923).

John Wilson, *A Life of Sir H. Campbell-Bannerman* (London: Constable, 1973).

HERBERT HENRY ASQUITH,
First Earl of Oxford and Asquith (1852–1928)

Cynthia Asquith, *Diaries* (London: Hutchinson, 1968).

H. H. Asquith, *Memories and Reflections*, 2 vols (London: Cassell, 1928).

Margot Asquith, *Autobiography* (London: Butterworth, 1920).

M. and E. Brook, eds., *H. H. Asquith's Letters to Venetia Stanley* (London: Oxford University Press, 1982).

Winston Churchill, *Great Contemporaries* (London: Butterworth, 1937).

Hansard, Parl. Deb. XXIV 1221.

Roy Jenkins, *Asquith* (London: Collins, 1964).

DAVID LLOYD GEORGE,
First Earl Lloyd George of Dwyfor (1863–1945)

Margot Asquith, *Autobiography* (London: Butterworth, 1920).

Richard Lloyd George, *Lloyd George* (Frederick Muller Ltd, 1960).

Lucy Masterman, *C. F. G. Masterman, A Biography* (London: Nicholson & Watson, 1939).

K. O. Morgan, *Lloyd George: Family Letters 1885–1936* (University of Wales Press and London: Oxford University Press, 1973).

Sir Oswald Mosley, *My Life* (London: Nelson, 1968).

Lord Riddell, *Intimate Diary of the Peace Conference* (London: Gollancz, 1933).

Peter Rowland, *Lloyd George* (London: Barrie & Jenkins, 1975).

A. J. Sylvester, *The Real Lloyd George* (London: Cassell & Co., 1947).

A. J. P. Taylor, ed., *Lloyd George, A Diary by Frances Stevenson* (London: Hutchinson, 1971).

ANDREW BONAR LAW (1858–1923)

Lord Beaverbrook, *Politicians and the War 1914–1916*, 2 vols (London: Thornton Butterworth, 1928).

Robert Blake, *The Unknown Prime Minister* (London: Eyre & Spottiswoode, 1955).

Violet Bonham Carter, *Winston Churchill as I Knew Him* (London: Eyre & Spottiswoode and Collins, 1965).

Lord Sysonby, *Recollections of Three Reigns* (London: Eyre & Spottiswoode, 1951).

STANLEY BALDWIN,
First Earl Baldwin of Bewdley (1867–1947)

A. W. Baldwin, *My Father, The True Story* (London: George Allen & Unwin, 1955).

Lord Butler, *The Art of the Possible* (London: Hamish Hamilton, 1971).

Dictionary of National Biography (London: Oxford University Press, 1975 edn).

Montgomery Hyde, *Stanley Baldwin* (London: Hart-Davies, 1973).

R. R. James, *Memoirs of a Conservative*: J. C. C. Davidson's memoirs and papers (London: Weidenfeld & Nicolson, 1969).

K. Middlemas and John Barnes, *Baldwin* (London: Weidenfeld & Nicolson, 1969).

Harold Nicolson, *Diaries and Letters*, 3 vols (London: Collins, 1966–8).

Nourah Waterhouse, *Private and Official* (London: Jonathan Cape, 1942).

Duke of Windsor, *A King's Story* (London: Cassell, 1960).

JAMES RAMSAY MACDONALD (1866–1937)

Malcolm Macdonald, *Titans and Others* (London: Collins, 1972).

Ramsay Macdonald, *Margaret Ethel Macdonald* (London: Hodder & Stoughton, 1912).

Ramsay Macdonald, *Wanderings and Excursions* (London: Jonathan Cape, 1925).

Ramsay Macdonald, Column in *Forward*, 6 December 1924.

N. Mackenzie, ed., *The Letters of Sidney and Beatrice Webb*, 2 vols (Cambridge University Press, 1978).

David Marquand, *Ramsay Macdonald* (London: Jonathan Cape, 1977).

Harold Nicolson, *Diaries and Letters*, 3 vols (London: Collins, 1966–8).

ARTHUR NEVILLE CHAMBERLAIN (1869–1940)

Winston Churchill, *The Second World War*, 3 vols (London: Cassell, 1948).

Keith Feiling, *The Life of Neville Chamberlain* (London: Macmillan, 1970).

Montgomery Hyde, *Neville Chamberlain* (London: Weidenfeld & Nicolson, 1976).

R. R. James, *Chips, The Diaries of Sir Henry Channon* (London: Weidenfeld & Nicolson, 1967).

Iain Macleod, *Neville Chamberlain* (London: Frederick Muller, 1961).

Countess of Oxford and Asquith, *Off the Record* (London: Frederick Muller, 1944).

WINSTON LEONARD SPENCER CHURCHILL (1874–1965)

Violet Bonham Carter, *Winston Churchill as I Knew Him* (London: Weidenfeld & Nicolson, 1965).

Piers Brendon, *Winston Churchill. A Brief Life* (London: Secker & Warburg, 1984).

Winston Churchill, Four Faces and the Man (London: Allen Lane, 1969).

Daily Mail, 5 January 1932.

Lord Ismay, *Memoirs* (London: Heinemann, 1960).

Kingsley Martin, *Harold Laski* (London: Victor Gollancz, 1953).

Lucy Masterman, *C. F. G. Masterman A Biography* (London: Nicholson & Watson, 1939).

Lord Moran, *Winston Churchill: The Struggle for Survival* (London: Constable, 1966).

Harold Nicolson, *Diaries and Letters*, 3 vols (London: Collins, 1966–8).

Henry Pelling, *Winston Churchill* (London: Macmillan, 1974).

Lord Riddell, *Diary 1908–14* (London: Country Life Ltd, 1934).

Mary Soames, *Clementine Churchill* (London: Cassell, 1979).

CLEMENT RICHARD ATTLEE,
First Earl Attlee (1883–1967)

Clement Attlee, *As It Happened* (London: William Heinemann, 1954).

Kenneth Harris, *Attlee* (London: Weidenfeld & Nicolson, 1982).

Harold Wilson, *A Prime Minister on Prime Ministers* (London: Weidenfeld
& Nicolson and Michael Joseph, 1977).

ROBERT ANTHONY EDEN, *First Earl of Avon* (1897–1977)

R. A. Butler, *The Art of the Possible* (London: Hamish Hamilton, 1971).

David Carlton, *Anthony Eden* (London: Allen Lane, 1981).

Anthony Eden, *Another World* (London: Allen Lane, 1976).

Herbert van Thal, ed., *The Prime Ministers* (London: Allen & Unwin,
1975).

MAURICE HAROLD MACMILLAN,
First Earl of Stockton (1894–   )

Lord Egremont, *Wyndham and Children First* (London: Macmillan, 1968).

Nigel Fisher, *Harold Macmillan* (London: Weidenfeld & Nicolson, 1982).

Harold Macmillan, *The Blast of War 1939–45* (London: Macmillan, 1967).

Anthony Sampson, *Macmillan: A study in ambiguity* (London: Allen
Lane, 1967).

Sunday Telegraph, 9 February 1964.

ALEXANDER FREDERICK DOUGLAS-HOME,
Lord Home of the Hirsel (1903–   )

Cyril Connolly, *Enemies of Promise* (London: G. Routledge & Sons, 1938).

John Dickie, *The Uncommon Commoner* (London: Pall Mall, 1964).

William Douglas Home, *Mr Home Pronounced Hume* (London: Collins,
1979).

Anthony Howard and Richard West, *The Making of the Prime Minister* (London: Jonathan Cape, 1965).

JAMES HAROLD WILSON,
Lord Wilson of Rievaulx (1916–   )

Richard Crossman, *The Diaries of a Cabinet Minister*, 3 vols (London: Hamish Hamilton and Jonathan Cape, 1975–7).

Lady Falkender, *Downing Street in Perspective* (London: Weidenfeld & Nicolson, 1983).

Simon Hoggart, *Back on the House* (London: Robson Books, 1982).

Frank Johnson, *Out of Order* (London: Robson Books, 1982).

Anthony Howard and Richard West, *The Making of the Prime Minister* (London: Jonathan Cape, 1965).

Dudley Smith, *Harold Wilson* (London: Hale, 1964).

Woodrow Wyatt, *Confessions of an Optimist* (London: Collins, 1985).

EDWARD RICHARD GEORGE HEATH (1916–   )

John Boyd-Carpenter, *Way of Life* (London: Sidgwick & Jackson, 1980).

Patrick Cosgrave, *Margaret Thatcher* (London: Hutchinson, 1978).

Simon Hoggart, *On the House* (London: Robson Books, 1981).

George Hutchinson, *Heath* (London: Longman, 1970).

Margaret Laing, *Edward Heath* (London: Sidgwick & Jackson, 1972).

Observer Colour Magazine, 16 February 1966.

Andrew Roth, *Heath and the Heathmen* (London: Routledge & Kegan Paul, 1970).

Yachts and Yachting, 3 August 1971.

LEONARD JAMES CALLAGHAN (1912–   )

Barbara Castle, *The Castle Diaries* (London: Weidenfeld and Nicolson, 1984).

Richard Crossman, *The Diaries of a Cabinet Minister*, 3 vols (London: Hamish Hamilton and Jonathan Cape, 1975–7).

John Doxat, *Shinwell Talking* (London: Quiller Press, 1984).

Frank Johnson, *Out of Order* (London: Robson Books, 1982).

Marcia Williams, *Inside No. 10* (London: Weidenfeld & Nicolson, 1972).
Woodrow Wyatt, *Confessions of an Optimist* (London: Collins, 1985).

MARGARET HILDA THATCHER (1925–   )

Patrick Cosgrave, *Margaret Thatcher* (London: Hutchinson, 1978).
Simon Hoggart, *On the House* (London: Robson Books, 1981).
Frank Johnson, *Out of Order* (London: Robson Books, 1982).
Penny Junor, *Margaret Thatcher* (London: Sidgwick & Jackson, 1983).
Patricia Murray, *Margaret Thatcher* (London: W.H. Allen, 1980).
N. Wapshott and G. Brock, *Thatcher* (London: Macdonald, 1983).